The First Wor

A.W. Purdue

 macmillan education   palgrave

First published 2015 by
PALGRAVE

Palgrave in the UK is an imprint of Macmillan Publishers Limited, registered
in England, company number 785998, of 4 Crinan Street, London N1 9XW.

Palgrave Macmillan in the US is a division of St Martin's Press LLC,
175 Fifth Avenue, New York, NY 10010.

Palgrave is a global imprint of the above companies
and is represented throughout the world.

Palgrave® and Macmillan® are registered trademarks in the United States,
the United Kingdom, Europe and other countries.

ISBN 978–1–137–33106–9   hardback
ISBN 978–1–137–33105–2   paperback

This book is printed on paper suitable for recycling and made from fully
managed and sustained forest sources. Logging, pulping and manufacturing
processes are expected to conform to the environmental regulations of the
country of origin.

A catalogue record for this book is available from the British Library.

A catalog record for this book is available from the Library of Congress.

Typeset by MPS Limited, Chennai, India.

Printed in China.

To the memory of my grandfather,
William Borthwick,
who fought in the Great War

Contents

Preface

The centenary of the beginning of the First World War has been greeted by books, newspaper articles and TV programmes featuring the views of historians, commentators and politicians on the causes of the war, and the next four years will, undoubtedly, see a similar explosion of debate and controversy as, year by year and month by month, the anniversaries of the campaigns and battles follow each other. The amount of material available to students and to general readers is already enormous, so the purpose of this book is to provide a concise narrative and an introduction to the many debates among historians on subjects such as the war's origins. The aim is not to simplify but to guide and to encourage the reader to explore more specialist works.

A concise account of the war in around 80,000 words must inevitably prioritise. The main focus of this book is on the diplomatic, political and military history of the conflict and on the disagreements among historians on major issues such as: the causes of the war and the relative responsibilities for its outbreak; the strategies and war aims of the belligerents; the balance of strength in terms of military might, size of population, and economic potential ; the major campaigns and battles; the achievements and failings of military commanders; the reasons for the eventual Allied victory; and the reshaping of Europe and the Middle East at the end of the war. This approach will provide, I hope, the essential framework for an understanding of the war and a context for those who wish to go on to explore, in greater depth than space has permitted, such subjects as the effects of the war upon social and cultural change or its influence upon the development of science, technology and medicine.

The history of the First World War is a subject I taught for many years as a member of the Open University's history department, a department well-known for its successful and innovative courses on the world wars of the twentieth century. My knowledge of the war owes a great deal to my then colleagues, many of whose works are referred to in this book. The debates and discussions I had with them and with academics from other universities at successive summer schools have contributed much to this book, though not all will agree with the interpretations and conclusions contained in it.

This study is an interpretative synthesis, drawing on the works and views of many historians, but bearing the stamp of my own explanations of the course of events. It can be seen as a companion volume to my previous book, *The Second World War*, also a volume in Palgrave's European History in Perspective series, and, like it, aims to show how views of its subject have changed over time.

My thanks are due to Jeremy Black as General Editor of the *European History in Perspective* series and to Palgrave's excellent editorial staff, Sonya Barker, Lucinda Knight and Alec McAulay.

List of Maps

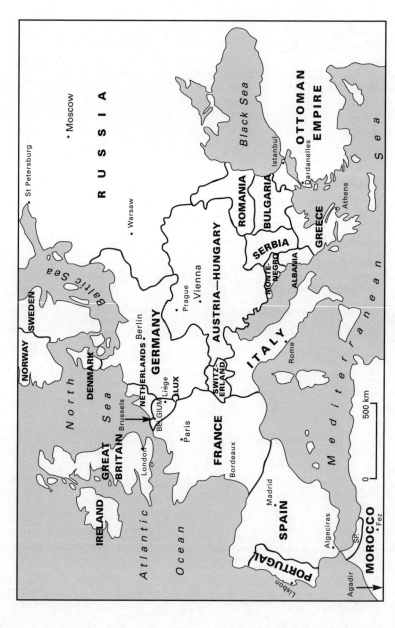

Map 1 Europe in 1914 (from Lowe: *Mastering Modern World History*)

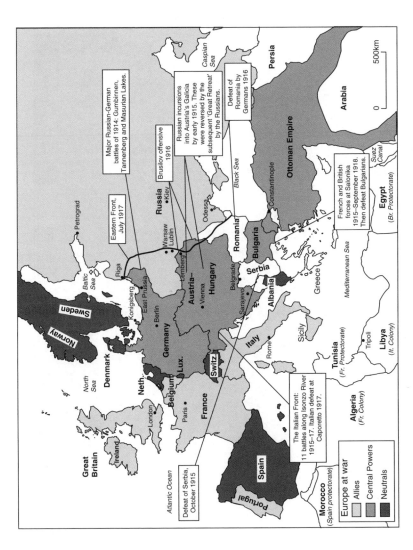

Map 2 The War in Eastern Europe (adapted from Lowe: *Mastering Modern World History*)

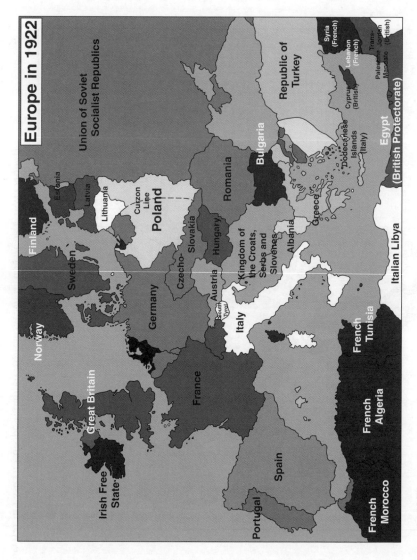

Map 3 Europe in 1922

Territory lost by Germany

Former territory of tsarist Russia

Austria-Hungary until 1918

●●●●●●●●●●●● Curzon Line – proposed by Britain (Dec. 1919) as Poland's eastern frontier. Russian territory east of the line was seized by Poland in 1920

Map 4   European frontiers after WW1

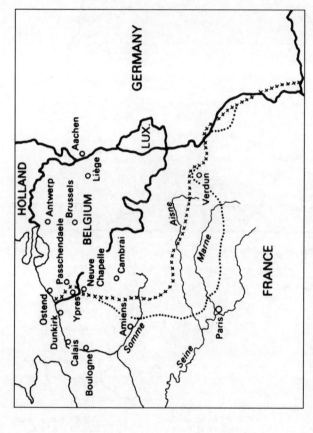

...... Limit of the German advance in 1914

×××××× The trench line for most of the war

Map 5   The Western Front (from Lowe: *Mastering Modern World History*)

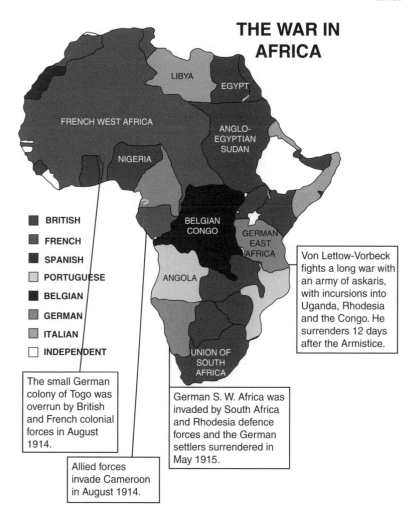

THE WAR IN AFRICA

LIBYA

EGYPT

FRENCH WEST AFRICA

ANGLO-EGYPTIAN SUDAN

NIGERIA

BELGIAN CONGO

GERMAN EAST AFRICA

ANGOLA

UNION OF SOUTH AFRICA

- BRITISH
- FRENCH
- SPANISH
- PORTUGUESE
- BELGIAN
- GERMAN
- ITALIAN
- INDEPENDENT

Von Lettow-Vorbeck fights a long war with an army of askaris, with incursions into Uganda, Rhodesia and the Congo. He surrenders 12 days after the Armistice.

The small German colony of Togo was overrun by British and French colonial forces in August 1914.

Allied forces invade Cameroon in August 1914.

German S. W. Africa was invaded by South Africa and Rhodesia defence forces and the German settlers surrendered in May 1915.

Map 6   The War in Africa

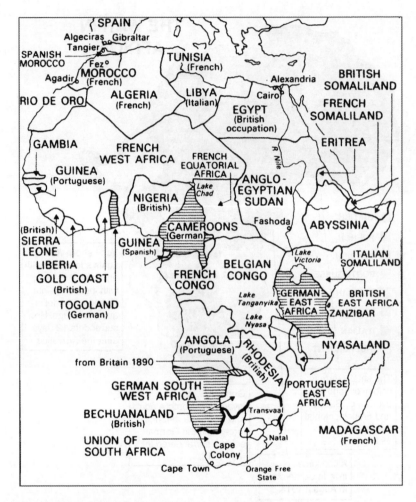

══ German colonies taken away as mandates by the
══ Versailles Treaty, 1919

Map 7 Africa and the peace treaties (from Lowe: *Mastering Modern World History*)

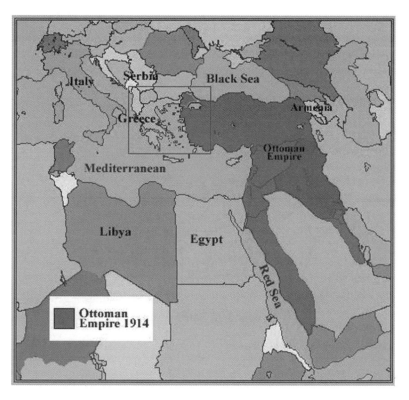

Map 8   Ottoman Empire 1914 (from National Archive)

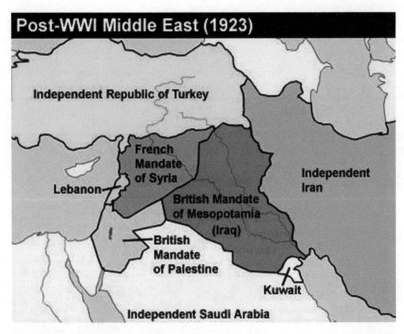

Map 9   Post-WW1 Middle East

Introduction

More books have been written and more theories propounded about the causes of the First World War than about any other war in world history. This is not surprising as the horrors of the conflict continue to shock, while its long-term effects changed the structure and balance of power in the world, and we are still living with the consequences.

It might have been expected that interest in the war would evaporate over time: that after the Second World War, interest in the previous war would dwindle; or that once the last servicemen who had survived the conflict had died its place in the memory and national consciousness of the combatant nations would fade. Yet, interest in the Great War, in what was to those who lived through it, has continued to grow: novels, films and TV documentaries dealing with the war attract large audiences, while thousands visit the graves of those buried close to where they fell in battle, tour the battlefields, visit war museums, or research the war records for evidence of grandparents' or great-grandparents' part in the war.

My own fascination with the First World War began in one of those treasured days experienced by every schoolchild, when they are kept at home by some mild illness. I discovered on my parents' bookshelf the numerous volumes of *The Great War Illustrated. Album de Luxe,* one of the many such series published during the war. What intrigued me was not just the photographs of trenches, mud, tanks, artillery, and men in grey or khaki uniforms, but the images of cavalry with swords and lances and of kings, emperors and generals in plumed helmets. I preferred the latter group, for these images of war were more attractive. In retrospect, I realise that what I had been attracted to was the end of one form of warfare and the emergence of the distinctly less glamorous and harder, more ruthless, technological wars of the twentieth century; perhaps, as well, the replacement of an old world by a greyer successor.

The First World War marked both the end of Europe's dominant position in the world and the eclipse of a Europe in which national states had competed, but also cooperated. Neither development was envisaged by the statesmen who led their countries to war in 1914, nor were they apparent in 1918, but when Sir Edward Grey saw 'the lamps going out all over Europe' he was watching, though he little realised it, the dying flickers of an imperfect, though in many ways admirable, civilisation. The nineteenth century had seen the apogee of European power and influence and it was, for better or worse, the First World War that made the twentieth century the 'American Century'.

The term, 'First World War', I used to assume, had come into use to replace the 'Great War' during and after the Second World War; in fact, though not often used, it was extant before 1918. Although it can be argued that in terms of the campaigns which determined the war's outcome it was essentially a European war which spread to the continent's periphery and the colonial possessions of the belligerents, and brought in the United States, it was a *world* war in its impact and the *first* to have such a worldwide effect. In world-political terms it was probably more important than the Second World War in that it began the decline of Europe's position and because we can see the two world wars as, basically, one great war of the twentieth century.

The combination of the war itself, the peace settlement, and the wars and civil wars in its immediate aftermath did much to create the world of the twenty-first century. In the long run it did much to bring about the end of the great European empires, to imbue a new national consciousness in the British dominions, and to prepare the way for America's future role as a world power. The relevance of the war to the contemporary world can be seen by a glance at the political map of the world as it is today, for so many of the lines demarking states and their boundaries are the result of it, as are the trouble spots. Three of them, the Balkans, the Middle East and the frontiers of Russia effectively make the case for the relevance of the First World War to the problems of the present.

The Balkans, where the conflicting aspirations of ethnic groups interacted with the ambitions and fears of the great powers to provide the scenario which led to war in 1914, continue to be a European fault line, as crises in Bosnia and Kosovo demonstrated in the 1990s.

Perhaps more serious threats to international stability are the contested frontiers of Russia. The defeat of Tsarist Russia and the consequent Russian revolutions led to the Treaty of Brest-Litovsk of 1918, which redrew the map of Eastern Europe at the expense of Russia's frontiers and, although the Second World War largely reversed these changes, the 'after-glow' of Brest-Litovsk was visible when, with the implosion of the Soviet Union in 1991, several hitherto constituent parts, including Latvia, Estonia, Lithuania and Ukraine, achieved independence. Many observers have seen Vladimir Putin's policies, particularly with regard to the Crimea and the Ukraine as a whole, as an attempt to reverse Russia's loss of territory.

The map of the Middle East, one of the world's major trouble spots, remains much as it was arranged by the war and the Versailles Settlement in the wake of the dissolution of the Ottoman Empire. Without the First World War it is unlikely that Israel, Jordan, Syria, Lebanon or Iraq would exist, at any rate in their present, or recent, forms. The exception is Turkey, yet, although the rise of Turkey as a national state owed most to its own endeavours and success in defying Versailles and repelling Greece, much of the impetus came from defeat in the Great War. The division of the Middle East at the end of the war may not have been edifying, but, as the work of Sykes–Picot, T.E. Lawrence, and Gertrude Bell falls apart, the world trembles.

Of course, it may be asserted that all subsequent historical developments cannot be put down to the First World War, but if we see the First and Second World Wars and, indeed, the Cold War as inextricably linked, then Thomas Mann's view that with its beginning 'so much began that has scarcely yet left off beginning' is compelling. What he wrote in 1924 is still true today.

Chapter 1:   Why Did It Begin?

The First World War was not the *first* great European war for, since the Thirty Years War of the seventeenth century, there had been several major wars involving all the great powers of Europe, and some had spread from Europe to involve the overseas possessions of the combatants. But it was the first fratricidal and general European war since the French Revolutionary and Napoleonic Wars. Those wars had lasted more than two decades, interrupted by only a brief period of peace after the Treaty of Amiens.

The First World War was, by comparison, a relatively short war, but it came after decades of respite from a general European war and after nearly forty years of peace with their neighbours for the populations of Western Europe. It did not, of course, seem a short war to those who fought in it, and, indeed, was only such if we consider it as a discrete and a separate war from the Second World War. Many historians now, however, consider the two wars as one, and essentially, a 'Thirty Years War' of the twentieth century, a war interrupted by 21 years of peace.[1]

The proclivity of Europe for major wars can be exaggerated for, despite the ambitions of monarchs and nations, there were always brakes on the temptation to resort to arms and obstacles in the way of any one power achieving hegemony. As A.J.P. Taylor wrote, the continent 'has known almost as much peace as war; and it has owed these periods of peace to the Balance of Power'.[2] Always threatened by the rise of a power with the potential to become dominant, the see-saw's balance was maintained time and time again by alliances whose combined weight re-established it. Thus, the wars of the eighteenth century and the French Revolutionary and Napoleonic Wars had seen coalitions formed against France, then the most powerful state in Europe.

4

Although there was an ideological dimension to the wars between 1792 and 1815, there were continuities between the Seven Years War and those fought against the French Republic and the Napoleonic Empire. One was the position of France as the most formidable and populous of European states – one in five Europeans in early nineteenth-century Europe was French – and the way that the other great continental powers combined against French ambitions. Another was the position of Britain as a maritime and successful colonising power with wide extra-European interests which supported continental coalitions against France, sometimes with armies in Europe, but, perennially, by reinforcing its allies and weakening its enemies via its naval and economic power.

The perception of France as the power most likely to strive for European hegemony lasted until its defeat by a Prussian-led coalition of German states in 1870, but this period did not see a major war between states. Europe survived the year of revolutions of 1848 without a war between states; the Crimean War was fought on the continent's periphery, and such major developments as Italian unification and Prussia's defeat of Austria did not lead to pan-European conflict.

The victory of Germany in the Franco-Prussian War and the proclamation of the German Empire profoundly altered the European balance of power. France's defeat surprised contemporaries, as it had continued to be regarded as the most powerful state in continental Europe as well as the most aggressive. It is indicative that British expenditure on defence was at a nineteenth-century peacetime high in the 1860s largely because of distrust of French ambitions. After 1871 it was clear that it was the newly unified Germany that had the population, the military strength, and the economy to make it, potentially, the greatest power in continental Europe. Yet, the view that European peace was endangered by the replacement of France by Germany as the foremost continental power has been much influenced by retrospective thinking. Russia was seen by many British statesmen as a bigger threat than Germany to British interests and to European stability, and the idea of a German threat has to be set against the fact that 1871–1914 was a peaceful period for most of Europe; a time in which wars and crises were contained by the capacity of the great powers to reach agreements. Why, then, did the European powers go to war in 1914?

It has become conventional to make a distinction between the long-term and the immediate causes of the war, or between the 'structural' and 'contingent' causes, but such divisions are simplistic and some of what are usually seen as immediate causes were manifestations of enduring problems.

An Unstable Europe?

The concept of a structurally unstable Europe, its instability made more dangerous by the opposed alliances it produced, is not only the factor usually cited as the main long-term cause of the war, but it acts as an umbrella for other factors placed in the same category of long-term causes: nationalism, imperialism, the arms race and economic rivalry.

Germany's defeat of France in 1870–71 and the emergence of a powerful German Empire certainly altered the European balance of power but did not necessarily make a general war more likely. The loss of Alsace and Lorraine to Germany after the Franco-Prussian War may well have meant that France would be permanently hostile to the new German state, but Bismarck's recognition of this, along with his claims that Germany had no further territorial ambitions, led to a German foreign policy that aimed at French containment. By no means confident in the strength of Germany's position, he sought security in alliances and declared that it was his intention to 'try to be one of three as long as the world is governed by an unstable equilibrium of five powers', which he clearly believed to be Germany, Austria-Hungary, France, Russia and Britain. The *Dreikaiserbund* or Three Emperors' Agreement of 1873, put into practice Bismarck's policy of isolating France and bound his trio, Germany, Austria-Hungary, and Russia, to consult together on differences that might arise between them and on what action to take in the event of an attack on any one of them.

The Dreikaiserbund had a basic contradiction in that two of the partners, Austria-Hungary and Russia, had major differences with each other, and it was allowed to lapse after Russia felt that she had been badly let down by her allies at the Congress of Berlin in 1878, at which Russia lost many of the gains she had made after her war with Turkey. The Dual Alliance with Austria in 1879 seemed to suggest that Bismarck had finally chosen between his erstwhile partners and was prepared to support Austria in the event of a future Austro-Russian war, but he continued to believe that good relations with Russia were essential for German security and achieved the near-impossible by drawing Russia into a renewed Dreikaiserbund in 1881 and further extending his system of alliances with the Triple Alliance, which brought Italy into alliance with Germany and Austria-Hungary in 1882 with Romania becoming a rather uncertain partner in the following year.

Italy's decision to ally itself with Austria-Hungary, the power which had been the main opponent of Italian unity and which still ruled territory (the Tyrol, Trieste, and Fiume) which Italian nationalists saw as *Italia irredenta,* may seem surprising, but as well as the desire for Austro-Hungarian territory, Italy had ambitions in the Mediterranean and North Africa, which conflicted with those of France. To some extent the Triple Alliance was engineered by Bismarck to give security to his most reliable ally on its southern frontier by encouraging Italy's Mediterranean ambitions and distracting her from her similar desire for Austrian territory. The Reinsurance Treaty of 1887 between Germany and Russia, in which the two states promised not to attack one another, though benevolent neutrality would not apply if Russia attacked Austria or Germany attacked France, may well have been an act of 'political bigamy' or 'a fraud on the Russians'[3] by a Germany wedded to Austria, but it indicated Bismarck's desire for peace and was a warning to Austria to act with caution.

One authority has seen the result of Bismarck's alliance system as building a European peace resting, 'not on a balance but on a complex system of alignments that eventually bound all the powers, except for France, directly or indirectly to Bismarck's Germany'.[4] Another view is that it, 'achieved two essential objects: it effectively deprived France of any continental ally and it established the German Empire as a 'responsible and respectable state, eager to uphold the new *status quo*'.[5] It was essentially conservative in that its main aim was to preserve the Germany the Chancellor had done so much to create. Its weakness lay in the reliance upon Austria-Hungary; for a strong state to rely upon a weaker partner can result in the strong becoming entangled in the problems of the weak.

Germany's *Weltpolitik*

Bismarck's system was dismantled after Kaiser Wilhelm II came to the imperial throne, dismissed his Chancellor in 1890, and with his new Chancellor, Count Leo von Caprivi, and a permanent official of the foreign ministry, Friedrich von Holstein – who is often seen as the real architect of policy until 1906 – initiated a 'new course' in foreign policy which reflected a basic change in the nature of Germany's self image. While Bismarck had seen the German Empire that he had done much to create as a strong but conservative and satisfied power with no expansionist ambitions, the new course in foreign policy which developed in the 1890s envisaged the Reich as a power which had not yet achieved a place commensurate with its economic and military strength, and which needed to find dynamic and radical means to realise its potential. The two main planks of Bismarck's policy, the need to keep France isolated and the maintenance of good relations with Russia, were discarded. When the Reinsurance Treaty was not renewed, Russia, seeing its position in Eastern Europe threatened by Germany's commitment to Austria-Hungary, came to welcome approaches from France. By 1894, a formal alliance between republican France and conservative tsarist Russia had brought about the very situation that Bismarck had sought to prevent.

The new German foreign policy can be seen as, like the Kaiser himself, febrile, erratic and disastrous in that it resulted in bringing into being an alliance between an implacable enemy and the most populous state in Europe. It thus exposed Germany to the danger of a war on two frontiers, with only one firm ally, Austria-Hungary, widely considered a power in decline with major problems which threatened its stability. Could Germany win such a war? The first commanders-in-chief of the German Great General Staff, Helmuth von Moltke (the Elder) and Count Alfred von Waldersee, had considered the possibility of a war against both France and Russia and had concluded that, rather than an attack against a heavily fortified France, the best plan would be a defensive war in the west and an offensive against Russia. Count von Schlieffen, who succeeded von Waldersee in 1891, began to consider the alternative strategy of an offensive against France. Coming up against the near-impossibility of an assault upon France's massive frontier defences, he proposed in 1894 a scheme for outflanking them by advancing through Luxembourg and the southern tip of Belgium, the genesis of his 'Great Memorandum' of 1905 and what became known as the Schlieffen Plan.

German policy from 1892 was consciously based on the possibility of a war with France and Russia, though this did not mean one was intended. There was, however, no expectation by German policy-makers of a war in which Germany was opposed by Britain as well as France and Russia and, indeed, it was implicit in this scenario that an understanding with Britain would at least ensure British neutrality. It is important, therefore, not to read the *neue Kurs* from the viewpoint of 1914–15 and Britain's entry into the war on the side of France and Russia, together with the defection of Italy from the Triple Alliance. German policy was, in the 1890s, based on the expectation that conflicting Italian and French ambitions in the Mediterranean would keep Italy in the Triple Alliance, that Anglo-French disputes over North Africa would militate against any understanding between Britain and France, and, above all, that Britain's opposition to Russia's imperial ambitions in the Near East and central Asia would endure and might even bring Britain into the Triple Alliance. Such expectations were optimistic but not unreasonable. Indeed, the main question throughout the 1890s was whether Britain's policy of isolation could be maintained in the face of her many commitments and seemingly endemic conflicts of interest with France and Russia, or whether a need for allies would result in entry to the Triple Alliance, a question which divided the cautious and pragmatic policies of Lord Salisbury from that of the restless and adventurous approach of Joseph Chamberlain.

Some of the rhetoric of the new German foreign policy suggested aims that went far beyond the search of a major continental power for security, and some of the pronouncements of German politicians had a neo-Darwinist tone, with talk of 'a struggle for survival' and fears that Germany, surrounded by enemies, might be weakening. For instance, there was the comment of Bernhard von Bülow (Foreign Secretary 1897–1900 and Chancellor 1900–1909) in a speech to the Reichstag in 1909, that, 'in the coming century Germany will either be the hammer or the anvil'. Admittedly, a similar tone can be detected in the views of some British politicians and diplomats. The language of German policy-makers has been seen as reinforcing other evidence gathered by those historians who have seen the new course in German foreign policy as a grasp for world power by an inherently expansionist nation prepared for war,[6] but exactly what *Weltpolitik* or the pursuit of *Weltmacht* (world power) was meant to achieve is uncertain. It has been described as 'the antithesis of *Realpolitik*, in substituting grandiose and ill-defined aims for limited definable gains'.[7] It was the demand for colonies and for a strong navy, energetically pursued by von Bülow and Admiral von Tirpitz, that created British fears of German ambitions. The passage of a Navy Bill through the Reichstag in 1898, which provided for a massive long-term construction programme, seemed to suggest to British statesmen that Germany was bent on becoming an imperial and maritime rival. As Norman Stone has argued, 'The last thing that Germany needed was a problem with Britain, and the greatest mistake of the twentieth century was made when Germany built a navy designed to attack her.'[8] British suspicions of Germany were exacerbated by the Kaiser's love–hatred for his grandmother's kingdom and empire, which resulted in his vociferous support for the Boers, the settlers of mainly Dutch descent with whom Britain fought the South-African War of 1900–1902.

The Anglo-French and Anglo-Russian Ententes

German confidence that British problems and interests would ineluc-tably result in Britain coming to an understanding with Germany was confounded. Anglo-French and Anglo-Russian differences were resolved and the entente with France of 1904 and that with Russia in 1907 left Germany and the Triple Alliance facing a much stronger combination of potential enemies than Bismarck had ever envisaged. This was only partially due to the resolution of Britain's differences with France and Russia, for what turned 'ententes', largely aimed at resolving imperial problems, into firmer understandings with an anti-German thrust were the policies of Weltpolitik and, in particular, Germany's naval building programme. German policy-makers made the fatal mistake of believing that the best way to bring Britain into the Triple Alliance was to frighten her with a menacing show of strength.

The ententes, as the agreements Britain came to with France and Russia are called, were not, originally, made with any anti-German intentions on Britain's part, but were, rather, a recognition by British statesmen that the Empire's multiple commitments and interests were, increasingly beyond Britain's military and economic strength. Britain was concerned to limit her commitments and the agreements were exercises in appeasement, designed to ward off potential crises.

The entente between Britain and France tends to be given more attention by British historians than the subsequent agreement with Russia, but British statesmen in the 1890s were far more worried about the implications of Britain's poor relations with Russia than about those with France. Anglo-French enmity centred on North Africa and on Britain's control of Egypt and although the Fashoda incident, when the sending of a French expeditionary force into the Sudan in 1898 nearly led to a clash between British and French troops, aroused bellicose language in Paris, the view from London was largely that disputes with France were a nuisance rather than a threat as the military balance in the Mediterranean and North Africa was very much in Britain's favour. Russian ambitions in the Near East and Central Asia were a more serious matter: Could Britain deal with a Russian advance into Persia or an invasion of India? Did Russia's penetration of Manchuria and designs on Korea threaten vital British interests in the Far East? Should Britain, while Russia's century old designs on Constantinople and the Straits were still extant, stick to or revise her traditional policy of propping up the Ottoman Empire?

Britain's problems with Russian expansionism in the Far East were largely solved by the unexpected emergence of an Asian state, Japan, as a formidable military and naval power. Despite not believing that the Japanese were strong enough to triumph in a war with Russia, Britain had negotiated an alliance with Japan in 1902, which relieved some of the pressure on the Royal Navy as it strove to fulfil manifold global commitments. Russia, however, persisted in its forward policy in the Far East, which resulted in the Russo-Japanese War. The defeat of Russia by Japan in 1905 effectively discredited those in Russia who had been arguing that the country's future lay in expansion in the Far East and Central Asia. Japan's destruction of the Russian Baltic Fleet at the Battle of Tsushima, in which the Japanese Imperial Navy bene-fitted from British naval advice, left Japan in undisputed command of the sea vis-á-vis Russia and was followed by an extension of the Anglo-Japanese Alliance, which included India and promised British support for Japan if she was attacked by Russia, a prospect that was, however, made less likely by the moderate terms of the 1905 Treaty of Portsmouth which ended the Russo-Japanese war, and by Russia's weakened state. Christopher Clark has seen the defeat of Russia in the Russo-Japanese War as, 'The Great Turning Point' in that it marked the end of Russia's expansionist policy in Asia and the Far East and made her more amenable to settling differences with Britain. In addition, it certainly inclined Russia to view better relations between France and Britain in a more positive light.[9]

The entente between Britain and France, signed in 1904 and negotiated while the Russo-Japanese War was still continuing, was not an alliance and it was not directed against Germany. Its subsequent importance has obscured its purpose and its significance at the time. Its original purpose was the settlement of a wide range of colonial disputes, the most important of which concerned Egypt, where British control had long been opposed by France, and Morocco, where the French aspired to hegemony. The agreement did much to improve Anglo-French relations, but the view taken of it by the Balfour govern-ment has been described by John Charmley as 'a welcome limitation of Britain's liabilities, but by no means a vital or indispensable part of a new course in British foreign policy'.[10]

It was the blundering handling of the Moroccan Crisis of 1905 by both the German and French governments which moved the entente closer to something approaching an alliance. By 1905, German attempts to form new relationships with Russia and Britain had made no progress. The attempt by the Kaiser to secure a Russo-German agreement by monarch-to-monarch talks with the Tsar at Bjorko had been overruled by the Russian government, and the expansion of the German navy had provoked Britain into building more powerful warships, rather than being forced into an alliance with Germany. Overestimating the importance of the Anglo-French agreement, von Bülow reacted to attempts to strengthen France's control over

Morocco by persuading the Kaiser, while on a Mediterranean cruise, to land in Tangier and make a declaration of support for Moroccan independence. Having substantially got the better of the crisis and even caused the dismissal of Delcassé, the French foreign minister, von Bülow threw away the chance of an agreement by insisting on an international conference, which, when it met at Algeciras in January 1906, came down largely on the side of France. Most importantly, by the end of 1905, not only had German overtures to Russia failed, but Britain had come much closer to making the entente a tacit alliance by agreeing to military discussions with the French general staff.

The French had been satisfied, but Russia, even after the Russo-Japanese War, was a greater threat to British interests. The Anglo-Russian agreement of 1907, like the Anglo-French entente, was a settlement of long-standing differences and was even further from being an alliance. It was a cautious and partial attempt to reconcile the two powers' interests in central Asia. It did, however, undermine, as Gordon Martel has observed, 'the foundations of German strategy, which had assumed that Britain and Russia would remain enemies and that this would eventually take one or other of them into the German camp as a subordinate ally'.[11]

The main driver of German policy since the dismissal of Bismarck had been frustration with the limitations of the Germany which he had done so much to create. Germany was by far the strongest European power in military and economic terms, though successive German leaders were often as conscious of what they saw as the state's vulnerability as its strength. Bismarck's policies were designed to reinforce security by keeping potential enemies isolated. Germany was a central European power and a power in the centre must necessarily be surrounded, though not necessarily by enemies; the centre is also a difficult place from which to expand. It can be argued that the policies of Wilhelm II and von Bülow were illogical. Germany did not wish to expand at the expense of its immediate neighbours, but German leaders felt constrained by the Empire's central European position, while other powers, with their colonial possessions, exercised a greater international influence. The expansion of the German navy has been seen as part of a desire to project German power world-wide, but the fleet built by Tirpitz was relatively short-range and designed to operate in the North Sea. It was widely seen by the British as a challenge to the Royal Navy, and many historians have, like William Mulligan, argued that Weltpolitik aimed to challenge Britain's position as the leading world power'.[12] To some extent the foreign policy of Bismarck had been in the interests of the conservative landed class of Prussia, satisfied with a Germany which dominated central Europe, while the radical world power policy can be seen as popular with business and urban interests which became more influential as the nation industrialised. These interests played a prominent part in the organisation and support of the Navy League and the Colonial Society.

By 1907, it was becoming clear that Germany's new course in foreign policy had failed. Arguably the failure was inevitable and, as a continental power, Germany's influence lay in its having the most efficient European economy and most modern army, while a more sensible policy would have been to mend relations with Russia. The attempt to rival Britain as a naval power, which was pursued even more enthusiastically after Algeciras, failed, and the Kaiser's comment, intended to suggest to the French that they should not rely upon Britain, that 'navies don't have wheels', might have been turned round as a comment upon the misdirected nature of German policy.

By 1907, the relative fluidity of the late 1880s had been replaced by a bipolar Europe separated into two alliances. That a great war would follow was far from inevitable, for several minor crises had been settled by diplomacy, but the danger that a crisis involving the essential interests of one or more great powers could, if mishandled, lead to a major conflict had increased. None of the great powers was bent upon war, never mind a cataclysmic war, and all laboured under the impression that were weaker than their rivals, whose strength they overestimated. German policy may have been clumsy, but if, other powers reacted to German moves, equally Germany reacted to the moves of others. The Agadir crisis of 1911 is an example of this. Germany had a good case as the cause of the crisis was the tightening of French control over Morocco, contrary to the terms of the 1906 Treaty of Algeciras, but the German response, the dispatch of the gun-boat, *Panther*, to Agadir in 1911 could be seen as provocative. Germany's aim was not to prevent Morocco falling under full French authority, but to demonstrate that Germany could not be ignored, nor the French violate international agreements unilaterally, and to gain concessions, but the action backfired. When the Germans demanded nearly all the French Congo as an exchange for their interests in Morocco, the British government interpreted it as an attempt to browbeat France and a demonstration of German power. What became an international crisis was more about Franco-German relations and a test of the strength of the Anglo-French entente than whether France should control Morocco, a country in which Germany had only a minor interest. The British attitude was influenced by the anti-German clique in the foreign office, although the foreign secretary, Sir Edward Grey, was more

cautious. The intervention by David Lloyd George, hitherto regarded
as a radical opponent of bellicose foreign policies, in a speech at the
Mansion House, in which he warned that British interests should
not be ignored, marked a stiffening, indeed a new interpretation, of
British support for the agreement with France of 1904 and a hostility to Germany influenced by Germany's challenge to British naval
supremacy. In the end, Germany was awarded two fairly useless strips
of the French Congo in return for recognising a French protectorate
in Morocco, while the price they paid was pushing the loose entente
rather closer to an unofficial alliance.

The hostility between Germany and the Entente powers had thus
increased, but options had not closed. Relations between Britain and
Germany appeared to improve between 1911 and 1914, while Anglo-
Russian relations deteriorated as a consequence of disputes over
Persia. It seemed clear, however, that the great powers were unlikely
to go to war over colonial disputes.

Nationalism, Imperialism and Economic Rivalry

A concentration upon diplomacy, international politics and alliances
may, many would argue, distract attention from fundamental forces
and developments which drove the ambitions and fears of states. By
the late nineteenth century, monarchs, presidents, and ministers
could no longer treat foreign policy as a cool game of chess in which
the fortunes of dynasties and states were directed until a check-
mate provided the occasion for a strategic retreat. Even in the least
democratic of states public opinion and popular emotions had to be
taken account of, while in France and Britain they were a formidable
influence on foreign policy, often for the worse. Lord Salisbury, who
probably had the best mind of any contemporary statesmen, despised
public opinion and democracy but, ever the realist, recognised
their power: 'We live no longer, alas, in Pitt's time ... the aristocracy
governed then and we were able to form an active policy, which
made England after the Congress of Vienna the richest and most
respected power in Europe. Now democracy is on top.'[13] The most
effective brake upon rash actions lay, ironically, in the community of
interests in foreign offices and diplomacy, perhaps the last area of
cosmopolitan aristocratic influence. Most diplomats saw their duty
as to further the interests of the nations they represented within the
bounds of realistic advantage, and within the limits of the pursuit of
reasonable settlements which would maintain international peace.

Unfortunately, the world of diplomacy was increasingly subject to national politics, political and military intervention, political appointments and the influence of domestic pressure groups.

As one authority on the war's origins has put it, 'Among the tectonic plates shaping the context of international politics, none loomed as dangerous and irrational as rampant, virulent, passion-filled nationalism.'[14] Nationalism had emerged as an important force in the first half of the nineteenth century. It has been seen as a result of improved physical and printed communications which created what one authority has called 'imagined communities';[15] people were able to relate to societies wider than their village, town or region as state education and military service ironed out linguistic differences and national languages emerged. Until late in the nineteenth century, nationalism was generally seen as in tune with economic and political liberalism but, as mass societies developed, it became more aligned with ideas of race, more dependent on opposition to alternative nationalisms, and more inclined to replace free trade with protectionism. In states which encompassed several national groups, of which Austria-Hungary is the prime, but not the only, example, and where borders conflicted with national or racial boundaries, it posed a threat to stability.

Norman Angell's argument that Europe's economies were too interlocked and interdependent to permit a war between the major powers[16] was persuasive to contemporaries and indeed seems sensible in retrospect. The only problem with it is that, of course, a war did start. The contrary view is that of Lenin and other Marxists: wars between capitalist states are the consequence of imperialist economic rivalries and are caused by capitalist interests or, as Frederick Ebert, the German Social Democrat, put it at the Stuttgart Conference of the Second International in 1907, war would result as 'the result of their rivalry for world markets'.

That economic interdependence did not prevent the war does not, however, mean that economic rivalry was responsible for it, nor does the fact that there were business and industrial interests, particularly armaments manufacturers, iron and steel manufacturers and shipbuilders, which could be represented as likely to profit from war, prove that they were able to impel governments towards war (even if some of them were organised in lobbying governments). Bankers and financiers were appalled at the prospect of war and feared a general conflagration would end international trade; further, many businessmen and industrialists had interests across national frontiers.

If imperial rivalry had been likely to cause a war, then we may ask why the most acute of such rivalries, Franco-British in North Africa and Anglo-Russian in Asia, had, far from ending in war, been settled by diplomatic means, while Britain had largely appeased Germany in the latter's search for colonies and German sabre-rattling over Morocco had ended in grumbling acquiescence at French control. It could, alternatively, be argued that it was the very settlement of colonial disputes that moved tensions away from the periphery and back to east-central Europe in the immediate pre-war years.

Arms Race

Sir Edward Grey in his memoirs[17] wrote that, 'great armaments lead inevitably to war', and this was a popular view after 1918, though, as an alternative cliché has it, 'guns do not go off by themselves'. Perhaps it was not so much armaments as war planning which made for the war. Weapons and the uses planned for them are subject to strategy, though the development of new or improved forms of weaponry can alter strategies. Military planning became ever more a profession during the nineteenth century. During peacetime, general staffs and admiralties had to justify their existence by planning for future wars whether they sought to launch them or not. Staff colleges and military academies were dedicated to the training of officers within the parameters of such planning and in the tactics and the use of weapons with which they were to be pursued. High commands and governments were influenced by geopolitical philosophers and historians who put forward views on the rise and fall of nations and the relative importance of sea power and armies.

Then, there is the question as to whether military and the political approaches to national security and national aims became too closely associated, with the attendant question of whether the civilian governments were really in control of the general staffs. In Germany the direct relationship of the Kaiser with armed forces came dangerously close to endangering the control of the government over foreign affairs; Annika Mombauer has argued that senior army officers exercised too much control over political decisions.[18] Yet, despite the Emperor's ostensible leadership role there was little co-operation on policy even between the army and navy, and William Mulligan has concluded that until 1914: 'The evidence suggests that the civilian leaders, from Bismarck to Bethmann Hollweg, were able to prevent the generals from taking crucial decisions.'[19]

The notion of a Europe in the grip of militarism may well be largely a myth. Only in Serbia, where the military continually intervened, and in the Ottoman Empire, where, after the 'Young Turks' led a revolution in 1908, the army was always a significant political factor, can we see policy dictated by generals. In Britain, the only major power to eschew conscription and where army officers did not wear uniform off duty, continental societies could appear obsessed with their armed forces, but in no major power were the generals in charge. There were military plans for possible wars, but little in the way of a co-ordinated national policy bringing together governments, foreign offices and the armed services in most states, and this lack of co-ordination may have been a greater problem than military influence. Britain's Committee of Imperial Defence (CID), an advisory body set up in 1902, was the nearest any state came to providing a forum in which ministers and senior officers discussed military planning, but the ministers who belonged to it kept its discussions secret from other cabinet members, while the Royal Navy stood aloof from its proceedings.

Since the Dreyfus affair, French politicians and army officers had viewed each other with suspicion, while: 'the ministry of foreign affairs protected its independence through habits of secrecy. Sensitive information was only rarely released to cabinet ministers. It was not unusual for senior functionaries to withhold information from the most senior politicians, even from the president of the Republic himself.'[20] In Russia, foreign policy changed constantly as the influence of ministers waxed and waned. In theory the Tsar was in control, but in practice the foreign minister, the prime minister and ambassadors, conservatives, pan-Slavists, and liberals jostled for influence. Ambassadors, in particular, were a threat to coherence, with those in Constantinople and Belgrade pursuing their own initiatives, while in Paris, Alexander Izvolski, the previous foreign minister, still pursued an agenda contrary to the policies of his successor, Sergei Sazonov.

The impact of geopolitical pundits was considerable. One highly influential writer was Alfred Thayer Mahan, a US naval officer and naval historian. In his *The Influence of Sea Power upon History, 1660–1783* (1890), he argued that the rise of British power demonstrated that command of the seas was the key to world power status. It was the Royal Navy which had enabled, by its control of the seas, what had been a relatively minor European power in the seventeenth century to become a great empire and a leading world power by the nineteenth century. Powerful navies were thus, according to Mahan, essential to great powers as they provided them with the ability to control sea lanes and to mount blockades.

A contradictory thesis was put forward by the geopolitician, Halford J Mackinder, who argued that, although sea power had indeed been the key to success in a period of European expansion overseas, this period was drawing to a close. The expansion of European influence and power into the rest of the world continued with almost all of Africa carved up, China seemingly about to share its fate and the American continent under the control of Europeans who had emigrated there, but this 'Columbian period' of history was about to end. In a paper, 'The geographical pivot of history', read to the Royal Geographic Society in 1904, he expressed the view that the end of Europe expansion would see a dominance of continental powers, with the advantage going to the larger states in terms both of geography and population and those who were most efficient in harnessing their industry and resources.[21]

One implication of Mackinder's thesis was that such a development would see Europe bringing its rivalries home instead of fighting wars overseas. Defeats and setbacks far from home could be swallowed and result in compromise; not just minor humiliations at the hands of Zulus or in North Africa, but even a major defeat such as that of Russia by Japan. Wars in Europe might, conversely, become struggles for survival. The later Leninist view of the First World War as an imperialist war can, if we follow Mackinder's logic, be turned on its head: the war is then seen as a result of the first episodes of a waning of imperialism. For Mackinder, the future would see the dominance of the largest states in terms of geography and population and those which were most efficient in harnessing their industry and resources. The great strategical 'pivot area' of the world was central Russia which, before the age of overseas expansion and colonisation, had been the 'heartland' and, with industrialisation, railways and more efficient agricultural development, would become so again.

The impact of these two contrary theses on naval and military planning had consequences.[22] The USA, with little fear of invasion, would, no doubt, have opted for a strong navy and a small army without the benefit of its admiral's thesis, and Mahan confirmed, rather than initiated, Britain's traditional reliance on its navy; but in Germany Bülow and Tirpitz were influenced by Mahan's view that naval strength and in particular the concentration of sea-borne might in battle fleets, was the key to world power, with results that were deleterious to Germany's position. Indeed, as a central continental power Germany might have found the Mackinder thesis more suited to its interests. The result of the Weltpolitik policy was to alienate Britain and result in a naval building competition, which Germany lost, and the consequent diversion of resources from the army.

War Plans

It is the duty of general staffs to make plans for all contingencies, and, inevitably, senior commanders conceive of strategies for the most likely scenarios, wars with their countries' most obvious possible opponents, The German general staff had for long been aware that a war with France and Russia would mean a war on two fronts in which Germany would not necessarily have the largest armies. The plan of the elder von Moltke had, as we have seen, been to fight a defensive war against France, while aiming to crush Russia, but his successors as Chief of the General Staff, von Waldersee and then von Schlieffen, reversed this. 'We can only', Waldersee argued, 'be strong and superior in one place; the defeat of France and her western allies is the most important.'[23] The plan drawn up by the long-serving General Count von Schlieffen reflected this analysis: it provided for a rapid offensive against France while German armies in the east were to fight defensively against Russia, prior to full-scale offensive once France had been defeated. The snag was France's formidable frontier forts, and the answer was to violate the neutrality of Luxembourg and Belgium and thus outflank these fortifications. By 1905, he had decided that almost two-thirds of the German army should be dedicated to a vast wheeling movement which would advance through Holland and Belgium and cross the Franco-Belgian frontier. This force, a preponderant right wing, would eventually envelop Paris and drive the French armies towards the weaker German left wing, which would advance from Alsace-Lorraine; the French forces would then be crushed in a decisive battle after a six-week campaign.

That there ever was a 'Schlieffen Plan', in the sense of a single and formally adopted military plan, has been questioned, and one military historian has argued that Schlieffen's 'Great Memorandum', far from being a blueprint for an offensive against France as part of a two-front war, was in reality designed to make the case for expansion of the German army by demonstrating the difficulties of even a war against France alone.[24] Nevertheless, the military movements launched by the nephew of the 'elder' von Moltke in August 1914 do have a broad resemblance to those mooted by his predecessor.

Certainly, later critics of Schlieffen have pointed to the inconsistencies in the 'Memorandum', and John Keegan has cited its author's admission that 'we are too weak to bring the plan to a conclusion'.[25] Despite the image of Germany as a highly militarised nation, the Germans eschewed the massive armies of their putative opponents and were more selective in their conscription policies. The Schlieffen

Plan was essentially the result of the perception by the German General Staff of the growing military strength of France and, in particular, Russia. Von Schlieffen wrestled with the problems and contradictions of his plan until his death. It needed more men, and more men were provided for by conscription laws in 1911–13; but larger numbers made for greater logistical problems – how were they to make their way on foot to Paris once they had been decanted into Belgium by rail, when the intervening road network was inadequate for their numbers?

All the continental great powers had made war plans. The French Plan XVII, its very title pointing to the many plans it superseded and the many changes of mind thus indicated, envisaged an all-out offensive into Alsace and Lorraine despite the strength of the German defences. Ironically, the genesis of the Schlieffen Plan had lain in the Count's quite logical conviction that the French command would never consider such a rash idea. The head of the Planning Bureau of the General Staff, Colonel Louis de Grandmaison, summed up the French approach when he declared that the defensive was cowardly and only the offensive worthy of a virile nation: a sudden attack would paralyse the enemy; 'he can no longer manoeuvre and very quickly becomes incapable of all offensive action'.[26] In 1911, General Joseph Joffre, a leading advocate of the offensive, was appointed chief-of-staff. Although French Intelligence had received reports that in the event of war the Germans intended to advance through Belgium, Joffre refused to believe that a German invasion would go west of the Meuse. His Plan XVII was a means of getting all his forces in place and then 'proceeding to battle'. The plan did not prescribe a particular direction of attack but, as a pre-emptive advance into Belgium was ruled out, an invasion of Alsace and Lorraine was implicit.

Considering that Germany's war plan depended upon being able to fight a defensive war against Russia and that assistance from Austria-Hungary was seen as essential if a Russian attack was to be successfully resisted, it is remarkable that there was so little coordination between the allies. Annika Mombauer, in her study of von Moltke, comments that, despite the desire of the German commander-in-chief from 1906 'to lead an "alliance war"', ignorance of Austro-Hungarian military affairs was a striking shortcoming in German military planning' and 'there was even surprise in Germany when it was "discovered" that not all soldiers in the Austro-Hungarian army spoke German'.[27] The assumption was, however, that Germany could leave it to the Austro-Hungarians to do the bulk of the fighting in the East, leaving only about thirteen German divisions on the eastern frontier while the main German force dealt with the French.

Russian generals had had little option but to plan a defensive strategy, given the weakened state of the Russian army after the defeat by Japan, and, indeed, to go on to the defensive and allow German and Austrian armies to founder in Russia's great open spaces before counter-attacking would have probably been the best option, even after the Russian army had recovered and been reorganised. However, Vladimir Aleksandrovich Sukhomlinov, minister for war from 1909, and leading generals had become converted to the general rage for the offensive, and this, together with French pressure, meant that in 1912 they were promising the French that Russian forces of 800,000 men would be available to attack Germany some two weeks after their cumbersome mobilisation had begun, and that massive offensive thrusts would penetrate East Prussia and Austrian Galicia.

The view that Europe stumbled into war as monarchs and statesmen lost control to generals, who in turn became captives of their or their predecessors' war plans, plans which had to be hastily implemented because of mobilisation timetables, has been out of favour for several decades, but recent works have reconsidered the importance of the arms race as a cause of the war,[28] while Christopher Clark has provided new support for the concept of slide towards war in which the protagonists were 'sleepwalkers'[29] and, as we shall see, re-opened the question of who, if anyone, was in charge in the countries which went to war in 1914.

The combination of the alliance system, preparations for possible wars and uncertainty as to who was in charge of foreign policy did make for a dangerous mix in the event of a crisis which affected the essential interests of any two powers belonging to opposing alliances. The emphasis must, however, be on what were *essential* interests. European peace had survived clashes over imperial interests, and only a crisis in which national integrities or fears of humiliation and impotency came into play could provide the context for a great war. The seeds of such a crisis had already been sown.

The Balkans: Europe's Fault-Line

Historians have conceived of several roads to war. One which has received enormous attention concentrates upon Germany, often seeing it as inherently expansionist and a major threat to European stability; rather Western-centric, it concentrates upon Franco-German and Anglo-German relations, German probing in North Africa, and, above all, on German military planning. Another pays more attention to Russia, to Russo-German relations and to Russian territorial ambitions in Eastern Europe and the Middle East.[30] Overarching both is the thesis that it was the opposing alliances and military plans which made Europe systematically unstable, so that any crisis which threatened the interests of a major power might lead to a major war. If the latter is true then, it can be argued, the particular events of June to August 1914 can be seen as merely the sparks, which ignited a bonfire composed of the dry timbers of a divided continent. However, the overestimation of the significance of such 'structural' factors has led to an accompanying underestimation of the importance of the supposed 'sparks'.

None of these approaches in itself necessarily provides us with a complete reason for the catastrophe of August 1914, and, indeed, it was their conjunction which led to it, but it is clear that it is the Russo-German and Russo-Austrian dimensions, and above all the perennial 'Eastern Question', that have been most neglected.

If most contemporaries were puzzled as to how the murder of an Austrian archduke could lead to a major European war, and generations of history students have wondered at the way the crisis which followed Sarajevo is often downgraded to, at best, an immediate cause of the conflict, this is because of a failure to recognise the salience of the Balkans to European stability. It may be, however, that the most important reason for the outbreak of war was the great issue that had dominated international relations since the late eighteenth century, the 'Eastern Question'. The long-drawn-out decline of the Ottoman Empire and its possible demise had proved to be the major cause of tension and instability throughout the century. The ebb of Turkish power in the Balkans had poisoned Russo-Austrian relations; while the suspicion that Russia had designs on Constantinople and wished to control the Black Sea Straits and thus threaten British influence in the Mediterranean had led to Britain taking on the role of the protector of the Ottoman Empire. The Crimean War had been followed by the great Eastern Crisis of 1875–8, which had ended with Russia, after a successful war with Turkey, being forced to relinquish much of its gains at the Congress of Berlin.

A great war was more likely to be the result of a crisis in erstwhile Ottoman Europe than one occurring elsewhere because any change in the balance of power in the Balkans was uniquely dangerous. A.J.P. Taylor wrote that, 'In retrospect it is difficult to believe that there was ever a serious danger of war in Europe on a great scale at any time between 1878 and 1913'.[31] The two dates he chose were times at which the disintegration of the Ottoman Empire appeared imminent. Recent works have tended, while not denying the unstable nature of pre-1914 Europe, to have modified the balance between the structural framework of great power dissension and the disputes on Europe's Balkan fault-line as causes of the war by placing the latter centre stage.

What gave Sarajevo the seismic implications that led to a European conflict, Christopher Clark has argued, was the way 'the loose network of the continental alliances became interlocked with conflicts unfolding on the Balkan peninsula'.[32] Sean McMeekin has gone much further and, in a revisionary work that puts the war's origins in the context, not just of the Balkans, but in that of the wider Eastern Question, argued that the First World War might well be called the 'War of the Ottoman Succession'.[33]

By 1914 the balance of power in the Balkans, established in the wake of the Treaty of Berlin, had been unstable for many years. The overthrow of the pro-Austrian Obrenović dynasty in Serbia, with the brutal assassination in 1903 of King Alexander and his consort, Queen Draga, changed the balance of power as the new regime inclined towards Russia. Incompetent, corrupt and dictatorial as King Alexander had been, the successor regimes lacked direction and leadership. Serbia became what would today be considered a 'failed state' as the new Karadjordjevic monarch, King Peter, the army, militias, secret societies and politicians struggled for control in an atmosphere in which none dared question extravagant pan-Serbian nationalist aims. The Serbs now looked to Russia for support in their aim of a greater Serbia, an aim that directly threatened Austria-Hungary, with its Croatian and Slovenian subjects.

Russian support for Serbia could not, however, be taken for granted. Bulgaria had for long been Russia's closest ally in the Balkans and a greater Serbia could only be achieved at the expense of Bulgaria as well as of Austria-Hungary, for Serbia laid claim to Macedonia, whose inhabitants the Bulgarian government considered to be Bulgarians. At the same time, Russia's defeat by the Japanese had turned its attention away from the Far East and back, not only to the Balkans, but to the aim, pursued throughout the nineteenth century, of control of Constantinople and the Black Sea Straits. Russian foreign policy was quite capable of ignoring Serbian interests and even pan-Slavist pressure in the interests of the great prize of control of the Straits, as was demonstrated by the initiative of the Russian foreign minister, Alexander Izvolski, when he proposed to the Austro-Hungarian minister in July 1908 that Russia would support an Austro-Hungarian annexation of Bosnia-Hercegovina in return for support for the Russian aim of having the Bosphorus Straits opened to warships in peacetime. Austria-Hungary pre-empted matters by formally incorporating the provinces, which were already under Austrian rule, leaving Russia, her aim unrealised, outwitted and resentful.

The significance of the unprovoked Italian invasion of the Ottoman province of Libya in 1911 has often been underestimated by historians of the First World War. In fact, it was a major step towards the world war as it raised the prospect of the final dissolution of the Ottoman Empire. France and Britain demonstrated little of their traditional concern for the preservation of the Empire and, in fact encouraged the Italians. Preponderant sea-power ensured that the Libyan ports and coastline were soon taken and, although the Italian army enjoyed little success, pressure from Russia forced the Turks to give way and sign a peace treaty by which they lost Libya in October 1912.

The Italian action had, however, emboldened the Serbs and Bulgarians, encouraged by Russian ambassadors, to make a tactical alliance. It seemed to the Balkan states that this was the time to divide up Turkey in Europe. Sazonov, the Russian foreign minister, did not want a Balkan war, but pan-Slavist opinion in Russia made it difficult for him to rein back the alliance. Despite an Austro-Russian note warning that no change in the status quo would be permitted, an echo of the old partnership by which the two powers had co-operated in the Balkans, the Balkan states were out of control: tiny Montenegro declared war on Turkey on 8 October 1912 and was quickly followed by Bulgaria, Greece and Serbia; within weeks Turkish armies had been defeated and the Ottoman Empire expelled from all but a toe-hold in Europe.

The attitude of the great powers to the Balkan upheaval was muddled and confused. Austria-Hungary failed to intervene. Britain abandoned its traditional role as supporter of the integrity of the Ottoman Empire, while Germany, which, with its strong commercial interests in Turkey, had appeared to be replacing Britain as the defender of the Empire, played a neutral role. Russia's main interest was Constantinople and the Straits. When it looked as if the Bulgarians might take Constantinople Russia signalled that it was prepared to go to war to prevent this, though, in reality, its concern was to prevent any state but itself controlling the city and the Straits.

The conference of the powers in London agreed that the Turks should now be confined to a rump of their previous European possessions and that the Serbs, who had conquered much of Albania, should withdraw in the interests of an independent Albanian state. However, victory could not end the mutual antipathy and conflicting territorial ambitions of the Balkan states, and a Second Balkan War followed in which Serbia attacked Bulgaria and was joined by Greece, Romania and even Turkey. The defeated Bulgaria was deprived of most of its earlier gains by the Treaty of Bucharest of August 1913, which enlarged Serbia, Romania and Greece, while Turkey recovered some of the territory lost to Bulgaria in the Treaty of Constantinople in September.

The wars left the Balkans more volatile than ever, and Austria-Hungary determined that in a future crisis it would act more firmly. The Triple Alliance had not come well out of the crisis. Italy had been revealed as unpredictable, while Romania had aligned herself with Austria-Hungary's enemies. For Germany, the outcome was worrying. To the Kaiser, the new chancellor (Theobald von Bethmann Hollweg) and generals, the Reich seemed in a dangerous situation, hemmed in by enemies. Overtures to Russia had come to nothing, the naval challenge had failed to frighten Britain into conciliation, and France remained an implacable enemy. Only Austria-Hungary could be relied upon as an ally; however, from the Austro-Hungarian viewpoint, the question was whether Germany could be relied on.

Austria-Hungary is often relegated to a secondary role to Germany in the slide towards war, but, as Samuel Williamson has demonstrated, it pursued an independent policy.[34] The Hapsburg Empire's fragility, imparted a degree of recklessness to its policies and, in particular, to the desire of the Chief of the General Staff, Conrad von Hötzendorf, and the foreign minister, Count Leopold von Berchtold, for a preventative war against its enemies. Germany was led by its ally as much as it led.

Faced with the growing hostility of France and Russia, Germany had little choice but to assuage Austria-Hungary. Another possibility was to find an extra ally, and the moves towards a close association with the Ottoman Empire presaged a future alliance, one far from incompatible with that with Austria-Hungary, for the Habsburg and Ottoman Empires had common interests in the Balkans and both feared Russian ambitions. There was no reason why Germany should not seek to increase its already considerable economic interest in Turkey: the French had already a major stake in the country's finances, and the appointment of a German general, Liman von Sanders, to train and command the Ottoman army could be said to merely balance the fact that a British admiral performed a similar role in its navy, while schemes for railways from Berlin to Baghdad could be seen to be an economically progressive step. All of these moves together could, however, be seen by Russia, paranoid about any other power exercising too much influence over Constantinople and the Straits, as a major threat to its influence and ambitions.

Germany's concern about being surrounded by enemies seemed to its leaders to have become a reality. After Agadir, it seemed that Britain would support France, even when France was in the wrong, and after the Balkan Wars it became clear that the French interpretation of its understanding with Russia went beyond a purely defensive alliance. Germany could not allow Austria-Hungary to be humiliated. The great error of dropping the Reinsurance Treaty and being shackled to the Habsburg Empire was coming home to roost.

There was no certainty that the 'Balkan powder-keg', as the explosive potential of rivalries in eastern Europe was so often referred to, would ignite and lead to a major war, but of all the areas that might possibly see a concatenation of events that would lead to a general conflagration, the Balkans was by far the most likely.

Chapter 2: How It Began

The visit of the heir to the throne of Austria-Hungary, Archduke Franz Ferdinand, and his wife to Sarajevo on 28 June 1914 was always going to be risky in view of Serbian hostility to Austrian rule over Bosnia-Hercegovina, and was made more so by the absence of adequate security precautions. The result was the most notorious assassination of all time. It almost did not happen, for the seven terrorists, in town with connivance of elements close to the Serbian government, were as bungling as those in charge of security. Nevertheless, after a chapter of accidents, a bomb thrown at the open car and a subsequent wrong turn by the driver, one terrorist, Gavrilo Princip, was given his opportunity and murdered the Archduke and his wife by firing his revolver twice at point-blank range. Princip was one of those angry figures, a man who had moved from anarchism to Serbian ultra-nationalism in the search for a cause that would give meaning to his life, but he had obviously received help from groups close to the Serbian government.[1] His bullets did not start the First World War, but began the sequence of events which led to it.

The timing of the assassination was fatal. The hackneyed view that, without the assassination other events, sooner or later, would have produced the First World War underestimates the 'perfect storm' that the Archduke's death produced. The lesson that Austria-Hungary had taken from the Balkan Wars was that Serbia, which had doubled in size, was not a state that could be negotiated with and was only to be dealt with by the threat of force or force itself. Berchtold and Conrad saw the single success of the Empire's policy to have been the ultimatum to the Serbs to withdraw from Albania, and were convinced that a punitive war against Serbia was necessary. What was required was a suitable *casus belli*. A draft memorandum which Berchtold had had his foreign office officials draw up two weeks before the assassination can be seen as providing the outlines of an ultimatum prior to the event which provided the occasion for it.[2]

It had been far from clear, previously, that Berchtold and Conrad had the necessary support for a forward policy against Serbia. Franz Ferdinand himself had been strongly opposed to an aggressive policy, as was Count Tisza, the Hungarian prime minister, who considered the Empire had more than enough Slavs and was against any acquisition of Serbian territory, while any move was dependent on German support. Germany had given less than solid support to Austria-Hungary during the Balkan Wars and, indeed, had consulted with Russia in the interests of limiting the conflicts. Austria-Hungary's survival as a great power was a vital German interest and it was clear that Germany would come to its ally's aid if it was attacked by Russia. What was much less certain was whether such support would be forthcoming in the event of a war started by Austria-Hungary.

The assassination of Franz Ferdinand gave Berchtold, Conrad and a group of foreign office officials led by Alexander von Hoyos, who were pressing for strong action against Serbia, a perfect opportunity. Not only could the problem of Serb nationalism be solved by firm action against a state which was clearly complicit to some degree in the assassination, but Germany was now supportive of action to crush the Serb threat to Austria-Hungary's integrity. Moreover, all of the great powers expected Austria-Hungary to take some form of action against Serbia, while even Russia could hardly be expected to give total support to a state rejoicing at the murder of the heir to an imperial throne.

The big question as to how an Austro-Serbian crisis led to a world war is whether it was a consequence of the dilatory nature of the Austrian response, which allowed time for the attitudes of Germany and Russia to harden, or whether the German high command deliberately used the crisis to engineer a major war. The July crisis was an Austro-Serbian and then an Austro-Russian crisis, which eventually became an expanding European crisis because Russia was prepared to go to war in support of Serbia and Germany was prepared to do the same in support of her only firm ally. Paradoxically, the best chance of preventing Vienna's determination to punish Serbia leading to a wider crisis lay in immediate unilateral action by Austria-Hungary. Serbia might have had to accept an early ultimatum, or, if not, a quick, small war might have headed off a great war. As John Keegan has argued: 'Had Austria moved at once [...] without seeking Germany's endorsement, it is possible, perhaps probable, that the Serbs would have found themselves as isolated strategically, as, initially, they were morally, and so forced to capitulate to the Austrian ultimatum.'[3]

Instead of seizing their opportunity, the Austrians dithered. Nothing better illustrates the arthritic nature of decision making in the Austro-Hungarian Empire than that Franz Ferdinand was killed on 28 June and Austria's ultimatum to Serbia not delivered until 23 July. Those responsible for deciding on the Austro-Hungarian response were divided. Perversely, the removal of Franz Ferdinand, a strong opponent of those determined to crush Serbia, strengthened the war party, but Count Tisza, though in agreement with confronting Belgrade with an ultimatum, was opposed to imposing terms so strong that a Serbian acceptance would amount to humiliation.

Most importantly, it was clear that Austria-Hungary lacked the self-confidence to proceed unilaterally and was awaiting promises from Berlin before proceeding further. Much, therefore, depended on the German reaction. Count Hoyos, Berchtold's chief-of-staff, was sent to Potsdam in July to secure German support. The promises he secured from the Kaiser and the Chancellor had a decisive effect on the Austro-Hungarian decision to issue an ultimatum which, Vienna assumed, was too tough for Serbia to accept. The promises that Hoyos was given on 5 July have been seen as a 'blank cheque' to Austria-Hungary, and as handing over control of the crisis to the weaker partner: 'Germany, by its pledges had surrendered the direction and pace of the July crisis' to Austria-Hungary'.[4] What remains a subject of controversy was whether the Germans were encouraging Austria-Hungary in the interests of a diplomatic victory or, at most, a limited third Balkan War, either of which would at once strengthen the multi-national empire, attach it firmly to Germany and change the balance of power in the Balkans in Austria's and Germany's favour, or whether they were preparing for a wider war. It soon became clear that, however much Conrad wished to take firm and decisive action, the Austro-Hungarian army was in no position to carry it out in the immediate future; it had been starved of resources, largely because of prolonged financial and political differences between Austria and Hungary, and although a reform programme had begun, it was not expected to be completed until 1916.[5] It has, indeed, been suggested that the Kaiser and his entourage 'actually doubted whether their Austrian allies, whom they regarded as rather weak, would be able to manage any sort of action against Serbia'.[6] The result was that the option of confining the crisis to a limited Austro-Serbian confrontation faded in the latter half of July.

Since the publication of Fritz Fischer's *Griff nach der Weltmacht* (Grab for World Power)[7] a dominant view has been that Austria was encouraged to make unacceptable demands on Serbia, as the German government

and its military commanders perceived in the assassination of Franz
Ferdinand a cause for a war which could be seen as defensive and
which would gain the support of German public opinion. The German
government and its high command were, it is argued, increasingly
worried that the balance of military power was moving against them as
the strengths of the Russian and French armies increased.[8] To a large
extent this was the fault of the German military commanders themselves; they had refused to countenance a permanent expansion of the
army because it would reduce the percentage of officers who came from
the landowning Prussian (*Junker*) aristocracy and of men who came
from rural areas, who it was thought made more trustworthy soldiers.
Nevertheless, Germany's leaders believed they could win in 1914 or
1915, but might not be able to defeat the combination of France and
Russia thereafter. It has also been suggested that the German governing elite were concerned that the social democratic party, the SPD, had
become the majority in the Reichstag and that there was an internal
threat to their position; the implication is that war would consolidate
support for their regime and, hence, a war in the near future was pref-
erable to allowing their military and governing position to be gradually
eroded. Whether they were correct in believing any or all of this is
debateable. Germany had a bigger population than France and was
already taking steps to increase the number of conscripts and reservists;
further, even though the Russian army was growing apace, German
soldiers were far superior to their Russian counterparts; and the SPD
was increasingly reformist rather revolutionary.

Several historians have argued that the die had already been cast two
years previously at a 'War Council' of 8 December 1912 at which the
Kaiser met his military leaders. This meeting is often cited as evidence
that Germany planned a 'preventative war' before Russian military
strength increased further, to Germany's disadvantage. The conference
was secret; it was not made known until the 1960s when Fritz Fischer
produced the notes made by the chief of the Kaiser's naval cabinet,
Admiral Georg Alexander von Müller, as evidence that the Kaiser and
his military chiefs were planning to bring about a major European war.
General von Moltke is, nevertheless, quoted as saying, 'I believe a war
is unavoidable and the sooner the better' and the Kaiser as arguing
that Austria must 'deal energetically with Serbia' and that, if Russia
supported the Serbs then war would be unavoidable for Germany.[9] How
important this meeting was, is debatable; neither the chancellor nor any
other civilian statesmen was present and, although there was discussion
of a war in 1914, von Müller, in his diary, concluded that 'The result of
this conversation was more or less zero.'[10]

The conference was, indeed, inconclusive for, although the Kaiser and von Moltke spoke of the need for an immediate war, Tirpitz declared that the navy was not ready and even von Moltke argued that public opinion needed to be prepared for a war with Russia. This latter point is significant in the light of future events, as Germany had not previously been prepared to encourage Austria to launch an attack on Serbia, which could be seen as an unprovoked act of aggression, because support for such a war, carrying with it the likelihood of intervention by Russia, would not have been forthcoming from the German public or the SDP. The assassination of Franz Ferdinand, however, seemed to be the perfect opportunity to allow Austria-Hungary to threaten a war of retribution against Serbia, and this could be portrayed as justified and essentially defensive.

There is, thus, plenty of evidence of German concerns that their position was worsening and for a determination to give support to their ally, but whether this leads to the firm conclusion that Germany deliberately planned a major war is far from certain. If Austria-Hungary had been successful in gaining a diplomatic victory this might well have been sufficient to satisfy Germany. That this was not to be owed much to Russia's reaction.

German support for Austro-Hungarian action which might lead to a war with Serbia, combined with the long wait for such action, were clearly crucial in setting in motion the slowly evolving crisis that followed on the assassination; but equally decisive in the process of events which led to a world war was the attitude of Russia. It has been argued by Sean McMeekin that Russia deliberately used the crisis to bring about a war with Austria-Hungary and Germany by, first of all, encouraging the Serbs to reject the Austro-Hungarian ultimatum, and then by mobilising, knowing full well that once its mobilisation was under way, the Germans were bound to respond or lose any advantage their capacity to mobilise more quickly gave them.[11]

As McMeekin has argued in a later study, a striking aspect of the Austrian ultimatum was the way in which Berchtold had managed to keep its terms secret: 'not a single minister of Austria-Hungary's imperial government, nor her sovereign, nor the ambassador of her only real ally, signed off on Berchtold's text before he sent it off under seal'.[12] The most astonishing omission is the failure to show it to the German ambassador in Vienna. The Germans were beginning to discover the disadvantages of issuing a 'blank cheque' without retaining any control of the time or circumstances at which it would be cashed. As McMeekin graphically puts it, 'The Austrian noose rigged up by the Germans themselves, was slowly tightening around Germany's neck'.[13] In addition, as Annika Mombauer has observed: 'The one-sided nature of Germany's military planning began to impose restrictions, not just on Germany's options, but also on Austria's. In fact, it made a localised conflict impossible'.[14]

The ultimatum that Vienna delivered to Belgrade on 23 July was tough, deliberately so. Tisza had been persuaded to abandon his previous position favouring terms the Serbs might have found acceptable. Nevertheless, the Serbian government had few cards to play with, and initial Serbian reactions seemed to indicate the probability of a grudging acceptance. What changed this was news from St Petersburg on 24–25 July indicating Russian support and condemning the ultimatum as unacceptable. The Serbs were, nevertheless, advised to avoid any unnecessary provocation. The Serbian reply has been described as a 'highly perfumed rejection' of Austria's demands,[15] yet its moderate and constitutional tone and disingenuous disavowal of any links between the Serbian government and Serbian expansionism and terrorism convinced many, including, late in the day, the Kaiser, that Belgrade had accepted most of Vienna's demands.

The real crisis which led to war was brief and came a month after Sarajevo. On 28 July, Austria-Hungary declared war on Serbia. Russia's general mobilisation was announced on 31 July, but a secret mobilisation had been under way from 25 July, and Russia was fully aware that the Germans were bound to respond. Sergei Sazonov, the Russian foreign minister, who pressed strongly for war, was secure in the knowledge that he had the support of France, President Poincaré having been on a state visit to Russia when the crucial decisions that would lead to war were being made.

What lay behind the Russian decisions was not just the matter of the balance of power in the Balkans but the wider Eastern Question. Support for Serbia had certainly strengthened and was popular with pan-Slavist opinion but, to quote Christopher Clark: 'The robustness of the Russian response fully makes sense only if we read it against the background of the Russian leadership's deepening anxiety about the future of the Turkish Straits'.[16] Sean McMeekin goes further and is more revisionist in portraying Russia as intent on war, arguing that Russia's aims were no less than the destruction of the Austro-Hungarian Empire, seizure of Constantinople, the command of the Straits and, even more ambitiously, the domination of Persia.[17]

What appears to shift the blame back to Germany is the odd contrast between German preparations for a possible war and German encouragement of Austria-Hungary to go to war with Serbia. Austro-Hungarian preparations for war were ponderous, for, despite Conrad's bellicosity, the army was not ready early in July when the decisions for an ultimatum and probable war were made, nor even when the ultimatum was sent on 23 July, and it was not until 28 July, some three weeks after Hoyos had returned from Potsdam with his 'blank cheque', that war on Serbia was declared. Had Germany hoped for a short conflict that would have presented Russia with the *fait accompli* of a defeated Serbia and thus, perhaps, dissuaded her from intervening, then speed was of the essence, but there was insufficient urging from Berlin to Vienna to get on with it. Nor was there any co-ordination of military planning between the Dual Alliance partners. The Austrians prepared for a war with Serbia and not for one with Russia, while, once Russian mobilisation was under way, the Germans were preparing to implement von Moltke's modification of the Schlieffen Plan, which provided for a defensive war against Russia while France was dealt with.

The Austrian historian, Fritz Fellner, has pointed to Kaiser Wilhelm II's telegram to Emperor Franz Josef of 31 July in which he informed him of Germany's mobilisation and went on to state that, in the coming struggle: 'it is of the utmost importance that Austria directs her chief force against Russia and does not split it up by a simultaneous offensive against Serbia. This is all the more important as a great part of my army will be tied down in France'. He went on to write that Serbia played only 'a subordinate role which demands only the most absolutely necessary defensive measures.[18] The Kaiser's telegrams were not always carefully considered expressions of his government's positions, but in this case the missive does seem to reflect the plans of ministers and generals and reveals a complete disregard for the interests of Germany's alliance partner. It is, however, clear that from the time that Berchtold was given what appeared to be a blanket assurance of assurances of German support there was confusion and misunderstanding in the relations between the Dual Alliance partners, and a false confidence that Russia would stand by and permit either a diplomatic or military defeat of Serbia. The Austro-Hungarians and particularly Berchtold must take much of the blame for the impasse that faced both Vienna and Berlin at the end of July in that, emboldened by the prospect of German support yet tardy in their actions, they gave time to the factions in the Russian government who were prepared to risk a wider war. The declaration of war by Austria-Hungary on Serbia on 28 July was both unnecessary and toothless as the Empire's armies were unable to go into action for a further fortnight, but it had the effect of bringing Russian intervention close and was perhaps intended by Berchtold to head off the diplomatic initiatives of Sir Edward Grey, who was proposing a four-power conference composed of Germany, Italy, Britain and Russia.

The seriousness of the crisis dawned upon the Kaiser and Bethmann Hollweg as the German Emperor and his ministers and generals returned from their holidays. The prospects of keeping an Austro-Serbian conflict localised were now rapidly diminishing, Russian mobilisation had begun and the confidence that Britain would remain neutral was evaporating, thus setting up the worst scenario from Germany's viewpoint. The Kaiser met with Bethmann on 28 July. It was a stormy interview in which Bethmann offered his resignation, to which His Majesty answered, 'You've cooked this broth and now you're going to eat it.'[19] Had Wilhelm read the Serbian reply to the Austro-Hungarian ultimatum earlier, things might have been different. When he did read the response from the Serbian prime minister, Pasic, late in the evening of 28 July, he wrote 'all reason for war has gone', and added, 'I should never have ordered mobilisation.'[20] But it was too late: the Austro-Hungarian declaration of war had already been delivered to Belgrade and Russian mobilisation was accelerating. The German general staff could not permit Russia's mobilisation to continue and Germany's declarations of war on Russia and then France followed on 1 and 3 August.

Who was Responsible?

In *Europe's Last Summer: Why the World Went to War in 1914*, David Fromkin, in Agatha Christie style, has his detective summon the ghosts of the long-dead suspects to the library. He concludes, in agreement with what has been, for long, the dominant consensus among historians, that the crime was committed by Germany, and singles out the chief of the German general staff, von Moltke, as the individual at whom the detective points an accusing finger: 'There is the person who did it.' As we have seen, however, it is possible to build up a tenable case against another nation, Russia, and another individual, Sergei Sazonov, as some historians have done.

The propaganda battle as to which power or powers was responsible for the war has a long history. It began during the conflict and continued with the publication of selected documents after it. The arguments over responsibility for the war had, in the inter-war period, a contemporary as well as an historical dimension for the Treaty of Versailles both branded Germany as the aggressor, with the 'War Guilt' clauses, and imposed reparations in the light of that guilt. German historians strenuously denied that Germany bore the main responsibility for the outbreak of war, while historians belonging to the victorious allied nations gradually moved from an immediate post-war view, that Germany was solely responsible, to a consensus that responsibility was shared. American historians were prominent in this inter-war revisionism: Sidney Bradshaw Fay argued that no European country had wanted to go to war in 1914, while Harry Elmer Barnes went further and allocated the main responsibility for the war to the Entente powers. That the nations somehow slithered into war and that no nation alone bore a special responsibility was the generally accepted view until the 1960s and the publication of Fritz Fischer's revisionist works; Luigi Albertini's *The Origins of the First World War* had previously argued for German responsibility but, first published in Italian during World War II, it only found a wide readership when translated into English. Albertini and Fischer, followed by Imanuel Geiss[21] took the view that not only was Germany responsible but that Germany from the time of Bismarck to that of Hitler demonstrated expansionist aims, arguments that aroused great controversy amongst German historians.

The view of Germany's culpability, if not necessarily the full-blown Fischer thesis, has been the established view since the 1960s and it was possible for an authority in the field to write as recently as 2000 that, 'No historian today would argue that Europe had slithered into war accidentally.'[22] Revisionism, however, has been followed by further revisionism, the latest of which has questioned whether the search for a culprit is the right approach and has returned to the earlier view that no one power was responsible for the war.

Christopher Clark in *The Sleepwalkers: How Europe went to war in 1914* (2012) eschews the blame game and the search for a smoking gun. The obsession with finding a culprit, he argues, leads to an assumption that there were capable decision-makers who had coherent intentions. Instead, he argues, the war was caused by the lack of men with the power or capability to make decisions. Far from the statesmen and generals of any nation moving deliberately towards a great conflict, Europe sleepwalked towards one because there was no-one in the states that went to war who was really in charge. Policy and decision-making were fractured as 'competing voices' fought and conspired in support of different policies: the military competed with civilian governments, who were themselves divided, while there were factions within foreign offices and ambassadors often pursuing their own ends.

There is room in the Clark thesis for all the older views of a Europe stumbling into war, entangled by alliance systems, an armaments race, the plans of military strategists, mobilisation and railway timetables, and the difficulties of governing and constraining mass societies, but its originality lies in its emphasis upon the incoherent nature of command and control.

It was far from inevitable that the assassination at Sarajevo would lead to a major European war; as Margaret MacMillan concludes in *The War That Ended Peace*, 'Europe's steps could have gone in other directions but in August 1914 they led to the end of the path and now destruction faced it.'[23]

How and Why Britain Went to War

Few people in Britain had ever heard of Archduke Franz Ferdinand and even fewer could have placed Sarajevo on a map, while although the Balkan Wars had been covered in the quality press by that recent journalistic innovation, the defence correspondent, east central Europe was an area which, if it meant anything to most Britons, conjured up the Ruritania of Anthony Hope's novel, *The Prisoner of Zenda*. The major news items in the British press during June and July 1914 were mainly about Ireland and the Liberal Government's Home Rule bill, to which Ulster Unionists and the Conservative and Unionist Party were vehemently opposed. Yet, by early August Britain would be at war, a war occasioned by an assassination in the Balkans.

The process by which a presumably stable parliamentary democracy, with a prime minister and cabinet, responsible to a parliament elected on a mass franchise, came to declare war without a vote in parliament, on an issue never put before the electorate, and via agreements and promises made secretly long before, of which most of the cabinet and nearly all MPs were ignorant, constitutes an astonishing sequence of events and decisions.

The standard explanation is, of course, that it was the alliance system and the Anglo-French and Anglo-Russian agreements that brought about Britain's declaration of war on Germany on 4 August, but this is doubtful. Britain was not a member of any alliance other than that with Japan; the ententes between Britain and France and Russia were not alliances and there was no obligation on Britain to go to war if either of its entente partners were attacked. Both agreements had been made to settle disputes and avoid conflicts between the signatories, and neither was anti-German. The problem was that, by 1914, senior members of the government, influential officials in the foreign office and members of the General Staff had come to interpret the ententes in a very different way.

One factor which had a major influence in the process by which the British interpretation of the ententes became closer to alliances and increasingly anti-German was the appointment of Sir Edward Grey as foreign secretary in 1905. Another was the activities of group within the foreign office who were violently opposed to Germany and became influential over Grey.

It is a general principle of constitutional government that governments make policy and civil servants assist in the furtherance of it, but a clique within the diplomatic corps, whose leading members were Eyre Crowe, Francis Bertie, Arthur Nicolson and Charles Hardinge, played a considerable role in the years before 1914 in pushing British policy in an anti-German direction. It has often been said that there was continuity between the policies of the Conservative government and the succeeding Liberal administrations, and certainly Balfour and Lansdowne had moved away from Lord Salisbury's cautious neutrality towards closer relations with France. Grey's important move in secretly giving a military dimension to the Anglo-French entente, making it in practice closer to an alliance, took place via secret talks in 1905–1906 and 1911 and a naval agreement in 1912 which provided for the disposition of fleets in the event of war. It went far beyond the entente of 1904. Grey insisted that these talks with the French were unofficial; the cabinet was not informed of the 1905–1906 discussions, which took place during the Moroccan crisis, and even the prime minister, Campbell-Bannerman, was sent only an account carefully worded to conceal the promises made to the French.

Motivating these clandestine military arrangements was the general perception held by Grey, the influential foreign office lobby, and indeed many in the war office, that Germany was pursuing Napoleonic ambitions. All attempts at reconciliation with Germany in the years before the war foundered on these deep suspicions. John Charmley, an historian critical of British policy, has used the concept of 'Crowe's fork'[24] by which, not only hostile announcements or acts by Germany could be interpreted as anti-British or signs of German plans for European hegemony, but conciliatory moves could also be seen in the same way, on the grounds that Germany was simply trying to lull Britain into a false sense of security.[25] Such an argument does of course stand or fall on what German's intentions really were; paranoia can sometime be justified. Alternatively, British fears of German intentions can be seen as part of a collective paranoia, a spiral of ever-deepening and mutually reinforcing suspicions affecting all the great powers of Europe.

The military talks with France produced, a script 'that in fact was to be followed' in 1914.[26] It has been suggested by Niall Ferguson, 'to turn Fritz Fischer on his head', that the CID meeting of 23 August 1911 (rather than the notorious meeting between the Kaiser and his military chiefs sixteen months later) was the real 'war council' which set the course for a military confrontation between Britain and Germany.[27] Grey did not seek war but found his room for manoeuvre reduced by a combination of what the ententes came to represent, rather than what the actual wording of the agreements declared, and the military arrangements, which implicitly changed the nature of British commitments.

The British road to war in late July and early August was tortuous. Initially, public opinion, a majority in the cabinet, and most of the Liberal Party were opposed to getting involved. What was clear was that, as Grey had recently had to reassure the Commons on 11 June: 'If war arose between the European Powers, there were no unpublished agreements that would hamper the freedom of the Government or Parliament to decide whether or not Great Britain should participate in a war.' Technically, this was true, but it could be claimed, as it was by Paul Cambon, the French Ambassador and by the foreign office Francophile, Arthur Nicolson, that the understandings of the military talks meant that Britain had a moral duty to support France.

Grey was in a difficult position in trying to persuade the cabinet and the Liberal Party of the necessity for intervention, for to brandish promises made at military discussions that he had kept secret from all but a handful of colleagues was not likely to be effective. In addition, though war between France and Germany seemed inevitable in late July, this was because of France's alliance with Russia, a country viewed with considerable antipathy by most of the Liberal Party. Unsurprisingly, Grey failed to get support at cabinet meetings on 27 and 29 July and, after a further meeting on 1 August, had to tell Cambon that the cabinet was opposed to intervention.

As the crisis worsened after the Austrian declaration of war on Serbia, and as Russian mobilisation became apparent, Grey did, of course, put forward plans for arbitration. These, however, were distinctly one-sided. As Clark points out, of the four powers Grey suggested as mediators at a cabinet meeting of 24 July – France, Italy, Britain and Germany – 'Only one was likely to defend the interests of Austria-Hungary', while Grey's later call for mediation by Germany between Austria and Serbia was little more than a request to the Germans to rein in Austria. By concentrating on the Austrian ultimatum to Serbia and not involving Russia, Grey's proposal ignored the fact that it was Russian support for Serbia that threatened to turn a Balkan conflict into a wider war. That he made little of the process of Russian mobilisation may well be due to the fact that the communications he received from the British ambassador in St Petersburg, Sir George Buchanan, merely reiterated the official Russian line, or it may be that the alternative explanation of Russia's actions was unwelcome. Grey dithered: forced to pretend neutrality and with opposition at home, he neither sent a clear signal to Germany that in the end Britain would side with France and Russia nor made proposals that were in line with his pretended neutrality.

What then led to the British declaration of war on Germany three days after Grey had told Cambon that the British cabinet was opposed to intervention? One factor was that Conservative politicians and the Conservative press began to press for British intervention. Another was the steps taken on 1 August, when the cabinet authorised Winston Churchill to proceed with full naval mobilisation, and on 2 August, when Germany was warned that if a German fleet came into the Channel to undertake operations against the French coast or French shipping the Royal Navy would give the French full protection. Although they could be held to be precautionary or preventative measures, these moves started a momentum which favoured the interventionists. Perhaps more importantly, the majority of the cabinet, who wanted to keep Britain out of the approaching war, played their hand badly, while those pressing for war were both more united and more astute. Supporters of non-intervention failed to find a leader. Lloyd George was the obvious candidate, and Lord Beaverbrook recollected that, 'practically everything depended on the attitude of Mr Lloyd George'; those opposed to intervention were gravely weakened when he changed sides at the eleventh hour.[28]

It was not Lloyd George's finest hour. Though some historians have praised him for unifying the cabinet and finally doing what they considered the right thing by backing the interventionists, Keith Wilson characterises his change of policy as 'just one more in the long line of self-interested manoeuvres', with Lloyd George acting opportunistically with 'his eye on the main chance'.[29] While one of his biographers has described him making up his mind in 'an agony of conscience',[30] another has, in a recent study, argued that it may be more accurate to suggest that it was 'an agony of advantage'.[31]

That internal British politics and the fate of the government played a part is obvious, for by 3 August, it was clear that a failure to support France would mean the resignation of Grey, Churchill, Haldane and even Asquith and the fall of the Liberal Government. The majority of Liberal MPs were probably still against intervention, but were leaderless after Lloyd George's desertion and knew full well that the Conservatives were prepared to take office.

The oft-repeated view that Britain went to war because of the German violation of Belgian neutrality has little substance, but the German demands on Belgium did enable Grey and those committed to the ententes to win the struggle within the government and take Britain into the war. It was debateable whether the 1839 treaty guaranteeing Belgian neutrality did bind Britain to uphold such neutrality in any circumstances or alone among the signatories, and even Lloyd George, who later claimed its violation to have been the most important reason for bringing the cabinet and public opinion round to support for war, is said to have argued earlier that the Germans would pass through only a small part of Belgium and 'pay for any damage that they do',[32] thus implicitly suggesting that this might be acceptable. Germany's fatal error, had she wished to avoid Britain's entry into the war, was the German ultimatum to Belgium demanding unheeded passage through the whole country in order to put into action the plan of von Schlieffen as modified by von Moltke. The 'dead hand of von Schlieffen', in Niall Ferguson's words, 'helped save the Liberal Government'.[33]

Controversy continues, however, over what might have been the basic reason for Britain's decision to align herself with Russia and France against Germany and Austria-Hungary. At the centenary of the start of the First World War approached, the standard arguments for Britain's declaration of war were dusted off. The journalist, Ben Macintyre, writing in *The Times*, summed it up: 'Germany was a militarist, imperialist autocracy, bent on European domination ... Britain had little choice but to fight',[34] while Max Hasting in *Catastrophe*, in similar mode, wrote of the dire consequences of a Europe under the autocratic control of Germany. This, of course, was the essence of Sir Edward Grey's justification for Britain's involvement, the view of Eyre Crowe and the anti-German foreign office group, and, indeed, of most historians' accounts of the reasons for Britain's decision for war. It has been directly challenged by Niall Ferguson, who characterises the view of Germany's war aims put forward by Grey and his supporters at the time, and subsequently reinforced by the Fischer thesis, as exaggerated. He argues that what Germany wanted was a German-dominated European customs union, an outcome Britain could have tolerated, and would indeed in the future have to live with.[35]

Further criticism of Britain's decision to go to war has come from John Charmley, who considers that the desertion of Britain's traditional policy of keeping out of continental wars whenever possible, and of Lord Salisbury's policy of eschewing alliances with European powers, was a tragic mistake with long-term implications for the decline of Britain as a world power.[36] Britain, in short, moved from a globalist strategy primarily concerned with maintaining her position as a world and imperial power to a continentalist policy which was preoccupied with the balance of power in Europe, thus abandoning the traditional strategy which Britain had followed since the eighteenth century. It may be claimed in opposition to this thesis that Britain had often combined continental alliances with her maritime and imperial strategies, but an essential difference was that, unlike the wars of the eighteenth century or the Revolutionary and Napoleonic Wars, Grey and the pro-French elements in the foreign office were advocating a continentalist strategy without a great army, for Edwardian Britain and the Asquith government were totally opposed to conscription.

Some recent studies have introduced a very different dimension to the reasons for Britain's entry to the war, that of Russian intentions and Britain's view of them. Christopher Clark argues that British policy was at least as preoccupied with Russian ambitions as those of Germany when making its decision to go to war. Like Niall Ferguson and, indeed Paul Kennedy,[37] Clark sees British foreign policy from the late nineteenth century as one of appeasement. Suffering from imperial overstretch with its manifold interests and limited military resources, Britain was concerned to appease the United States, France, and particularly Russia, by seeking to resolve differences in the many corners of its vast empire. It was prepared to appease Germany too, particularly in Africa, but despite the reasoning of Grey and sections of the foreign office, and even senior officers in the army, Germany could be seen as less of a menace to British interests than Russia. Clark argues that there were two different British security paradigms, the continentalist view, which stressed the centrality of the European balance of power and saw Germany as the danger, and the more globalist or imperial viewpoint, from which Russia appeared the more fundamental threat. Despite the Anglo-Japanese Alliance and Russia's defeat by Japan, and even despite the Anglo-Russian entente, the problem of Russia had not gone away: 'in fact it was resurfacing during the last year before the outbreak of war. At that time, the extremely high-handed and provocative behaviour of the Russians in Persia and Central Asia encouraged some policy-makers in London to believe that the Anglo-Russian Convention might be on its last legs, and others to press still harder for an alliance with St Petersburg.[38] Clark quotes that implacable enemy of Germany, Sir Arthur Nicolson, who wrote that 'it would be far more dangerous to have an unfriendly France and Russia than an unfriendly Germany'.[39] Clark considers that it is misleading to overstate the tension between the two viewpoints for, as with Nicolson and Eyre Crowe, they were often blended in a desire to contain both Russia and Germany. Though it was to contain Germany rather than Russia that Britain went to war: 'British intervention on the side of Russia offered a means *both* of appeasing *and* tethering Russia and of opposing and containing Germany. In the conditions of 1914, the logics of global and continental security converge in the British decision to support the Entente powers against Germany and Austria.'[40] Sean McMeekin's view that the war was deliberately planned by Russia is a controversial exercise in revisionism, but he demonstrates that British appeasement of Russia had gone so far as to reverse Britain's traditional support of the Ottoman Empire and points to how quickly, once Turkey had come into the war on Germany's side, British approval of Russian ambitions for Constantinople and control of the Straits was forthcoming.[41]

Britain's path to war in 1914 was muddled and untidy, and was far from the directed will of a parliamentary democracy. Indeed, the way in which the momentous decision was made makes Britain a prime example of Clark's main thesis, 'sleepwalking' into war. The reasons for the decision to go to war will continue to be debated, but the decision was accepted by public opinion at the time with a reluctance which, as the war continued, hardened into an affirmation of the necessity of the war and a determination to win it.

Chapter 3:   War Fever?

One popular depiction of the social, cultural and political atmosphere of early twentieth century Europe is of a civilisation cracking
beneath a serene exterior as it was riven by divisive forces: nationalism, no longer in harmony with liberalism; socialist movements,
threatening class warfare; and rickety *ancien régimes*, desperate to find
ways of maintaining mass support. Voices were crying out for war,
and strikes and demonstrations in great cities pointed to the flimsy
construction of the 'proud tower' of Europe. Even in the arts, disso-
nance and violence were increasingly ubiquitous and many, like the
Italian futurists, yearned for a cleansing war which would sweep away
bourgeois peace. The outbreak of the First World War was, many have
claimed, welcomed with enthusiasm by the crowds which gathered in
every capital. As Barbara Tuchman wrote in her massively influential
book, *The Proud Tower*: 'The diplomatic origins, so-called, of the Great
War are only the fever chart of the patient: they do not tell us what
caused the fever. To probe for underlying causes and deeper forces
one must operate beneath the framework of a whole society and try
to discover what moved the people in it.'[1]

Discontents

It is certainly possible for those in search of the supposed fever to
build up a picture of a world bent on self-destruction and many writers
have done so. Assassination had been a threat to monarchs, presidents
and politicians since the 1880s and had led to many deaths: Tsar
Alexander, President Carnot of France, Empress Elizabeth of Austria,
two Spanish premiers, kings of Italy, Portugal and Greece, and, across
the Atlantic, President McKinley of the United States, while the best

known is, of course, that of Archduke Franz Ferdinand. Violent men in comfortable studies conceived of Utopias once monarchs, the ruling class, the bourgeoisie and governments had been destroyed, and provided the sanction for hungry and embittered men in attics, who found revenge in assassination. Anarchism provided only a minority of those dedicated to assassination and bombings in pursuit of what they considered virtuous aims: it was Russian populists who murdered Tsar Alexander, imagining that this would prompt a mass rising of Russia's peasantry; extreme nationalists, like the Irish Fenians, perpetrated more atrocities than anarchists; Gavrilo Princip, although he had an anarchist background, was, by 1914, a Serbian nationalist.

Many contemporaries saw the growing support for socialism in the period as the most serious threat to stability and the status quo, and some historians have shared this perception. The 1905 Russian revolution seemed to demonstrate the vulnerability of autocratic and monarchical regimes, and the violence of the disturbances shocked many, even in countries with more democratic constitutions. It was not only the rich who feared socialism; many a shopkeeper or clerk was kept awake at night by the image of revolutionaries storming up his suburban garden path, while strikes and demonstrations seemed to indicate a coming storm. In fact, however, socialist movements were deeply divided, with even formally Marxist parties like the German SPD being split between those who believed in revolution and whose aim was the overthrow of governments, and revisionists, who concentrated upon improving the wages and living standards of the working classes and getting representatives elected to parliament. The gradual improvement of wages throughout western Europe from the late nineteenth century assisted revisionists who sought to have a voice in government and those trade union leaders who saw the strike weapon as a means to economic ends rather than the overthrow of capitalism. It can be argued that socialism and trade unionism were, in advanced economies, increasingly a feature of political and economic life rather than a force bent on upheaval.

Some historians have seen a major source of instability in the continued political power and social and economic influence of anachronistic institutions and social groups. Arno J. Meyer in *The Persistence of the Old Regime* argued that 'Down to 1914, the steel frame of Europe's political societies continued to be heavily feudal and nobilitarian.' Essentially, Meyer's argument and that of others who point to the inconsistency of emperors, kings and aristocrats presiding over rapidly industrialising societies, is an expression of Marxist theory affronted by the incomplete ascendency of industrialists, businessmen and financiers. After all, the 'bourgeoisie' were supposed to sweep away the old order before making way for the triumph of the proletariat. This thesis has a particular problem in analysing Germany. The German Empire had been largely the creation of the ascendancy of Prussia, a state dominated by its landed, though not very wealthy, *Junker* aristocracy. The later decades of the nineteenth century saw the general development of both the middle orders and industrial working classes; Germany was becoming less rural and more urban, especially in regions where industrialisation was transforming the economy and society. But still, Europe's most modern economy was dominated politically by men in gorgeous uniforms who lived in castles and derived their incomes from agriculture.

A number of historians have, therefore, identified the disparity between the governmental structure of Germany and its economy and society as for the reason for a belligerent foreign policy intended to produce patriotic unity in the face of internal divisions. More loosely, this argument can be applied to Europe as a whole, the argument being that, although Germany was the extreme example, most countries, even Republican France, had ossified political and social structures. As Mayer has argued:

> The inner spring of Europe's general crisis was the over-reaction of old elites to perceived dangers to their privileged positions. In their siege mentality, they exaggerated the pace of capitalist modernisation, the revolt of the plebs, the frailty of the state apparatus, and the breakaway of the industrial and professional bourgeoisie.[2]

The opposite argument is, as we have seen, the more conventional Marxist one: far from being not 'bourgeois ' enough, in terms of the 'capitalist class' not having wrested sufficient power from the old regime, it was the very triumph of the bourgeoisie and consequent inter-capitalist competition for markets that led to war.

It is difficult to argue that the very peak of the ancien régime in early twentieth century Europe, the monarchies or the monarchical system, can be rated as a factor making war likely. Theoretically, the emperors of Germany, Russia and Austria-Hungary wielded considerable political power and had special relationships with their empires' armed forces, but much depended on the will, determination, consistency and ability of the individual ruler. The operatic bellicosity of Kaiser was on occasions a destabilising factor in international relations, but in July 1914 he, ineffectually, attempted to arrest the drive to war. Tsar Nicholas feared the prospect of war and agonised as his advisers unanimously pressed for the full mobilisation that was a crucial step towards the conflict, approving the order, then rescinding it, and then, 24 hours later, giving way. In Austria-Hungary, no great decision could be made without the assent of the aged Emperor Franz-Josef, but, equally, no great initiatives were to be expected from him. He had handled the affairs of the most complex of states with considerable skill for more than half a century and had presided over a managed decline in which, as one commentator famously quipped, the situation was, always 'desperate, but never serious'. Increasingly, however, he had become more of a revered institution than a ruler and, generally cautious, gave his consent to policies only when there was a consensus amongst his advisers. As for Britain, King Edward VII had felt strongly that he had a political and diplomatic role and he had played a prominent part in improving Anglo-French relations, but his successor George V was the first British monarch to consider his role to be largely symbolic and he, dutifully, went along with the advice of his governments; he was, 'no more than an anguished and impotent spectator' of the unfolding tragedy. Apart from the Kaiser's occasional impetuosity, the monarchs of the great powers were cautious in their attitudes to international affairs; any blame that attaches to them for the outbreak of war relates to sins of omission rather than commission.

The prevalent view before 1914 was that, far from making a future war more likely, the fact that most European states were headed by monarchs – and that the monarchies of Europe were a cousinhood – provided an effective barrier against war. How could 'Willy and Nicky', who seemed to enjoy a close personal relationship, go to war with each other? Was it likely that what seemed the extended family of European royalty would be torn apart by war? On the brink of war the Kaiser's daughter, Queen Victoria's grand-daughter, married Prince Ernst August, son of the Duke of Cumberland, who would have been King of Hanover had not Bismarck abolished that kingdom. The wedding brought the Tsar of Russia and the King-Emperor of Britain, along with a galaxy of other monarchs, to Berlin. Here was a royal and family occasion, yet one at which so many of the wedding guests were committed to opposing alliances.

The interrelated nature of Europe's monarchies failed to stop the slide towards war. The nation, its ambitions, fears and hatreds, prevailed over the cousinhood of the monarchs, but then it also prevailed over the theoretical internationalism of socialism and the working class, and business's interest in peace.

Other historians have identified a malaise that went beyond politics or economics and for which cultural developments provide the most important line on the fever chart. Again, Germany, this time its literature, philosophy, painting and music, provides the central case study for those who find deep currents of unrest in pre-war Europe, an unrest characterised by sexual liberation, violence, and a revolt against cultural and social traditions. It has been argued that:

> Germany, more extensively than any other country, represented the aspirations of a national avant-garde – the desire to break out of the 'encirclement' of Anglo-French influence, the imposition of a world order by a Pax Britannica and French *civilisation*, an order codified politically as 'bourgeois liberalism'.[3]

Modris Eksteins' argument thus draws a parallel between Germany's *Weltpolitik* and a cultural attempt by German *Kultur* to break out of the suffocating embrace of *Zivilisation*. His argument is, thus, the anti-thesis to the view that the war represented a conflict between conservative, monarchist reactionary forces represented by Germany and more modern national democratic forces represented by Britain and France; rather, the war was a 'cultural confrontation between a revolutionary modernist Germany and a conservative England'.[4]

Germany's cultural *avant-garde* can be depicted as extreme in its opposition to both prevailing artistic conventions and social mores, as with the sexuality and violence of Frank Wedekind's 'Lulu plays' and Richard Strauss's *Salome*, while the influence of Friedrich Nietzsche's philosophic writings, with their emphasis upon the will to power and view of morality as a restraint upon freedom, is often seen as pervasive. In fine art, the works of Franz Marc and other early expressionists of the *Der Blaue Reiter* school are often cited as prophetic of war.

Yet, the cultural crisis or 'birth of modernism' was a pan-European phenomenon which took many contradictory forms. In Germany, and to some extent in Britain, the cult of the open air and nature encouraged youth organisations, hiking, and camping and a distrust of the urban and the modern, while the Italian Futurists were enthusiasts, not just for the modern in the shape of the latest technology or the speed at which the racing car or the aeroplane could travel, but for modern war. Filippo Tommaso Marinetti, author of the 1909 Futurist Manifesto, wrote that 'We will glorify war – the world's only hygiene' and liked the idea of it so much he became a war tourist during the Balkan Wars and wrote a very noisy poem, 'The Battle of Adrianople', in which words and sounds imitated artillery fire.

Some aspects of Futurism found an echo in the work of Wyndham Lewis and the British Vorticist movement, and there are contradictory views of Britain in the pre-war years: many viewed nostalgically the Edwardian period as a serene Indian summer of peace and, but this was to be challenged by G. Dangerfield's *The Strange Death of Liberal England* (1936), which portrayed a country in crisis as industrial unrest increased, suffragettes mounted a campaign of violence, and a constitutional crisis and even civil conflict seemed likely to result from the passage of a bill providing for Home Rule for Ireland.

Early twentieth-century German high culture had a particular rebellious intensity, but European culture in general shared a rest-lessness of spirit as old conventions in music art and literature were challenged. The comment by Virginia Woolf that, 'On or about December 1910 human nature changed' is absurd but thought-provoking, in that it is representative of the view of many intellectuals that human relationships, traditional morality and the nature of art were all changing rapidly in the years before 1914. A more popular choice for a symbolic date was 9 May 1913, the date of the opening night in Paris of Igor Stravinsky's *Rite of Spring*. To many, the music marked the abandonment of harmony and structure and the ballet a conscious primeval challenge to civilised art. Tuchman considered that with its performance 'all the major tendencies of the next half century had been stated'.[5]

David Fromkin sums up the view of a European civilisation in crisis:

> It may well be that the European sense of frustration – the sense of stalemate in life, art, and politics – led to a violent sense of aban-don, of letting go: a sense that the world ought to be blown up, and let the consequences be what they may. Europe's Nietzschean mood seemed to play some sort of role in making the Great War possible.[6]

There is, however, a contradictory view which questions how pervasive this mood of frustration and fascination with violence was, the extent to which a crisis in high culture caused either jubilation or angst among the majority of Europeans, and how unstable the governments and societies that went to war in 1914 were. Early twentieth century Europe, whether characterised as 'bourgeois' or 'ancien régime' can contrarily be seen as peaceful and prosperous. Living standards for most sections of society had been rising steadily since the late nine-teenth century, and people had more leisure time than ever before, a fact that was evident from the vibrancy of popular culture with its magazines, theatres of variety and spectator sports. Seaside holiday resorts in all western European countries may well have fallen into separate categories, catering for the rich, the middle orders or the poor, but the more important fact is that, increasingly, workers and their families could afford holidays. A retail revolution had done as much to improve living standards as had wage rises and made better food, clothing and household furnishings available to all but the very poor. This, as Michael S. Neiberg argues in his study of Europe and the outbreak of war, was far from a frustrated civilisation with a death wish or appetite for a great war. He depicts a Europe enjoying a peaceful summer in the weeks before the war, a Europe on holiday, with even the Kaiser on his yacht. Few expected a war and far fewer wanted one. Each nation valued its sovereignty and individuality but there was, Neiberg asserts, a social and cultural unity.[7]

How, then, did the governments of so many states gain, within a few weeks, the assent of the majority of their populations to war?

Cheering Crowds

A familiar depiction of the reactions of the populations of the states that went to war is one of enthusiastic and irrational patriotism, cheering crowds in the streets and squares of capital cities, a new-found national unity as political divisions were set aside, and men eager to volunteer queuing outside recruiting centres. This view has been embedded in popular consciousness by novels, films and television programmes.

A number of historians have recently questioned the thesis of mass bellicosity and though they have not replaced the view that populations, faced with a war that had seemed unlikely only a few weeks earlier, largely rallied behind their governments, a much qualified and nuanced interpretation has emerged.[8] Public expressions of enthusiasm were inevitably an urban phenomenon, and rather too much emphasis has been placed on demonstrations of support for the war in capital cities and other large towns. Despite advances in communications, news that their countries were at war filtered only slowly to many rural areas and in *France profonde* ('deep' or rural France) the news had to be announced after the tolling of church bells had gathered local populations together; it was not received with enthusiasm. The reaction of Russian peasants seems to have been one of despair and anger. Even in the cities, several studies have pointed to the degree that flag-waving crowds seem to have included a large proportion of young white-collar workers while working-class suburbs remained subdued.

This does not mean that there was not support for the war, but rather that the view of excitement and exhilaration at its announcement has been exaggerated and was confined to certain social groups. General support developed more slowly as populations became convinced reluctantly that their governments were justified, that the enemy states were aggressors, and that the war had to be fought.

The supposed obstacles to a major conflict were quickly shown to be easily bypassed. Angell had not been wrong in thinking that a great war would be injurious to finance and trade and would be unwelcome to bankers and industrialists, but he had overestimated their influence and the ability of economic interests to obstruct political and military decisions. There was financial panic, but as Niall Ferguson has put it: 'Angell and the rest had got it the wrong way round: the banks could not stop a war – but war could stop the banks.'[9] Financiers and the owners of the means of production soon adapted to the impulse to put the national cause above the dislocation of international trade and turned to finding ways of financing the war effort and transforming industrial production in the interests of war economies. The widespread view that socialism and the labour movements were internationalist and that the solidarity of working-class movements would mean a united pan-European opposition to war was, similarly, almost immediately shown to have been wrong. The German Social Democrats (SPD), by far the strongest of Europe's socialist parties, was at first directed by its executive to demonstrate for peace, but, as the crisis worsened, the leaders assured the government that they were loyal Germans and, as Russia mobilised, SPD deputies in the Reichstag, fearful of exposing Germany to conquest by autocratic Russia and its barbaric hordes, voted for war credits and a domestic political truce. French socialists, influenced by the last speeches of Jean Jaurès, assassinated on the eve of war, argued that the defence of socialism and of France and French traditions were one and the same. In Britain, the Labour Party, which, though not a socialist party, was the parliamentary voice of the trade unions, also swung round to support for the war; a process that involved the ousting of its party chairman, Ramsay MacDonald, who, with a number of Independent Labour Party members opposed this policy. In 1915 Arthur Henderson, a leading Labour MP, joined the coalition cabinet.

Kaiser Wilhelm declared, as the great majority of German Social Democrats (SPD) voted for war credits, 'Henceforth I know no parties.' The President of the French Chamber of Deputies spoke in similar vein: 'There are no more adversaries here, there are only Frenchmen', while in Britain, the unifying effect of the declaration of war brought John Bull's other island back temporarily into the fold as even the fratricidal conflict in Ireland between Ulster Unionists and southern Nationalists was stilled.

For socialists at the time, affronted by the failure of a European working-class to display international solidarity against the war, and for leftist historians later, the concept of an emotional spasm which led to the war being supported by working people and labour leaders had an appeal, while it also provided, as Catriona Pennel describes in her study of the United Kingdom's response to the outbreak of war, a 'cathartic explanation' for pacifists, who believed that all wars were irrational and that people who supported war in 1914 were necessarily behaving irrationally.[10]

The recent reassessment of the notion of 'war fever', has not replaced it by an opposite in which there was widespread opposition to the war but by a picture of the populations of the combatant states coming, rightly or wrongly, to the conclusion that the war was necessary. They did so reluctantly, not because they were deluded or brainwashed but because they were convinced that *their* cause was just. A further consideration was the absence of an alternative, not just for individuals but for nations, for once the war had started any nation proposing peace might find itself at an immediate disadvantage.

Essentially, public opinion in all the states that went to war seems to have been satisfied that their country was fighting a just and a defensive war, a war that had been made necessary by the actions of devious and implacable enemies. In *Dance of the Furies*, Michael S. Neiberg quotes the Berlin correspondent of the Manchester Guardian reporting that 'Germany is really drifting into war against her will' and adds that this observation could well stand for 'an entire continent that was going to a war its people firmly believed they had no role in starting'.[11]

Europe thus found itself in a bloody cul-de-sac from which there was no easy means of escape. Later generations have expressed bewilderment that not only did the war continue without victory for either side, but that popular opinion continued to support the war as the death toll mounted and, even for civilians, hardships increased. But to hope for victory and press on was the obvious course, especially as most of the populations of the combatant states became convinced that the national cause was just, while the effect of ever-mounting casualty figures was to increase hatred of the enemy rather than a desire for peace.

Chapter 4:   Elusive Victory

It has become almost a cliché that the general expectation in August 1914 was that the war would be short, even 'over by Christmas'. Such optimism may well have been generally true of the attitudes of excited sections of the public in combatant states, of much of the press whose patriotic fervour urged men to recruiting offices, and of many of the government ministers who had led their countries to war, but the views of military commanders were mixed. War plans and strategies nearly all reflected the concept of mobile offensive campaigns in which enemy armies would be enveloped, great decisive battles be fought, and victory swiftly secured, yet even von Moltke, who was in charge of implementing his modification of the ambitious Schlieffen Plan, had prophesied a long and desperate struggle, while Lord Kitchener horrified the British cabinet with his conviction that the war would last for years.

The great myth was that an offensive by well-trained forces with high morale would be able to overcome defensive positions. The history of warfare and the technology of war had seen an oscillation between times when defence was more formidable than attack and times when the opposite was the case, and the early twentieth century was a period when, largely due to the machine-gun and barbed wire, defence had the advantage. There was, in 1914, little excuse for not realising how horrific modern war might be, or for failing to understand the way that technology favoured the defence; the American Civil War and the Russo-Japanese War had revealed the nature of industrialised warfare. Many generals did appreciate this, but, regarding the facts as inconvenient truths unsuitable for laymen and not wishing to appear defeatist, had failed to pass on their knowledge to governments or admit it openly. High commands held out prospects of rapid victories to governments, and the campaign plans they made were for great mobile advances that would envelop enemy armies, but these were contradicted by the secret fears many had as to what could go wrong. It was significant, however, that no power had prepared for a long war in terms of how to pay for one, how to replace the armaments and ammunition lost or used up, or how to maintain the living standards of its population. The illusion of a short, victorious war was soon dispelled and any hopes that it would not bring about enormous numbers of dead and wounded did not last much longer; by the end of 1914 each side had suffered a million casualties on the Western Front alone.

Military plans did not cause the war, but, once the brakes of foreign offices, governments and the cousinhood of monarchs failed, the plans, with their mobilisation timetables and the need to maintain advantages as troops and weaponry were moved into position, accelerated the move to war as much as the domino effect of the alliances with which they were entwined. All the states at war with the exception of Britain[1] had drawn up military plans to be put into practice in the event of war, but the Schlieffen Plan was not only the most detailed and the most worked over, but it carried with it not just military but diplomatic complications. It represented a disjunction between military planning and diplomatic policy. German foreign policy had aimed at securing agreement with Britain and, at the least, British neutrality in any war, but the plan's dependence on access to France through neutral countries and, in its final form, passage through Belgium, enabled the pro-war faction in the British cabinet to triumph. The German high command saw the military advantage gained by attacking France through Belgium as essential to the plan's success; Bethmann Hollweg had realised it might well result in a British declaration of war, but military necessity made the risk worth taking. Similarly, the timing of Germany's declarations of war on Russia and France, born of a mixture of diplomatic propriety and military pressure, released Italy and Romania from any obligation to come into the war on Germany's side as the terms of the Triple Alliance declared that they had no obligation to do so unless Germany was attacked.

By 1914, German military planning had become concentrated on a single option. Until 1913 an alternative to the Schlieffen Plan had been kept alive: an Eastern Option by which a defensive war would be fought in the west while there would be an offensive in the east, north of the Vistula. As Annika Mombauer has argued, such a plan might have provided a feasible alternative to the Schlieffen Plan when, at the end of the July crisis, it looked for a short time as if French neutrality was a possibility.[2] At any rate, the fact remains that by opting for a single plan, and failing to give the Eastern Deployment Plan its annual update in April 1913, the German high command boxed itself in and lacked the flexibility to respond to events.

Germany's Offensive in the West

Once Germany had declared war on France, German hopes of success in the west depended on the success of the deceased general's plan as modified by his successor, von Moltke. One of Schlieffen's main worries as he tinkered with his plan had been whether his armies were big enough for the tasks he had set them, though his other problem was how to enable armies of the size he had allocated to his strong right wing to advance rapidly along the roads available. It was all very well transporting these forces by rail to the German–Belgian frontier, but thereafter they would have to make their way on foot accompanied by horse-drawn transport.[3] His worry as to whether his forces were strong enough was, of course, in tune with the general German concern that the Reich's armies were being outmatched by the increases in the strength of the Russian and French forces. The numbers both sides had available for the coming confrontation in the west were disadvantageous: German forces of 1,700,000 men were outnumbered by the 2,000,000 on the French side, to which 100,000 Belgians and British were to be added.

Numbers were important, but the German army was a better trained and more efficient fighting force. French universal conscription for three years provided the army with large numbers of young men but at the cost of a reduction in the size of the reserve. The Germans, with their more selective form of conscription. were able to devote more resources to training and equipment: their army was superior in artillery and mortars, men served for two years and then went into the reserve, reporting for annual training, and they had three times as many NCOs as the French. One of the strengths of the German army was that, rather than having a chain of command in which orders came from the top and the duty of the lower ranks was simply to obey, junior officers and NCOs were encouraged to show initiative, something which was to prove effective in the confusion of battle.

German forces, having first taken control of Luxembourg, crossed into Belgium on 4 August. They did so four days after German mobilisation had begun, but a fortnight before that mobilisation was due to be complete. The hope was that in the light of German promises that, after the war, Belgium's frontiers would be recognised again and compensation paid for damage, the Belgians would put up only a token resistance. That hope was to be swiftly confounded for as soon as it was known in Brussels that German troops had crossed the border King Albert rushed to parliament and secured its support for resistance.

The first task for the German army was to take the great Belgian fortress of Liege, but the Belgian army had demolished most of the bridges across the Meuse and mounted a tenacious defence of the complex fortifications. The German attackers suffered heavy casualties but by 16 August the inner citadel had been taken and the defensive forts been reduced by heavy artillery. The Belgian forces withdrew to their fortified national redoubt at Antwerp. The siege of Liege had not been the most propitious start to Germany's war plan, but the way was now open for the three German armies, three-quarters of a million strong, who composed the right-wing to implement the Schlieffen Plan. They poured into France on 18 August marching at the extraordinary speed of twenty miles a day, while the left-flank stood on the defensive in fortified positions in Lorraine. Although the left flank was weaker than the attacking right flank, it was larger than had been intended by Schlieffen, and Moltke was criticised later for having made it needlessly strong.

Meanwhile, the French army had not been idle and the French commander-in-chief, General Joseph Joffre, had begun his own offensives. French forces had invaded Lorraine on 8 August and been driven back, but on 14 August Joffre put the first stage of France's Plan XVII into effect. The intention was to drive the Germans out of Alsace and Lorraine and back to the Rhine, an aim at once reflective of French patriotism and the belief that an offensive spirit could triumph over the defence. As the French armies advanced, the Germans initially fell back, but gradually their resistance stiffened and on 20 August French troops were mown down as they charged uphill against the German lines at Sarrebourg, after which the Germans launched a counter-offensive along the whole line. Very nearly enveloped on both flanks the French were lucky to withdraw behind the River Meurthe whence they had begun their advance. The Germans, should, in accordance with the Schlieffen Plan, have refrained from a further offensive by the left-wing, but von Moltke gave in to the demands of the commanders in Lorraine, Crown Prince Rupprecht of Bavaria and General von Dellmensingen, to renew their offensive – a mistake, as the French were now behind strong defences and easily withstood the German attack.

On 21 August, Joffre launched another attack. As the German right was evidently strong and the left had proved to be stronger than previously thought, he considered that the centre in the Ardennes was the place to attack. In fact German forces in the Ardennes were themselves advancing and were of equal strength to the armies Joffre sent against them. The French 3rd and 4th armies were defeated in fierce fighting in which the German artillery played a decisive role on 21–22 August. The French Plan XVII had come to a standstill and by the end of August 75,000 French soldiers had been killed and 200,000 were wounded or prisoners.

All was now in place for the main German attack. The retreat of the Belgians into their entrenched positions at Antwerp had opened the way for the German right wing and for the decisive battle which von Schlieffen had planned. Their forces, under Generals von Kluck, von Bülow and von Hausen, were advancing rapidly. Joffre seemed purblind to the danger and, confident that there was no serious threat in the north-west, had left only his 5th Army on the northern end of the French line, supported by the small British Expeditionary Force (BEF), to meet Germany's main thrust. Hard-pressed, the commander of the French 5th Army, General Charles Lanrezac, retreated before the main German advance and lost touch with the recently disembarked BEF under the command of Sir John French, which found itself faced with the main force of General von Kluck's 1st Army at the Mons–Conde Canal. The battle which followed is called the Sambre by the French and Mons by the British, after the two rivers around which the fighting took place.

The BEF, an army of experienced regulars, battle-hardened in the Boer War, acquitted itself well. The rifle fire from their Lee Enfields of one round every four seconds enabled two divisions to hold off six German divisions and to inflict three times the casualties to their own, which were 1,850. On the Mons–Conde canal their defensive entrenchments foreshadowed the digging in of all armies on the Western Front. Eventually forced to withdraw when the Germans brought up howitzers and by Lanrezac's retreat, the BEF's success in holding up the German advance was, as David Stevenson puts it, 'dwarfed by the comprehensive allied debacle in the "battle of the frontiers"' (as the engagements of 20–24 August are collectively known).[4]

The BEF had fought well, but whether Britain's only well-trained and experienced army was in the right place and put to the best use so early in the war has been questioned. The decision to send a British force to France as quickly as possible and to then place it in the French line was essentially political. The BEF was a well-organised and well-equipped professional army and Churchill, for one, thought at the time that it would have been better used as a decisive strategic reserve instead of being sent to the Belgian frontier on the left wing of the French 5th Army. Even its commander, Sir John French, had favoured a rear concentration in Amiens. It performed magnificently at Mons, the first of the costly battles it was to be called upon to fight, but by late September it was largely destroyed. Rather than placing this fine army in the front line so soon, it might have been wiser to have saved it so as to provide a nucleus and a training arm for the larger armies Britain would need to recruit for a long war.

That a well-managed retreat can be as important to the outcome of a war as a successful offensive was demonstrated by the 'Great Retreat' of the French and British Armies from the Meuse to take up positions for the defence of Paris. The Allied forces had a number of advantages, not the least of which was their control of the French railways, which enabled them to move troops far more rapidly than the Germans, who were advancing on foot, but disagreements between the British and their French allies, already fractious after Lanrezac's failure to keep Sir John French informed about the French army's intentions when it retreated to the River Sambre, were mounting. It took the intervention of the War Secretary, Lord Kitchener, to convey to Sir John the cabinet's instructions that he stay in the line and conform to the movements of the French army.

Faults intrinsic to the Schlieffen Plan were, however, becoming evident: railways and bridges in Belgium had been sabotaged, ammunition supplies were endangered as horses fell sick without proper corn, and troops, expected to march day-after-day, were exhausted. As the German armies advanced, communications and co-ordination became a problem. Von Moltke was directing operations from far behind the front and the inadequate telegraph and telephone lines were often intercepted by the French. The German aim had been a decisive and rapid victory over France while a defensive war was fought against Russia. The fear that lurked in the back of the minds of the German high command had always been that Russian might would be brought to bear more quickly than expected and that Germany would be invaded before France was defeated. It needed a strong and determined commander to proceed with the battle of France and not be deflected by such fears, and von Moltke was not such a man. By September, he was feeling the strain and was proving too susceptible to appeals for assistance from particular generals to stick firmly to the principles of the plan he had inherited from von Schlieffen. Thus, he took troops away from the decisive front and weakened the strong right wing by sending reinforcements to assist in the containment of the Belgian Army in Antwerp and other redoubts, and, becoming concerned about the position of the 8th Army far away in Prussia, where it was hard-pressed by the Russians, detached two corps to the Eastern Front, despite the fact that they were not needed there. Moltke compounded this weakening of the main thrust of the German advance by ordering his armies on the left wing to attack, which they did without success, an order which was in contradiction to the basic plan of leaving the offensive to the right wing.

In the last days of August the command structure of the German forces became increasingly dislocated; not only was the Schlieffen plan being abandoned, but no coherent strategy took its place. David Stevenson's view is that, 'Moltke's actions at this juncture suggest he was determined to protect Germany's territories, whether in East Prussia or Alsace, but willing to strike wherever the enemy seemed weak, rather than staking everything on the right flank'.[5] On 27 August he gave instructions for a general advance with his two right-wing armies under Bülow and Kluck moving south-westwards towards the Seine and Paris while his Fourth and Fifth Armies were to advance into French Lorraine. He then altered his instructions and ordered Kluck's 1st Army to move south-eastwards, which would take him east rather than west of Paris, thus abandoning the plan of sweeping west of the city.

Much now depended on Joffre. A very different character to Moltke, his composure and refusal to alter his peacetime routine disguised his determination and ruthlessness. He did not lose his nerve after his initial failures, but set about raising new armies from the French interior, shifting others from east to west and sacking 58 of his least competent generals. As Kluck's and Bülow's armies drove between Paris and Verdun, he saw an opportunity for a strike against Kluck's left flank and ordered an attack to begin on 6 September. However, Kluck was moving fast and fighting actually started on the previous day when Kluck's force clashed with the newly raised French 6th Army. This was the occasion on which French troops were conveyed by Parisian taxis to the battleground, something which has passed into legend as a great patriotic act, though taxi-drivers being taxi-drivers they kept their meters running.[6] The confrontation which began would become known as the battle of the Marne and would go on until 9 September.

The battle of the Marne has been seen as one of the most decisive battles in history. Certainly its outcome ended the German offensive and marked the point in the war in the west ceased to be a war of movement. It was not a concentrated battle but a long, strung-out affair, with fighting extending along a hundred-mile front from Paris to Verdun and from there to the Swiss frontier. It was not, perhaps, the battle itself that was decisive, however, but the orders from the

German high command on 8–9 September to break off the action. Luck plays a large part in warfare and, as Hew Strachan has argued, 'if the French line had broken anywhere – particularly between Verdun and Toul or south of Nancy – the battle of the Marne would have been lost as surely as if things had miscarried round Paris'.[7] But Moltke was not a lucky commander.

By 8 September the battle seemed to be going in favour of the Germans. The attempt to trap them by a pincer movement from Verdun had been unsuccessful, in the central sector around the St Gond marshes the German 2nd Army had halted an offensive by the newly formed French 9th Army under General Foch, while in the west, and along the Ourcq, Kluck's forces had repelled an attack by General Maunoury's 6th Army. The British had, however, had some success when, after seeing a gap between Kluck's and Bülow's forces, the BEF had been able to move forward against little opposition. This pointed to the difficulties faced by the German right wing to the west of Paris. Its strength had been eroded, in part by Moltke's decisions, but also by its loss of many men, the exhausted state of the rest after their long marches, and by a shortage of ammunition for the artillery. In the western half of the battlefield the Allies now enjoyed a numerical advantage, with some 30 divisions as opposed to Kluck and Bülow's 20.

It *was* a decisive battle in that the end-result was the withdrawal of German forces to secure defensive positions above the Aisne, but, it can be argued, it was called off by the German high command when their forces still had a good chance of winning. Moltke was by this time heading for a nervous breakdown and at his headquarters in Luxembourg was far away from and out of touch with his generals on the field of battle, Kluck and Bülow, who failed to liaise with each other. The orders to withdraw were given on the basis of reports from Lieutenant-Colonel Hentsch, foreign intelligence chief of Oberste Heeresleitung (OHL), the German High Command, who had been despatched by Moltke from Luxembourg as an intermediary between supreme headquarters and the commanders of the right-wing armies. Whether this comparatively junior officer exceeded the instructions given him by Moltke has long been debated. He discussed the situation with Bülow, who advised a withdrawal, but he did not visit Kluck's 1st Army headquarters. Hentsch's advice to Moltke appears to have been crucial in persuading the latter to order a general withdrawal to the Aisne. Whether this was a correct decision is another matter. As one distinguished historian of the war has argued:

Yet, even with superior numbers, fresh troops, and massive consumption of munitions, the French were still being forced back. Given a few more days the Germans could probably have seen off Joffre's counterstroke, ensconcing themselves within striking distance of Paris and of the trunk railway between the capital and Lorraine. But to the OHL the picture seemed much grimmer and on 8–9 September it resolved to break the action off. Moltke did not exactly snatch defeat from the jaws of victory, but almost certainly he could have secured a better situation by persisting.[8]

Whether or not von Moltke was justified in breaking off the action, another major study has concluded that, although tactically indecisive, 'the Marne was a truly decisive battle in the Napoleonic sense' and Germany had failed to secure the quick victory on which its war plan rested. From now on it was committed to a war on two fronts. 'With hindsight, some would say, Germany had already lost the war.'[9] After Moltke gave the order to retreat, the German armies retraced their steps over hard-won ground to the river Aisne and by 14 September had established themselves on a chalk ridge some 600 feet above the river. There they dug in and erected barbed-wire defences. This was the beginning of 'trench warfare' and ironically it was Moltke, now relieved of his command, a general who had sought to defeat France by a sweeping offensive, who initiated a form of warfare which in which the defensive had an enormous advantage. Attacks ordered by Joffre were easily repulsed and this part of the front experienced the stalemate that was soon to characterise the whole of the war in France and Belgium.

Now began the 'race to the sea' as General Erich von Falkenhayn, who was now, in practice, commander-in-chief of the German army, attempted to manoeuvre around the Allied left wing, thus initiating counter moves to the left by the allied armies, a slow waltz by which, from mid-September, the resultant clashes took the German right and the Allied left further and further to the north-west until a line of trenches extended to Nieuport on the Belgian coast.

A stalemate was emerging, but Falkenhayn perceived an opportunity for a major offensive in Flanders which would force the Allied forces out of Belgium altogether. German forces took Bruges and Ghent and began an assault upon Antwerp, a city with massive fortifications to which the bulk of the Belgian army had retreated. Utilising the great guns that had destroyed the fortifications of Liege to make breaches in Antwerp's defences before sending in the infantry, the German attack was successful, though held up for a time by a Royal Naval Division, which arrived by train to come to the aid of the Belgian defenders. After a week of fighting, Antwerp was surrendered on 10 October. Its fall released three divisions to add to the force assembled by Falkenhayn for his planned sweep to expel the Allied forces from Flanders and to take the Channel ports, while in addition he had four new army corps who had been in training since the start of the war. On the Allies' side, the BEF had been moved by train from the Aisne to the Channel coast to take up new positions to the north and west in Flanders.

The resulting clash was bloody. Its epicentre was Ypres, a town which the British troops were soon to call, without affection, 'Wipers'. The BEF pushed back the German 6th Army but were unable to advance far. North of the town the four new German corps were halted at the river Yser when the Belgians opened flood gates and created a five-mile wide flood plain. With relative immobility on both sides, fighting became channelled around Ypres itself. At and around the town a fierce battle took place between the five corps of the BEF, supported by Belgian troops, who defended the town, and a formidable German attacking force which included the new German corps, largely made up of volunteers who had received minimum training. The First Battle of Ypres lasted from late October until the middle of November and cost both sides some 130,000 casualties. This was the end of the old regular British army, which lost 60,000 men, and the Belgians lost a third of their remaining army. For the Germans, the great loss passed into national memory as the 'massacre of the innocents', those patriotic young men who had enlisted in August.[10] Some of the heaviest fighting took place in the 'Ypres salient' an area which jutted out beyond the town and which was tenaciously defended by the British, not for any serious military purpose but because its loss would have been seen as a setback and would have dismayed opinion back in Britain.

The end of the First Battle of Ypres came when the German high command decided to concentrate upon the war with Russia and to improve the defences of its armies in Belgium and France by extending and deepening their trenches along the whole of their front. This was to set the scene for the battles of 1915.

The Eastern Front

The Russian army, by far the largest in Europe, inspired French hopes and German fears. Not only had it recovered from the defeat by Japan, but its capacity to mobilise swiftly had been enhanced by expensive improvements to Russia's strategic railway system. The apparent military recovery of Russia made Germany's decision to concentrate on defeating France while going on the defensive to the east seem riskier in 1914 than it might have appeared a few years earlier, although apprehensions of that strategy caused the French to insist that their Russian ally should go on the offensive in order to take some of the pressure off France. The German strategy of concentrating its main forces in the west thus left it with a single army, the 8th, to defend East Prussia. In contrast, the numerical strength of the Russian army was so great that it could plan to send the bulk of its western forces, stationed close to Warsaw, south to the Carpathians and on into Austro-Hungarian territory and still find armies with which to invade East Prussia.

The Austro-Hungarian government, whose ultimatum of 23 July and subsequent declaration of war on Serbia of 28 July had done much to bring about the wider conflict, was tardy in formally joining its ally, Germany, in the war against its enemies, delaying its declaration of war on Russia until 5 August and, rather than declaring war on France and Britain, waiting for them to declare war on it, which they did on 12 August. This reflected Austria-Hungary's greater appetite for war against Serbia than for the wider conflict it was now faced with, an approach that was further demonstrated by its failure to co-ordinate its strategy with Germany's. It was almost as if the Austrians were reluctant to recognise that they were at war, not just with a small Balkan state, but with the Russian Empire. The German military leaders were as much to blame as their Austro-Hungarian counterparts for the lack of liaison between the two allies. Not only did von Moltke not share knowledge of German planning with the Austrians, but the German military seems to have been ignorant about the strengths and weaknesses of the Austro-Hungarian army, even to the extent of not realising its complex ethnic mix.[11] A co-ordinated strategy between the 'Central Powers', as Germany and Austria would become known, would have meant moving the greater part of Austro-Hungarian forces to the border between Austrian Galicia and Russian Poland (the Duchy of Warsaw) ready to resist the inevitable Russian invasion and take some of the pressure off Germany as it prepared to fight its defensive war in the east.

Conrad von Hötzendorf had, indeed, promised von Moltke that the greater part of his forces would be used against the Russians, and this was supposed to be the war plan: seven divisions against Serbia, the rest for Russia, but in the event he sent about a third of his army to deal with Serbia and instead of directing the force earmarked to face the Russians to the Galician frontier, ordered it to take up positions well behind the border close to the Carpathian mountains, while a third army intended to be used in whatever theatre it was most needed, was put on trains bound for the Balkans. Conrad's strategy seems to have been based on the hope that the Russians would be so slow in their advance that he would be able to crush the Serbs before he had to fight the much more formidable enemy. The German high command and the Kaiser himself, justifiably horrified at the Austrian desire to concentrate on defeating a small Balkan country when a wider war was developing, put pressure on Conrad, who had then to attempt to get troops bound for the Balkans turned round and sent to Galicia. The only solution, other than to doom the Austro-Hungarian railways to months of chaos, was for the troops to carry on to the Serbian frontier, get out of their trains, get back in again, and set off for the Russian front. Not a propitious beginning for Austria-Hungary's war.

While Austria-Hungary attempted to defeat the Serbs and dithered over its preparations to resist the Russians, the war between Germany and Russia had already begun. In accordance with their agreement with the French, the Russians had decided that if Germany's main effort was made against France their Plan A would come into operation: their south-western armies assembling on the borders of East Galicia would attack the Austrians and their north-western armies would invade East Prussia. In mid-August this dual offensive began.

Two Russian armies invaded East Prussia, the 1st Army under General Pavel Rennenkampf moving westwards between the Masurian Lakes and Königsberg, while the 2nd, commanded by General Aleksandr Samsonov, moved north from Warsaw, invaded from the south-east and moved towards Graudenz. The intention was to trap the German 8th Army, a smaller force than the combined Russian armies, in a pincer movement. Unfortunately the two generals, members of opposing factions within the Russian army's command,[12] failed to cooperate, a process made difficult in any case by poor communication systems and the nature of the terrain. The claws of the pincer became further and further apart as the two Russian armies, separated from the beginning as they had set off five days apart, lost contact with each other as they traversed the edges of the 50-mile-wide Masurian chain of lakes.

Things, nevertheless, went the Russian way at the first serious encounter when the German 8th Army mounted a frontal attack on the Russian 1st Army at Gumbinnen. The German General Hermann von François enjoyed initial success but then came up against troops in defensive positions sheltered by farm buildings and villages. The Germans suffered 8,000 casualties in a few hours and a panicked retreat began. Commander of the 8th Army, General Max von Prittwitz, lost his nerve and informed von Moltke, far away in Koblenz, by telephone that he would have to have to abandon East Prussia and fall back on the Vistula.

The thought of leaving East Prussia to its fate or rather, to the Russians horrified Moltke. Giving up any part of German territory would have been bad for morale, but East Prussia was the homeland of the army's elite, so Prittwitz did not survive as commander for long after his moment of panic. He was replaced by a retired general who had applied for re-appointment at the beginning of the war, Paul Ludwig Hans Anton von Beneckendorff und von Hindenburg – known universally as Paul von Hindenburg – while Erich Ludendorff, who had shown ability at Liege and had a reputation as a skilled organiser, was appointed chief-of-staff. This odd couple, a steady, if unimaginative, aristocrat and a ruthless, middle-class technocrat, were to work well together and were eventually to dominate Germany's war.

Von Prittwitz's desperate appeal rushed von Moltke into unnecessarily withdrawing two corps from the Western Front and sending them to the east. They were not needed, for the 8th Army's staff, and in particular its chief of operations, Colonel Max Hoffmann, had already salvaged the situation following Gumbinnen by transferring troops by rail and foot to the south-west and taking up positions on the west and east flanks of the Russian 2nd Army as it trudged northwards. This move drew on the experiences of pre-war exercises, which had suggested that the way to defeat two invading armies separated by East Prussia's chain of lakes and forests was to defeat one and then turn on the other. Rennenkampf had not been defeated, but François's impetuous attack had halted his advance and he was short of ammunition. He felt no great sense of urgency and, as he sensed fewer German troops in front of him, suspected a German withdrawal to Königsberg, rather than a removal to the south-west. The rudimentary nature of the Russians' communication system meant that the orders of the overall commander, General Yakov Zhilinski, who was several hundred miles away, were intercepted and the Germans knew full well that Rennenkampf would not pursue while the bulk of the 8th Army moved south to take on Samsonov.

On 24 August the Germans made contact with Samsonov's army and the Battle of Tannenberg began. Gradually, as the Russian columns pushed northwards, German attacks from both flanks increased and on 26 and 27 August cut through the Russian centre. On 29 August, German troops under François's command pressing eastwards met up with other German units fighting southwards and both realised that Samsonov was surrounded. What followed was what John Keegan has called a classic 'cauldron' operation, a rarity in the First World War, although common on the Eastern Front in the Second.[13] The Russians were encircled and demoralised, while their ammunition and rations were beginning to run low. They began to surrender; nearly 100,000 were taken prisoner and 50,000 killed and wounded. General Samsonov committed suicide.

Tannenberg (the name came from a nearby village where in 1410 the Teutonic Knights had been defeated by the Slavs) became celebrated as Germany's greatest victory in the war; it had saved East Prussia from conquest and prevented a dangerous advance towards Silesia. It also turned Hindenburg and Ludendorff into heroes, though they did not deserve credit for the battle plan which, as we have seen, had been devised by the 8th Army's staff officers and approved by the unfortunate von Prittwitz before his dismissal, while a vital role was played by General von François, who had not only led the eastward assault of the Russian army, but had, by disobeying Ludendorff's order to desist at a crucial point in the battle, ensured victory. The battle was, indeed, a great triumph for the Germans, but it was not the decisive victory it was made out to be. Tannenberg mattered, it has been argued,

> because of its propaganda effect, its effect on perceptions... the idea that it created of a decisive and historic success, helped obscure the absence of such a victory where it was actually wanted, in the West. The illusion of German military invincibility was fostered, not simply in the minds of the German press-reading public but also in those responsible for the direction of policy itself.[14]

Many of its gains were soon reversed, for when Ludendorff launched the 8th Army, reinforced by the corps transferred by Moltke from the west, against the Russian 1st Army, its commander, Rennenkampf proved himself to be a capable general. In the battle of the Masurian Lakes the Russians conducted a fighting retreat back across the border and, on 25 September, counter-attacked, driving the Germans back and recapturing much of the ground lost at Tannenberg.

Nevertheless, the Germans had had the best of the fighting in East Prussia and had done so with forces that were not only inferior in numbers, but were composed largely of reserve divisions, Landwehr units and garrison troops. The Russians were, however, to do rather better against their other enemy, Austria-Hungary. The main body of Russia's forces were deployed at the southern end of the salient of the Duchy of Warsaw which jutted out between the territory of the two Central powers, a spearhead for an attack towards Posen, Silesia and even Berlin, as Russia's commander-in-chief, Grand Duke Nicholas,

saw it, but also potentially vulnerable in the event of a pincer movement by German and Austrian forces.

As we have seen, the commander-in-chief of the Austro-Hungarian
forces, Conrad von Hötzendorf,[15] had failed to align his strategy with
that of Germany. Worse still, the plan for a quick victory over Serbia
had not only failed, but, by 19 August, the invasion of Serbia had been
humiliatingly repulsed, while the troops that ought to have been sent
to the frontier with Russian Poland had not yet arrived there after
their diversion to the Balkans. Conrad may have misled the Germans
with his promise to make war with Russia his first priority, but such
dissembling was also true of his German ally, for Moltke, finding that
the Austrians were not content with assurances that France would be
speedily dealt with, had promised support for an Austrian offensive
against Russia, a promise he must have known he could not fulfil.
Conrad had, in any case, wavered and ended up with the largest
part of his forces committed to the Serbian front, while operations
in Galicia were delayed. Nevertheless, two Austro-Hungarian armies
were in place in Galicia by late August, ready to launch Conrad's
planned offensive against Russian Poland, despite the fact that help
from the German army in East Prussia was far from certain.

Conrad has been described as representing the best fruits of the
nineteenth-century school of warfare and its worst defect, the failure to appreciate the part that material factors had come to play in
modern warfare: 'Lacking a sense of tactical reality, he would attempt
feats of strategic virtuosity for which his instrument was inherently
unfitted'.[16] Certainly, the instrument, the Austro-Hungarian Army,
was unfitted for his ambitious plan to defeat the Russian Army in
September 1914 and Conrad's armies were oddly situated for an
offensive as they were detrained well behind the frontier, which
meant a long and exhausting march before they met the enemy.

'From the beginning', a major authority on the Eastern Front has
commented, 'the Austro-Hungarian forces in Galicia were bedevilled,
not only by delays, but also by a fundamental uncertainty as to what
they were meant to achieve.'[17] For decades, the imperial government
had saved money by cutting back expenditure on the army, and the
first weeks of the war had seen confusion and mishaps. Nevertheless,
on 23 August Austrian forces went forward across the border into
Russian Poland along a 175 mile front with morale seemingly intact.
In engagements on the northern border with Russian Poland the
Austrians, led by their cavalry, advanced rapidly, while a Russian
advance into Austrian territory was repulsed with major losses before
retiring to the Russo-Polish town of Kraśnik. The Russians suffered

a further reverse at Komarów where they only escaped encirclement by retreating. On the eastern part of the front, however, the Austro-Hungarians attacked an immensely superior force, both in terms of numbers and of artillery and machine guns, near Lemberg and were soundly defeated and forced to retreat into Lemberg's great fortress, leaving the town to the Russians.

After Lemberg, Austro-Hungarian counterstrokes failed and a general retreat was ordered to the Carpathian line to the south and to the Dunajec river east of Cracow. The Austro-Hungarians were now on the defensive, a posture that in almost every corner of the war was proving to have advantages over the offensive, and the Russian armies had to advance via waterlogged roads, while in their way stood another great fortress, Przemyśl, garrisoned by 100,000 troops. The war in eastern Europe, like the war in France, was becoming a stalemate, although of a rather different kind. Not only was the front almost twice as long as that in France and Belgium, but the density of soldiers on either side was much lower. One reason for immobility on the Western Front was that whenever one side made a breakthrough, railways enabled the other side to rapidly bring up reinforcements, whereas in an area like Russian Poland, railway systems were sparse.

By the autumn of 1914, the great plans of the military commanders in all the combatant states had failed, revealing the truth of von Moltke the elder's statement that 'No plan of operations extends with certainty beyond the first encounter with the enemy's mass weight.' On 14 September his nephew paid the price for failure when he was dismissed as commander-in-chief and replaced by General von Falkenhayn, previously Prussian minister of war. What was becoming clear was that the German army was superior to the Russian in everything except numbers and that its professionalism was enabling it to get the better of its opponent in most encounters, but what was equally obvious was that Austria-Hungary was 'close to being unable to fight the Russians without German help'.[18] Norman Stone has referred to a 'more or less constant Austro-Hungarian crisis'.[19] What was perhaps surprising was that the Austro-Hungarian armies held together as well as they did, considering their multi-ethnic composition and the way they had been starved of resources for decades. It is, nevertheless, the case that their performance was very variable; units drawn from areas like Vienna or the Sudetenland could perform as well as German units, but Slav troops were unreliable when fighting Russians, although later in the war they fought well enough against Italians.

Falkenhayn continued at first with the policy of giving priority to the Western Front, which led to disagreements with Hindenburg and

Ludendorff, who had ambitions to repeat Tannenberg by encircling the Russians in another great battle. His aim of launching a major offensive in Flanders in order to break through to the Channel coast failed, but not before the first battle of Ypres had led to enormous French, British and German losses. At this point, in late October, he changed his strategy and, ordering his western forces to dig in and strengthen their defensive positions, switched his attention to the east. Taking three corps from the 8th Army, he formed a new 9th Army, put it under the command of Hindenburg with Ludendorff as chief-of-staff and Hoffman as head of operations, a veritable 'A team', and moved it south close to Cracow to assist the Austrians, from which position it and the Austrians began to advance in late September towards Warsaw. The Russians had plans of their own, however, and Grand Duke Nicholas had assembled the bulk of Russia's forces on the Eastern Front around Warsaw with the aim of mounting an offensive which would sweep through Silesia and take the war into central Germany. The battle of Warsaw began as Austrian and German armies advancing towards the city were met by a surprise attack ordered by the Grand Duke. Due in part to a bungled plan by Conrad, who had allowed the Russians to cross the Vistula in the hope of striking them in the flank, the Central Powers got the worst of it and were forced to retreat with heavy losses, but, as so often happened on the Eastern Front, where armies found it difficult to advance far beyond their railheads, the Russian advance petered out due to a shortage of ammunition and supplies.

What followed has been described as, 'a true war of movement, greater than any seen in Europe since the campaign of Austerlitz',[20] as two great armies endeavoured to outflank each other. Hindenburg, not realising the strength of the Russians around Warsaw, had ordered the 9th Army to march down the west bank of the Vistula so that he could encircle the Russians from the north, while the Russians were preparing to cross the Vistula from the east and march north of Warsaw from which they intended to outflank the Germans. At first the Germans, who had taken 136,000 prisoners in the early fighting, seemed about to encircle the Russians, thus realising Hindenburg's and Ludendorff's dream of another 'cauldron' victory, but then they seemed to be the ones about to be encircled The fighting culminated, as autumn turned into winter, in a desperate struggle around the fortress city of Łódź, which was eventually taken by the Germans in early December. By the end of 1914 the Russians had been pushed back well away from the German border, while a rare Austro-Hungarian victory at Limanova-Lipanow strengthened the Austrian line in Galicia.

The War at Sea: The First Phase

The importance of the war at sea is often underestimated. It can be seen as the war that did not materialise, in that expectations of great battles between mighty fleets were, with the exception of Jutland in 1916, confounded. Yet, that Britain retained command of the seas and the Royal Navy was able to mount a blockade, which resulted in the gradual attrition of the German economy, were as important to the war's eventual outcome as the fighting on the Western and Eastern Fronts.

Were admirals better prepared for the war that awaited them in 1914 than generals? One argument is that indeed they were, for, although often depicted as reactionary old sea-dogs, admirals had proved themselves far less resistant to change and new technology than generals, who had clung tenaciously to the cavalry, the lance, the sword and the bayonet. The Royal Navy, perhaps because its officers came from less aristocratic backgrounds than did army officers and received, even in the days of sail, more technical training, had displayed what John Keegan has described as 'a ruthless lack of sentimentality for the beauty of pyramids of canvas' and had adopted, successively, steam propulsion, wrought-iron and then composite quality armour, had moved guns from broadside to turrets, and, by 1914, had begun the change from coal to oil.[21] An alternative view is that, if admirals were more open to technical innovation than generals, 'most naval staffs saw technical advances as new facts to be fitted in to an older doctrine of naval war',[22] which is similar to the way their army equivalents viewed new weaponry. Just as generals still expected that great offensives could be made and enemies outflanked, so senior naval officers of all the large navies thought that command of the seas came from the ability of powerful fleets to win great battles with the consequences that they could then protect their own sea lanes and blockade enemy ports.

The battleships, the capital ships of 1914, may have been far more powerful than the wooden-hulled and wind-propelled ships of the line of Nelson's day, but they were given much the same task. They were expected to play the leading role in the great battles that were confidently expected, even if these huge gun-platforms would need the aid of faster more lightly armoured battle-cruisers and escorting destroyers. The launch of HMS *Dreadnought* in 1906, with its thick armour and ten twelve inch guns heavier than any previous battleship yet, with its steam turbine engines, faster than its predecessors too, had immediately made all existing battleships obsolete. All the belligerents in 1914 had made major investments in their Dreadnoughts, yet there was a downside to these formidable warships, and the position of the battleship as the ultimate expression of sea power was to last less than half a century, while their role in the coming war was to be less decisive than admirals and naval strategists expected. One problem was their range: their appetite for coal or, later, oil meant they had to return to port to refuel every few weeks, so that major naval powers needed bases dotted around the oceans. Another was the reverse of their great cost, the extent of the loss if one was sunk, which made them almost too precious to risk, the major reason why Jutland in May 1916 was the only great battle to be fought between the Royal Navy and the German High Seas Fleet. Battleships were not only vulnerable to fire from other battleships and battle cruisers, but, due to those other developments in the technology of naval warfare the mine and the torpedo launched from torpedo boats and submarines, they had, like the major pieces on a chess board, to be surrounded and protected by those lesser pieces, torpedo boat destroyers.

Admiral 'Jackie' Fisher is best known for having supported the building of Dreadnought battleships but his enthusiasm for the concept of the battlecruiser is just as important, though these hybrids of the battleship and the cruiser were less successful. Faster, because more lightly armoured, than battleships, but as well armed, their speed was supposed to be their protection. By 1914, the German and British navies had respectively five and nine battlecruisers. In the traditional reconnaissance role of the cruiser they were useful enough, though the many more lightly armed fast cruisers that could have been built at the same cost might have been more effective, but both navies had come to believe that the battlecruiser's speed would allow them to engage with battleships with relative impunity. That this was not so was to be amply demonstrated in the sea battles of 1914–16. All capital ships faced the choice between improving the speed at which they could fire their guns by keeping their ammunition close to gun turrets or of opting for safety by keeping ammunition separate and protected, but with battlecruisers the risk of making the former choice was greater because of their lighter armour, as the actions of Heligoland Bight, Dogger Bank and Jutland were to demonstrate. The vulnerability that came with lighter armour was more marked in British battlecruisers, which had, 'ominous flaws in their ability to survive punishment', due to Fisher's insistence on larger guns at the expense of armour plate, while the Germans, in accordance with Tirpitz's dictum that, 'a warship's first duty is to stay afloat' had accepted smaller guns and lower speed as the price of heavier armour.[23]

At war, Britain and Germany were asymmetrical, with Germany in possession of the most powerful army in the world and Britain the most powerful navy. Germany's decision from the 1890s to challenge Britain by attempting to build a powerful navy was based on the nationalistic exuberance of the Weltpolitik policy and the mistaken belief that Britain could be frightened into an alliance. If the naval arms race did not cause the war, it did much to ensure that Britain entered it on the side of France and Russia. Most importantly, Britain had clearly won the expensive race to which the balance of 29 to 18 battleships testified. But what could the predominant naval power do to achieve victory over the more powerful military power? In the long term, of course, the military potential of Britain and the British Empire was far greater than the small professional army of 1914 suggested, but it would take time before population size and economic strength could provide a large army. In the short term, however, Britain could follow her traditional policy of relying on her continental allies and their large armies to do the land fighting and utilise her command of the seas to blockade German ports. Churchill had ordered the full mobilisation of the fleet on 1 August and on 12 August a blockade was established to prevent merchant ships entering German North Sea ports, while the French navy introduced a similar blockade against Austrian Adriatic ports.

The Royal Navy's blockade was not the 'close blockade' by which ships were positioned outside ports but a more distant blockade which involved closing the southern and northern exits and entrances to and from the North Sea. To do so it was essential to maintain the superiority of the Grand Fleet, mainly based at Scapa Flow in the Orkney Islands. If Germany's High Seas Fleet could be defeated in some great Trafalgar of a battle, then well and good, but so long as it stayed in harbour, the blockade would deny Germany imports from outside Europe and gradually weaken its war effort. What could the German navy do in the face of an all-encircling blockade? Germany's geographical position limited its access to the seas to a short stretch of the North Sea coastline and the Baltic, and the major investment in its navy was a misreading of its strategic potential as a continental power, especially as money spent on the navy reduced expenditure on the army. It could, nevertheless, pose a threat to Britain with its powerful, if inferior High Seas Fleet, which could make sorties in the hope of catching elements of the Grand Fleet at a disadvantage, and aim to wear down the strength of the Royal Navy by small actions and the sinking of its ships by mines and submarines. Its policy was not to shirk a grand battle, but was to seek one only under favourable circumstances.

The German Navy employed all these tactics in the first months of the war. At the battle of Heligoland Bight in late August, destroyers from Harwich and Dover launched an attack on German patrols in the Bight. German cruisers came to their assistance but low tide prevented German capital ships from doing likewise. When the British destroyers signalled for help, Vice-Admiral Beatty with a force which included four battlecruisers joined the battle, sinking three light cruisers and escaping before German reinforcements could join battle. The Germans were more successful with mines and submarines: the war at sea claimed its first casualties with the sinking of the light cruiser *Amphion*, which struck German mines on 6 August. On 3 September, a German submarine sank a British cruiser HMS *Pathfinder* in the North Sea, the first warship to be sunk by a torpedo fired from a submarine, and on 22 September another submarine sank the British cruisers, *Crecy, Aboukir* and *Hogue*. A more serious loss, so serious that the British cabinet decided to keep it secret, occurred in October when one of the most modern battleships, *HMS Audacious*, was sunk by a mine off the north coast of Ireland. These losses were worrying intimations of the vulnerability of warships to mines and harbingers of the important role submarines would play as the war developed.

Although German naval policy was hyped as part of Weltpolitik, and much of German opinion saw it as a means of extending Germany's influence overseas, Tirpitz had always seen its central purpose as challenging Britain; hence, the German High Seas Fleet was concentrated in Germany's North Sea ports. There were also, however, a number of German warships scattered around the world to protect German colonies and interests. In August 1914 these consisted of a number of fast and well-armed cruisers which were to wreak havoc as raiders on Allied shipping in the early months of the war. In the pursuit of these German cruisers, the Royal Navy had the disadvantage that, with the concentration of naval policy upon building dreadnoughts, the production of fast light cruisers had been neglected, but one factor in its favour was that wireless communication between German ships was vulnerable to interception. In their role of raiding Allied shipping and, occasionally, the shelling of British and French colonial ports, the German cruisers were, otherwise, difficult to find in the vastness of oceans, though their main problem was finding neutral ports where they could refuel.

They enjoyed mixed fortunes. The SMS *Königsberg* had a short career attacking shipping off the African coast near to Dar-es-Salaam before seeking refuge in the Rufigi delta, where although blocked in by British warships she was able to hide until July 1915, when she was sunk,[24] while another light cruiser, the *Karlsruhe*, exploded in mysterious circumstances off Barbados. The most important German naval force outside the North Sea was, however, the East Asiatic Squadron based at Tsingtao (or Qingdao) which consisted of two armoured cruisers *Scharnhorst* and *Gneisenau* and the light cruisers, *Emden* and *Nürnberg*. Without a base after the loss of Tsingtao, its commander Admiral Graf von Spee was joined by the *Dresden* and the *Leipzig*, which had previously been attacking Allied ships off the Californian coast. He decided to keep the squadron together, with exception of the *Emden*, whose captain was given permission to proceed to the Pacific and Indian Oceans where it was for a while the bane of the Allies, shelling Madras and Penang and sinking a Russian cruiser, a French destroyer and sixteen British merchantmen, until sunk by the Royal Australian Navy cruiser, *Sydney*.[25]

Spee's decision to keep the bulk of his squadron together went against textbook practice for the use of cruisers in his situation, which was to disperse and scatter. Individual ships would find it easier to refuel and could attack soft targets like merchant ships while avoiding any battle with a superior force, which would itself have to disperse to seek out the individual cruiser-raiders. Spee, however, had a powerful squadron which might well be the match for any British fleet he might come across and, as Hew Strachan puts it, his 'temperamental preference was to keep his squadron united and under his own control, and to dominate the seas while he could'.[26] After shelling French possessions in the Pacific, Spee, with his two armoured cruisers and the *Nurnberg*, rendezvoused with *Dresden* and *Leipzig* near Easter Island. The admiral commanding the Royal Navy's South American Station, Rear Admiral Christopher Cradock, had been informed that von Spee was proposing to move from the Pacific to the Atlantic and, obliged to divide his command, rounded the Horn with a cobbled-together squadron consisting of two ageing cruisers, *Good Hope*, (his flagship), and *Monmouth*, the light cruiser, *Glasgow* and an armed merchantman, *Otranto*. The Admiralty had belatedly sent the pre-dreadnought battleship, HMS *Canopus* to strengthen his force but the old ship was slow and still lagged behind in the Atlantic. The battle of Coronel, which took place off the coast of Chile, should never have happened, as it was foolhardy of Cradock to take on a squadron which had faster and more heavily armed ships than his own ragbag collection. The outcome was the first defeat of the Royal Navy in a hundred years; both the *Good Hope* and the *Monmouth* were sunk and Craddock went down with his flagship.

The Admiralty viewed the situation after Coronel with apprehension, fearing that von Spee might wreck havoc in the South and even the North Atlantic, and, therefore, ordered that a major reinforcement of ships be sent to the Atlantic. These included the battlecruisers, *Invincible* and *Inflexible*, ships that could not easily be spared from the North Sea, which were sent to the South Atlantic under the command of Vice-Admiral Sir Doveton Sturdee. That, shortly after their arrival at the Falkland Islands, they were to destroy Spee's squadron and avenge Coronel was due to British good luck. Spee had no knowledge that Sturdee's ships were at the Falklands, when, on 8 December, having decided to proceed back to Germany, he detoured to attack the wireless station coal stocks there. Hesitating to attack Sturdee's ships, he turned away but was pursued by the battlecruisers, which were much faster and had more powerful guns than any ship in his squadron. *Invincible* and *Inflexible* sank *Scharnhorst* and *Gneisenau*, while Sturdee's cruisers sank the *Leipzig and Nürnberg; Dresden* escaped but was later scuttled.

The Admiralty had taken a considerable risk in despatching two battlecruisers to the South Atlantic, thus depleting the force available to deal with the German High seas Fleet. The decision had paid off with the battle of the Falkland Islands, but the Germans were able to take advantage of the diminished strength of the Grand Fleet to bring the war home to the British public. On 16 December, a German battlecruiser squadron commanded by Rear Admiral Franz von Hipper bombarded the east coast ports of Scarborough, Whitby and Hartlepool on 16 December, killing 122 civilians. The High Seas Fleet was also at sea, ready to give Hipper support, and the action was intended to provoke the Royal Navy, perhaps unaware of this, into venturing forth with capital ships. Jellicoe knew from intercepted wireless messages that Hipper was at sea, but not that the High Seas Fleet had left port, and fell into the trap. He sent out Beatty's battlecruisers and six battleships, thus providing the High Seas Fleet with a chance of a major victory. It was lucky for Britain that Admiral Frederich von Ingenohl, not realising that he had superiority in ships and fearing that he might be facing the entire Grand fleet, turned away, while Hipper's cruisers slipped back to the German coast. The German cruiser squadron, nevertheless, persevered with its forays; the next encounter with British was to be the battle of the Dogger Bank on 24 January 1915.

The opening stages of the war at sea had already demonstrated that one of the German navy's weaknesses was its communication systems; its wireless messages were often intercepted by the Royal

Navy. Foreknowledge of German intentions led to Hipper's squadron being ambushed by Beatty's battlecruisers while reconnoitring the fishing grounds of the Dogger Bank. Hipper was commanding three battlecruisers and an armoured cruiser, the *Blucher*, but Beattie had brought a superior force of four battlecruisers. Rather than a confrontation, the battle of the Dogger Bank was a chase, with Beattie's flagship, HMS *Lion*, leading his other battlecruisers at top speed and exchanging fire at long range with Hipper's squadron. The vulnerable *Blücher*, an elderly ship, was sunk by a concentration of fire from Beattie's battlecruisers, and the leading German battlecruiser, the *Seydlitz*, caught fire, but was saved by a deliberate flooding of her magazines. The battle could be seen as a British victory but Beattie's ships had not come too well out of the running battle, having only sunk one of Hipper's ships, while the *Lion* had suffered extensive damage. After Dogger Bank, the High Sea Fleet remained in its home ports and did not come out again for another year. The first stage of the war at sea was over.

The Balance at the End of 1914

By the end of 1914, every army engaged, whether on the Western or Eastern Fronts had suffered enormous losses of men, killed, wounded or captured. None of the planned offensives had succeeded and on neither front had any side made a decisive breakthrough, while the great sea battle that had been expected had not taken place. The Germans had been held at the Marne, but nearly all of Belgium and part of France were under German control. To the east, the great Russian 'steamroller' had been less effective than Russia and her allies had hoped and the Central Powers had feared. East Prussia had been defended and Austria-Hungary had survived, though her own offensive, the invasion of Serbia, had failed.

Winston Churchill considered that the First World War was decided in its first twenty days and there is a case for this if one sees the failure of Germany to make a knock-out blow in France as predicating the future course of the conflict. If we take a slightly longer timescale to take account of the Eastern Front, then it is certainly true that by the end of 1914 the main parameters of the war until late 1917 or the Spring of 1918 had been set: a tight stalemate in the west and a looser one in the east, with Germany doomed to the two-front war it had hoped to avoid and the Allies unable to budge the Germans from the territories they had occupied.

The outstanding feature of the first five months of the war had been the failure of the attack. This was not due only to the machine gun and barbed-wire, which made assaults by cavalry or infantry over open ground suicidal. Other factors included the roughly equal size of the armies on each side on the Western Front and, on all fronts, the primitive nature of communication systems, which made it difficult for generals to direct their forces on the battlefield (it has been estimated that it took eight to ten hours for a message from divisional headquarters to reach the front), and reliance on railways, which meant that an army which advanced beyond its railheads quickly ran out of ammunition and supplies and could only be reinforced by marching men to battle.

In France and Belgium what followed after the first battle of Ypres was a much more static war with increasingly effective defensive systems. Earth, experience had shown, provided the best form of defence against artillery, whether troops were situated in holes in the ground, behind embankments, or in complex underground networks. Both sides began to develop increasingly sophisticated lines of trenches in the shape of zigzags, so as to avoid bullets and shells sweeping along the line, and with front-line troops living in underground quarters. The Germans had some advantages in this new form of warfare: in most areas they held the higher ground, which meant their trenches tended to be drier and they were able to dig deeper. They also had the great psychological advantage in that, although their great offensive had been halted at the Marne, they had conquered a great deal of French and Belgian territory. Thus, though stalemate and the superiority of the defence might have suggested that both sides remain largely on the defensive, the onus to attack was on the French and British. The German high command was largely content from November 1914 until the spring of 1918, with the exception of Verdun, to defend its positions, while the Allies were pressed by public opinion into offensives, often resulting in great numbers of casualties.

By the end of 1914, there was a stalemate on both the Western and Eastern Fronts. In the west the formidable and increasingly sophisticated lines of trenches reified the impasse with millions of men dug in to their earthen security only perhaps a hundred yards apart. In the east the front was much longer and the density of troops much lower, but, nevertheless, trenches were dug by both sides in central Poland, and for the moment great offensives had ground to a halt. From the soldier's point of view, the great advantage of this was that it made life safer. For generals and governments the conclusion was less clear: wars could not be won, or so it was thought, by a defensive strategy, but, equally, wars could not be won by armies whose high casualty rates made them smaller than the enemy's; if the defensive posture was defeatist but the offensive thinned the ranks, then the optimum policy was, either to remain on the defensive until the other side had weakened itself in failed offensives and then mount devastating counter-attacks, or to find new ways of mounting attacks, which would be more successful. Staff college training determined that most generals would favour the latter and, as Germany occupied Allied territory in the west, it was especially incumbent upon British and French commanders to find new ways of mounting offensives.

The war at sea had been no more decisive than that on land. The great battleships had largely remained, except for nervous forays and skirmishes, in the safety of Scapa Flow or Germany's North Sea ports. Britain's blockade exerted a stranglehold on German exports and imports, but Germany was moving towards a war economy, and the factories which had produced exports went over to the production of weaponry. In the longer term the blockade would come to threaten the German war effort and depress civilian morale. Efforts to contain it would change the nature of naval warfare, but, for the moment, there was stalemate at sea as well as on land.

It is one of the myths of the Great War that casualties were the greatest after trench warfare had become the norm on the Western Front along the line that stretched from Switzerland to the sea and were at their peak during the major confrontations of Verdun, the Somme and Passchendaele. It was in fact the first five months of the war, a period of relatively open warfare, which saw the highest number of war-related deaths: 1914 saw 25 per cent of all French war-related deaths and 14 per cent of German.

To posterity and to a limited number of contemporaries, the obvious answer to the failure of either side to gain a decisive victory in 1914 was a peace settlement. The plans of generals had proved flawed and the technology of warfare had been revealed to favour defence over attack. Above all hundreds of thousands had been killed, wounded or captured for little or no gain; surely now was the time to go back to diplomacy.

A major reason that there were no significant calls for compromise and negotiation were those same casualty figures; the sacrifice of blood made it more difficult to make the case for peace, because peace without victory might suggest the sacrifice had been in vain. Whether combatant states were democracies or autocracies, all were to a greater or lesser extent mass societies and governments, newspapers and civil societies had combined to retain popularity by imbuing the war with the character of a crusade. A further obstacle to peace was that the German public believed that Germany had won at least a partial victory in the west, while an inflated impression of the success of Tannenberg could be seen as presaging victory in the east. France and Britain would demand the evacuation of conquered French territory and the reinstatement of Belgium's frontiers as the price of any settlement, a price the German government and German public opinion would not be prepared to pay.

There were, in short, many negative reasons why the war continued, summarisable as the difficulty of halting a war which had already demanded sacrifices from the populations of the combatant nations and resulted in the demonisation of enemies. But what were the positive reasons? What were the war aims of the powers involved? It has been claimed that Germany had detailed and Napoleonic ambitions and that they were revealed in the memorandum or programme set out by Bethmann Hollweg in September 1914, a document which remained secret for some forty years. This listed German aims: annexations of territory, which included Luxembourg, Liege and Verviers, and the French iron ore field of Briey, German control of the Belgian coast, a customs union which would ensure German economic dominance of Europe, and the acquisition of further colonies in Africa to create a continuous German African empire. It is clear that, if these were indeed the aims for which Germany went to war, then they were entirely unacceptable to the Allied powers and prove that Germany indeed went to war with Napoleonic ambitions. How seriously the September Programme should be taken has been the subject of much debate. It was written while the battle of the Marne was still going on and a complete German victory still seemed possible, it contrasts with the assurances given as to Belgium's integrity in late July and early August, it says nothing about Britain and is vague about demands on Russia, and it was not an official document, while Bethmann himself discouraged talk of war aims at the time. Can it be dismissed? David Stevenson argues that 'its significance must be qualified. Yet it remains an essential guide to Bethmann's thinking'.[27] It has to be seen in the context of the interplay between forces within Germany, the army, industrialists and pressure groups, at a time of euphoria. Bethmann was to change his views as victory proved elusive and, though the document cannot be ignored, changes in fortune as the war progressed were to see German war aims change with them. What the September Programme does not prove is that Germany went to war with the aims it describes.

The great powers had stumbled into war rather than made a conscious choice to launch the conflict. Only Russia had consistent aims, territorial gains at Austria-Hungary's expense, which it pursued from the beginning, and command of the Straits and Constantinople, which it had long wished for and energetically sought as soon as the Ottoman Empire was in the war, but it is debatable whether such aims impelled it towards war. France had not sought war to regain Alsace-Lorraine, but that was bound to be a primary ambition in any war with Germany, and other aims were added as the war proceeded. Britain found itself at war committed to the defence of France and Belgium, but, like France, soon acquired a list of other objectives. Those who joined in later stages, like Turkey, Italy or Bulgaria, 'exercised choice [and] sold their services to the highest bidder'.[28] Indeed, none of the powers went to war with specific aims – their war aims emerged as the war continued.

The one piece of radical re-thinking came from the German commander-in-chief, General von Falkenhayn, who, despairing of victory on two fronts, suggested coming to terms with Russia so that Germany could concentrate on the war in France. This rather sensible proposal, redolent of Bismarck's view of the necessity of Germany and Russia being partners, was howled down as defeatist in Germany, where those in power were beguiled by the prospects that Hindenburg and Ludendorff held out for victory in the East, while Russia's generals still clung to the belief that the Central Powers could be defeated. Other than peace negotiations, options were to plough on with great offensives and find new ways of mounting them, or to go on the defensive and hope that the enemy might exhaust itself in expensive attacks, a course that had little appeal for generals who refused to consider abandoning the belief that decisive and absolute victory could still be won.

One further avenue was to use diplomacy to find new allies, thus widening the geographical spread of the conflict and opening up the prospect of new fronts and new offensives.

Chapter 5:   The Widened War

That the war would expand beyond the war zones of Europe was almost inevitable as several of the combatant powers – France, Britain, Germany and Belgium – had overseas empires and ambitions to expand them. There were precedents in that the Anglo-French and Anglo-Spanish conflicts of the eighteenth century had spread to the West Indies, North America and India, while the French Revolutionary Wars had seen French troops in Egypt and the British naval victory at the battle of the Nile. That more states would join in the conflict was probable as rulers and governments weighed up the progress of the war, decided which side was likely to win, and what advantage could be derived from an alliance with the putative victors.

The expansion of European influence and rivalries to the furthest corners of the world was reflected in that the first power to join in the war after the early days of August 1914 was Japan, which issued an ultimatum to Germany on 15 August. It was no burning quarrel with Germany, nor an automatic result of her alliance with Britain, that impelled Japan's ultimatum. The terms of the Anglo-Japanese Alliance did not make it obligatory for Japan to go to war, as Germany did not directly threaten Britain's colonies in Asia, but there were modest advantages to Britain if she did so – assistance against German naval detachments in the Pacific and the ability of Britain to safely switch naval forces to the Atlantic – and Grey asked for Japanese naval assistance. In Tokyo, the urge to join in the war was inspired by interests nearer home, the desire to take over German colonies, some of their Pacific islands and the territory and naval base of Qingdao, which Germany leased from China. The latter acquisition was in line with Japan's expansionist ambitions in China, which aimed at direct control over the Shantung peninsula and southern Manchuria.

The extent of the British Empire, which encompassed 9 million square miles and contained 348 million people, ensured, by itself, that the war had a global nature from the beginning. All the colonies, the Empire of India and the self-governing dominions were, constitutionally, automatically at war once Britain was, but there was little need to consider the constitutional legality as, throughout the empire, with the partial exception of South Africa, there was enthusiastic support for Britain's decision to go to war. The dominions' main contribution to the war was to be in fighting alongside and as part of British forces, but New Zealand also seized the opportunity to occupy Samoa, while Australia laid claim to the Solomon Islands and New Guinea.

Colonial War in Africa

It was in Africa where lay the greatest potential for war between the powers, with colonies sometimes adjacent to each other. France was the only state to deploy African colonial troops in the European war, bringing Zouaves, African infantry, Spahis and a Moroccan brigade[1] to fight alongside units from metropolitan France, something which outraged German opinion. If the idea of using colonial troops against Europeans could seem questionable, there were some who hesitated to export Europe's war to Africa. Indeed, there had been a loose pre-war understanding to exempt Africa south of the Sahara from hostilities in the event of a war between European powers, and British policy was that, on the whole, operations in Africa should be defensive; but Germany, unable to attack Britain directly, saw opportunities in forays on British colonies which might disrupt its trade and undermine its financial position. Many settlers and colonial administrators viewed the prospect of using colonial troops to fight those of other colonies as likely to weaken colonial rule in general as well as disrupting economic development. As, in the final analysis, the wars in and among the African colonies made little difference to the outcome of the greater war, it might have been better if such views had prevailed. Nevertheless, the three areas of German colonisation, West Africa, South West Africa and East Africa were all to see fighting.

In West Africa the tiny German colony of Togo had been overrun by British and French colonial forces and its important wireless station destroyed by 27 August and by the end of the month Allied forces drawn from Nigeria, Gold Coast (now Ghana) and Sierra Leone and including French African infantry and Belgian forces from the Congo were invading German Cameroon. To take this German colony proved a much more difficult task; the British colonial units in particular suffered heavy losses and German resistance did not end until early in 1916.

German South West Africa (present day Namibia) saw a very different type of conflict for it was a Whites-only affair. The Germans, who had subdued the native population with considerable ruthlessness, had a garrison of 3,000 men and there were some 7,000 German settlers. British troops had been withdrawn from the neighbouring Union of South Africa on the declaration of war, while, alone among the self-governing dominions, South Africa was far from united behind the British cause and a rebellion of Afrikaans-speaking Boer settlers had broken out. The South African government was thus in the position of having to put down a rebellion and at the same time invade the German colony, while its only military resource was its local defence forces, some of which were largely composed of Boers, who might not be reliable. The rebellion failed, however, and South Africa was free to respond to the British request to seize the wireless stations and harbours of German South Africa. Taking over the German colony also appealed to the South African defence minister, Jan Smuts, who had plans for the expansion of the Union. Despite the resignation of the commandant of the defence forces and most of his staff, four mainly mounted columns, a mixture of Boers, British South Africans and Rhodesians, were formed to take the capital of South West Africa, Windhoek. They moved on Windhoek from the coast, from the Orange river and from Bechuanaland and, although German resistance was stout, captured it on 12 May 1915.

By far the most formidable resistance the Germans put up was in East Africa, larger than France and Germany put together and Germany's most important African possession. The war in German East Africa (now Burundi, Rwanda and the mainland part of present-day Tanzania) can be said to have begun with a bombardment of Dar-es-Salaam by a British cruiser on 8 August, though there was then a pause, largely because neither the governor of the German colony nor the British governor of Kenya had much enthusiasm for fighting his neighbour, while neither had armed forces of any size to fight with. The impulse for war came from local settlers, British and German, and on the German side from Colonel Paul von Lettow-Vorbeck, who had recently been appointed by Berlin to command the *schutztruppe* or protection force.

John Keegan describes Nairobi, 'filling up with bellicose young settlers and white hunters' and forming their own military units, 'with outlandish names – Bowker's Horse, the Legion of Frontiersmen'.[2] The war, which resumed in September, was to outlast the Great War itself, finishing days after the Armistice of 11 November 1914. Lettow-Vorbeck began with little by way of an army, some 2,500 native troops or *askaris* and 200 white officers, though at its peak his force consisted of 12,100 Africans and 3,000 Europeans. An ingenious commander, he salvaged the guns from the German cruiser the *Königsberg*,[3] sunk by the British, and converted them into field artillery. The number of troops in Lettow-Vorbeck's force was far less than the numbers of bearers, which was 45,000 for, in the absence of roads or railways, bearers were armies' transport systems over a difficult terrain. The British who had around 50,000 askaris, needed more than a million bearers, some 100,000 of whom are estimated to have died from disease.

A recent study of the war in East Africa is entitled *Tip and Run*,[4] which describes Lettow-Warbeck's tactics well. Having had the conventional training of a German officer, he was no enthusiast for guerrilla warfare and would, no doubt, have preferred to seek out the enemy and meet it in pitched battle, but he realised that he lacked the resources to do so and adopted the type of fighting that could bring success in the great spaces, rivers and bush of East Africa. The forces that the British sent against him failed again and again. A combined Indian and British force was defeated in November 1914 and driven back to the beaches leaving behind hundreds of rifles and thousands of rounds of ammunition, which the Germans' askaris were desperately short of. In March 1916, Smuts arrived with a South African force and far too many mounted men for a region where horses were notoriously prone to sickness. Von Lettow-Vorbeck ambushed them and then disappeared into the bush where his askaris could live off the land. In 1918 he was still active, and, though largely confined to Portuguese territory, still a threat.

Whether the fact that the war spread to Africa and even the Far East made it a global or world war is a matter on which historians disagree. Hew Strachan argues on the basis of the war in Africa, that to suggest that the First World War was 'a sort of European civil war', which only became global after the entry of the United States, is an 'arrogant use of hindsight'.[5] There can be little doubt, however, that, despite the great loss of life there, the fighting in Africa was essentially a side-show, which made little difference to the outcome of the war in Europe. Far more important in 1914 and 1915 than clashes in Africa or in the Pacific was whether the Central Powers and/or the Allies would gain the support of new entrants to the war.

New Allies

Both the Allies and the Central Powers had, from the beginning of
the war, hopes that further states would come in on their side. At first
sight the Central Powers might have seemed to have more securely
based hopes for, after all, Germany and Austria-Hungary were part of
a Triple Alliance of which the third partner was Italy, while Romania
was also attached to the Alliance by a secret treaty. Relations between
Austria-Hungary and Italy were, however, always fraught, due to
Italian claims on Austrian territory, while Romania had claims on
Hungary's Duchy of Transylvania, where three million Romanians
lived. Neither Italy or Romania were likely to be eager to go to war
with France or Russia, but Bethmann Hollweg made it almost certain
that Italy and France would not join the war on Germany's side by
declaring war on Russia and France before German mobilisation was
complete. By treaty, Italy and Romania were both obliged to come to
Germany's aid if she was attacked, but by being the first to declare
war Germany gave them the opportunity to be neutral. Another state
that Germany and Austro-Hungary had reason to believe might join
them was Bulgaria, which, having been worsted in the second Balkan
War and lost much territory to Serbia, was thirsting for revenge and
held in check only by fear of its erstwhile patron, Russia. In the short
term, however, Italy, Romania, and Bulgaria found it convenient to
be neutral, while viewing the progress of the war and listening to the
promises and inducements of both the Allies and the Central Powers.

The Ottoman Empire

A late entrant to the war in 1914 was the Ottoman Empire, a state
which the German government had good reason to believe might
come into the war on its side, for a treaty of alliance between the
two powers had been negotiated in late July. A German–Turkish alliance was at once a nightmare scenario and a golden opportunity for
Russia, the former in that it raised the prospect of a closure of the
Black Sea Straits to ships carrying Russia's imports and exports, and
the latter in that with France and Britain on its side it could hope to
gain the Straits and Constantinople.

The 'sick man of Europe', had struggled to reform his economy,
institutions and armed forces throughout the nineteenth century, while
gradually losing most of his European territory as the result of the insur-
rection of the Empire's Christian subjects and the eastwards expansion

of Russia. The Ottoman Empire was faced with the problem and choice common to all of the Islamic world; should it attempt to defeat the west by remaining true to its own traditions or by modernising itself upon Western lines? It was the army which felt the need to modernise most acutely, and the officer corps became the best educated and most Westernised section of society, an intelligentsia under arms. It was army officers who formed the 'Young Turk' movement or Committee of Union and Progress, which had the aim of forging a new Turkish nation, and which staged a revolution in 1908. That had been followed by defeats at the hands of Italy and the Balkan states, but after a coup in 1913, the Young Turks were back in key ministerial positions. In 1914 Turkey faced the problem that its main defender throughout the nineteenth century, Britain, seemed less and less prepared to continue in that role, while its consistent enemy, Russia, seemed to have increased its ambitions to the extent of planning to gain control of Constantinople and the Black Sea Straits, so vital to its economy, and was even considering the dissolution of the Ottoman Empire.

Germany seemed the power that threatened Turkey the least, and Turkish-German relations had become close. A leading investor in the Turkish economy and builder of the Berlin to Baghdad railway, Germany had secured the appointment of General Liman von Sanders as head of a military mission and when he became effectively commander of a Turkish army corps in charge of defending the Straits Russian reaction was inevitably hostile as it appeared access to the Mediterranean was now under the control of her greatest enemy. Control of the Straits was indeed a Russian priority in the months before the war, and Sergei Sazonov, the foreign minister, had ordered plans to be drawn up in the summer of 1914 for an amphibious strike on Constantinople. He was aware, however, that, although British support for the Ottoman Empire was waning, such a strike might push Britain back into the stance of its defender and replay the situation of 1853 or 1878, so he preferred that it should take place after the outbreak of a general European war. The events of July and August 1914 provided the perfect scenario and outcome for Russia's plans.

A fundamental weakness in Russia's position with regard to Turkey was her inferiority as a naval power in the Black Sea and in 1914 this appeared about to get worse, for, in the early summer, the state-of-the-art dreadnought battleships, *Sultan Osman 1* and *Reshad V*, two of four destined for the Ottoman navy, were nearing completion in Tyneside shipyards. The *Sultan Osman 1*, which would mount more guns than any other ship afloat, would, by itself, alter the naval balance between

Russia and Turkey in the Black Sea, rendering the capital ships of the Russian navy obsolete. The two ships were due to arrive in Ottoman waters in July and when Russia requested that the British government block or delay the delivery of the *Sultan Osman 1*, the request was turned down by Grey, the foreign secretary and Churchill, First Lord of the Admiralty (naval minister). On Friday 31 July, as it became apparent that war was imminent, Churchill ordered British naval crews to board and seize the two dreadnoughts, as much to increase the strength of the Royal Navy as to pre-empt a strengthening of the Turkish navy.[6] Germany was, however, in a position to give a nudge to Turkey that would both largely negate the effect of Churchill's action and bring her into the war.

On Tuesday 4 August, just as Grey was being authorised by the cabinet to send an ultimatum to Berlin, the German battleship SMS *Goeben*, together with the support cruiser, *Breslau*, commanded by Admiral Wilhelm Souchon, came into range of the guns of HMS *Indomitable* and *Indefatigable* in the Mediterranean. Because Britain was not yet at war they could not open fire and Souchon proceeded eastwards at top speed, slipping out of range, just as the British ambassador was delivering Britain's ultimatum in Berlin and only hours before war began. On arrival at their destination, Constantinople, the ships formally entered Turkish service, running up the Ottoman ensign and their crews donning the fez. At a stroke, Turkish naval supremacy in the Black Sea was ensured.

Gradually, Turkey edged towards war with Russia and, though the government remained divided, the Young Turk ministers were increasingly in charge. Enver Pasha (war minister) and Talaat Bey (interior minister) played the leading role in seeking the German alliance, an alliance which they considered might assist the empire to become a modern national state. They were tough negotiators and in the agreement of late July they secured a guarantee of the empire's territorial integrity in return for promises of neutrality as between Austria-Hungary and Serbia and a vague undertaking to support Germany in a war against Russia. It has, indeed, been argued that Turkey got the better of the bargain from the signing of the alliance till the end of the war.[7] The mining and complete closure of the Dardanelles in September cut off Russia's only year round warm water access to the world's markets. Russia's ambassador in Constantinople, M.N. Girs, reported to Sazonov that: 'Turkey is being flooded with German officers, enlisted men, guns and shells'[8] and, as a further inducement to the Turkish government to enter the war, two German trainloads of gold, each of value one million pounds sterling, arrived in Constantinople during October. Finally, Enver Pasha and other pro-German colleagues, without telling fellow ministers, allowed the two capital ships under the command of Ottoman Vice-Admiral Souchon to bombard Russian ports with the aim of forcing Russia to declare war, which it did early in November. The Ottomans declared war on Russia and its allies eight days later.

The entry of Turkey into the war had momentous consequences. It presented Russia with the possibility of old ambitions being realised in the Near East; now, not only could it hope to dominate the Balkans by putting an end to Austria-Hungary as a great power, but, by destroying the Ottoman Empire, it could aspire to control the Straits, have access to the Mediterranean, and dominate Central Asia. For Tsar Nicholas II, it opened up 'Russia's path towards the realisation of the historic task of her ancestors along the shores of the Black Sea'.[9] For Britain it meant the end of her long support for the Ottoman Empire against Russia's desire to destroy it, even though such a switch of policy brought the risk of giving advantage to its major rival in the Near East and Central Asia, but for those in Britain who were pessimistic of the opportunities for victory on the Western Front it held out the enticing prospect of a new sphere of war in which British naval power could be brought to bear, while advancing and strengthening the British Empire's position in the Middle East at the expense of Turkey. For Austria-Hungary, it brought the hope of some weakening of the Russian onslaught on its northern borders, and for Germany it provided a new ally and to some in Berlin, like Arthur Zimmermann, under-secretary at the foreign ministry, it seemed that the alliance was the 'strategic crux of the German war effort',[10] though Germany was never in practice able to make the most of it. Turkey's entry into the war also greatly increased the significance of the southern Balkans, for Turkey depended on supplies brought overland from Germany and both sides made great efforts to cajole Bulgaria and Greece either to maintain neutrality or enter the war.

The Ottoman Empire, which, under the stress and strain of war, was to become transformed from a multi-national and Islamic empire into a national Turkish state, was at once stronger and weaker than it appeared. Its administrative and financial structure was ossified and inefficient and its armies were often to be defeated by their misman-agement and poor supplies, but, just as often, they demonstrated that the Turkish soldier was not to be underestimated when it came to hardy endurance and fighting ability. The Sultan, Mehmed V, had been sidelined by the Young Turk ministers and was now something of a cipher; nevertheless, he was also Caliph and as such could claim to be leader of the Muslim world. He proclaimed a Holy War, calling on Muslims in British, French and Russian territory to rebel. Britain had concern that the appeal might have some success with Muslims in India, but, although there were some minor troubles with largely Muslim regiments, the 'Holy War' found little support, in part perhaps because of the anomaly of combining it with support for one European alliance at war with another. The Turks, who increasingly saw themselves as a nation, rather than pan-Islamists, were in fact to have trouble maintaining the loyalty of their own subjects, not just Christian Armenians, but even fellow Muslims like the Kurds and the Arabs, who were beginning to have their own nationalist ambitions.

The Turks began their war badly. The main Turkish offensive was directed against Russia, Enver Pasha ordering a 150,000-strong army to invade Russia via the Caucasus in late autumn. This was a disaster even though the Russians were outnumbered. The whole exercise had been badly planned and the hope that the Islamic populations of the area would rise in support of the Turks was confounded. Enver seems not to have taken account of the fact that as winter set in his troops would have to advance and fight in freezing temperatures, and his supply line was weak, while the mountainous region favoured the defence. Two-thirds of the invading army died of disease or cold before it withdrew. Nor did things go better west of the Caucasus, for in February 1915, a Turkish force based in Damascus tried to cross the Suez Canal, which had been closed by the British to ships of enemy belligerents, but was repulsed by a larger British army while a hoped-for Egyptian rising against the British and support from desert Arabs failed to transpire. Turkish territory had already been penetrated at the end of 1914 when an Indian division was sent to the Persian Gulf and from there moved inland to Basra.

Nevertheless, the Russians had been unnerved by the invasion of the Caucasus; Grand Duke Nicholas had appealed for assistance, an appeal that found a response in Britain from those looking for an opportunity beyond the stalemate of the Western Front. One member of the British government to whom the idea of finding a new theatre of war in which to launch an offensive was attractive was Winston Churchill, First Lord of the Admiralty, whose restless mind became focused on the concept of forcing the Dardanelles with warships. He, like many others had become impatient with the lack of progress in the war. As hopes of a breakthrough in Flanders faded, the idea of mounting a surprise attack on Germany's ally was attractive. If Turkey could be knocked out of the war, a supply route to Russia would be opened up and Balkan neutrals, such as Romania and Greece, might be persuaded to join the Allies, thus opening up a new front against the Central Powers. What, moreover, appealed to the First Lord was bringing Britain's naval might to bear. The most powerful navy in the world had yet to make a significant contribution to altering the course of the war, but here was an opportunity to use naval power to dramatic effect.

Historians have usually seen the decision to attack the Dardanelles as an Anglo-French matter, but recent work has suggested that Russia's part in it has been underestimated. Control of the Straits and Constantinople were a major Russian concern in the early twentieth century and became a major war aim in 1914. Christopher Clark has seen control of the Straits as increasingly central to the Russian foreign minister, Sazonov's, thinking in the last years before the outbreak of war. Throughout the nineteenth century that aim had been thwarted and it was Sazonov's view that: 'Russia's claim to the Straits would only ever be realised in the context of a general European war, a war that Russia would fight with the ultimate aim of securing control of the Bosphorus and the Dardanelles.'[11] Russia's problem was that her naval weakness in the Black Sea made an amphibious operation questionable, while campaigning against Germany and Austria-Hungary in Galicia was requiring the attention of the bulk of the army. The answer was, Sean McMeekin argues, that, in view of Russian weakness, the 'age old dream of conquering the Straits would have to be achieved in the near future by her Allies'.[12]

That Britain offered the Russians control of Constantinople as she did in 1914 was, in itself, an astonishing reversal of a century of foreign policy; that she should have sought to present the Ottoman capital to Russia by taking the Dardanelles with British forces, and without any contribution of troops by the Russians, was to stand Britain's long held view of the Eastern Question on its head. Yet, it was perhaps the logical extrapolation of the appeasement of Russia which the British foreign office had been pursuing since 1907: 'And yet here were British statesmen openly advocating the total dismemberment of the Ottoman Empire so that Russia might have naval access to the Mediterranean – the urgent prevention of this had been a full-on British *casus belli* as recently as thirty-six years ago.'[13] The strangest aspect of the attempt to find a new front in the Near East is that the ally which stood to gain most contributed virtually nothing. Churchill stipulated in January that Russia must contribute both warships and amphibious landing force to the campaign and what he expected was an attack on the Bosphorus shore by both naval and amphibious forces, while the Royal Navy with French assistance forced its way through the Dardanelles. All that transpired by way of Russian action was a brief shelling of the Bosphorus forts by Russian warships.

There was, nevertheless a potential advantage to Britain if a quick campaign in the Dardanelles could knock Turkey out of the war. Churchill won over the Asquith government and got the grudging assent of the First Sea Lord, Admiral Lord Fisher, to his proposal to force the Straits with a fleet largely composed of old pre-dreadnought battleships and break through to the sea of Marmara, from where it would be in a position to bombard Constantinople and force Turkey to submit. The success of the plan had a lot riding on it when a purely naval attack began on 19 February 1915 against the shore batteries which barred passage up the Dardanelles to Constantinople as, immediately, there were indications that it encouraged Greece, Bulgaria and Italy to incline towards the Allied side, while the Russians announced that their Black Sea fleet would attack Constantinople from the Bosphorus. In the event the shore batteries proved difficult to destroy and the attempt to force the passage failed when half a dozen British and French battleships were blown up by a hidden minefield.

Whether the naval action should have been resumed is debatable. Churchill, who had wanted to press on with the naval action argued for the rest of his life that a further effort might have brought success, but, although the battleships may well have been 'expendable', no admiral likes to lose ships and the loss of life amongst the crews was considerable. Admiral John de Robeck decided after conferring with General Sir Ian Hamilton that the army was needed to deal with the shore batteries. Hamilton's force had to be brought from Egypt, so by the time military landings took place on 25 April the Turks had had plenty of time to reinforce the Gallipoli peninsula.

The failure of an attack by the Russian Black sea fleet on the Bosphorus forts after two of its destroyers were sunk by the *Goeben* put an end to any prospect that Turkey would be forced out of the war by naval actions. Now it was up to Hamilton's force, with the navy's guns to support it. In April, Allied troops, British, French, Australian and New Zealanders, landed at five beaches on the south-western tip of the peninsula, but the previous record of Turkish troops proved a poor guide to their potential when fighting close to their capital, with an advantage in numbers, and led by a commander of ability and determination, Mustafa Kemal, later Atatürk, the founder of modern Turkey. The landings suffered very heavy casualties and once on the beaches troops found themselves forced to climb upwards while under fire from Turkish soldiers on the higher slopes, while the

Australian and New Zealand force found what was to become known as 'ANZAC Cove' a particularly difficult challenge. No significant gains were made at the price of heavy losses, and trenches were dug by both sides. Further landings to the north at Suvla Bay were made by three fresh divisions in August, landings which at first found little opposition but did not get far from the beaches because the commander wanted to make sure that all supplies were unloaded properly before proceeding further. After 250,000 losses[14] had been sustained an evacuation of all allied forces took place between December 1915 and January 1916. The evacuation was the only part of the Dardanelles campaign which can be considered to have been successfully carried out.

A grim background to Gallipoli was the Turkish government's reaction to the perceived disloyalty of Turkey's Armenian minority. The combination of defeat in the Caucasus, British action in the Dardanelles and fears as to the stability of multi-ethnic Ottoman Empire, led to what some have seen as the genocide of Turkey's Armenian population. Some have seen this Christian minority as for generations loyal to the Empire and satisfied with the limited degree of liberty and economic prosperity it was permitted within an Islamic-ruled society, but there had been serious Armenian revolutionary activity in 1894–6 and Hew Strachan has written that 'the best that could be said of the Armenians' loyalty to the Ottoman Empire was that it was conditional'.[15] The Turkish assault on the Caucasus raised the question of Armenian loyalties, for there were Armenians in Russia as well as in Turkey and, just as the Turks had hoped to gain the support of Caucasian Muslim populations, so the Russians had expectations that Armenians might rebel against Turkish rule – there were appeals by the Tsar and the Armenian patriarch in Russian Armenia to this effect. After the Turkish defeat by the Russians at Sarikamish in late February 1915, a battle in which Armenian volunteers had fought alongside the Russians, the Turkish government, already concerned as to whether the Armenians could be trusted, came to believe that they were planning a united Armenia under Russian protection and, just before the British landings on the Gallipoli peninsula, ordered the expulsion of the Armenian population. Out of a Turkish Armenian population of between two and three million, roughly a third are thought to have died of hunger or disease while bring deported, another third to have been massacred and the remainder to have survived. Whether the appropriate term is 'genocide', 'massacre', or 'mass murder' remains open to debate, but the fate of the Armenians, although its specific origins lay in religious and nationalist hatred of what was perceived as an internal threat at a time of crisis for the Turkish state, was part the general increase in violence and brutality and the ignoring of the conventions of warfare that characterised the developing and widening war.

The attempt to find a new front or a 'soft underbelly' of the Central Powers as an alternative to the bloody stalemates in France and Eastern Europe had failed. A few precarious footholds on the Gallipoli peninsula had been secured at a great cost of lives and then had to be abandoned. Churchill, the most prominent supporter of the Turkish adventure, had to resign and the Asquith government was weakened. But the attempt to knock Turkey out of the war had been meant to deliver multiple benefits: to take pressure off Russia, both in the Black Sea and in Poland; and to encourage new states to enter the war on the side of the Allied or Entente powers. The prospect of the final dismemberment of the Ottoman Empire promised the distribution of great prizes or bribes to persuade Italy, Romania, and Greece to come off their neutral fences. Indeed so frenetic did the bargaining become that it was difficult to remember who had been promised which part of Ottoman territory and it became apparent that sometimes the same morsel had been promised to more than one party.

Italy

The state which kept everyone waiting, as it decided which side to join and when it would be opportune, was Italy. The Italian state which had emerged in 1870 was not really a great power either in military or economic terms, nor, indeed, was it a cohesive national entity as the differences between north and south remained wide, but it had great ambitions. Its membership of the Triple Alliance had always been something a contradiction as its most consistent ambition was to take over territory belonging to its alliance partner, Austria-Hungary. It was no great surprise, therefore, that Italy opted for neutrality in August 1914 and spent most of the next year listening to the inducements offered by the Central and Allied powers for joining their sides before finally deciding which had made the better offer. It was always more likely that Italy would join the Allies; only they could offer Austrian territory, and to have sided with the Central Powers would have meant putting the Italian navy at the mercy of the Royal Navy in the Mediterranean. Nevertheless, the Treaty of London of 26 April 1915, by which Italy 'undertook to use her entire resources for the purpose of waging war jointly with France, Great Britain and Russia' promised her a cornucopia of rewards: Trentino, the South Tyrol, Istria and a third of Dalmatia at Austria-Hungary's expense, a 'just share' of the Ottoman Empire in Asia, and compensation in Africa for British and French gains from German colonies – as an additional sweetener she was to receive a loan of £50,000,000 to be issued on the London market. The cautious but territorially avaricious Italians did not enter the war immediately, but Britain's naval action in the Dardanelles convinced the Italian government that to shilly-shally any longer might risk losing the promised gains. Even then, majority opinion in Italy was either hostile to or lukewarm about entering the war, and when Germany and Austria-Hungary offered the cession of the Trentino, plus free city status for Trieste, in return for Italian neutrality, there was a government crisis. The so-called 'radiant May' saw what has been called a 'bourgeois coup' in which the war party triumphed over the left and centre. The German-Austrian offer, if sincere, would have secured 'Italia-irredenta', and when Italy eventually entered the war on 23 May against Austria-Hungary, but not yet against Germany, it was clear that her motives were imperialist expansion and that the country was far from united.

The Balkans

One by one the states of south-eastern Europe entered the war. Since the end of the Balkan Wars Bulgaria had been thirsting for revenge for its loss of territory; Austria-Hungary's war with Serbia gave it a perfect opportunity. Nevertheless, King Ferdinand and the Bulgarian government hesitated, fearful that, if Greece and Romania joined the Entente powers and the British and French were successful in Gallipoli, they might find themselves on the losing side yet again. It was not until October 1915 that Bulgaria was finally persuaded by the promise of Serbian territory to join the Central Powers in the invasion of Serbia.

Lacking trust in the effectiveness of the Austro-Hungarian Army after its failure in its initial offensive against the Serbs, the Bulgarians made it a condition, when they signed a military convention on 6 September, that the main thrust of a new attack upon Serbia be made under German command and should come from the north, Bulgarian forces then to follow with an invasion from the east. August von Mackensen, who was given command of the combined Austro-German force, crossed the Danube in early August despite the river being swollen by heavy rain. Belgrade fell to the Austrians for the second time, and, before the Serbs could counter-attack, the Bulgarian Army hit their eastern flank.

About to be encircled, the Serbs began an arduous retreat across the mountains to Albania. It was not just an army that retreated but a sizeable part of the population for Serbian soldiers took their families with them, and the journey over snow-covered passes, during which hunger, disease and the attacks of Albanian tribesmen took their toll, resulted in the deaths of 20,000 civilians. Of the 200,000 troops who had set off, however, around 140,000 made it to the Albanian coast where they had to survive bombardment from the Austro-Hungarian Navy before being evacuated to Corfu and thence to Salonika in British and French ships.

Other than surrender, there can be no more complete a defeat than when an army evacuates its country, yet a Serbian Army remained, albeit in exile. Nevertheless Serbia had suffered enormous losses, the worst in relation to size of population of any participant in the war. Of an original strength of 420,000 men in September, 94,000 had been killed or wounded and 174,000 were captured or missing.[16]

For the Allies the defeat of Serbia and Bulgaria's entry to war were great setbacks, but there were hopes that they might persuade Greece to enter the war. Earlier in the year Lloyd George had nurtured such a hope and proposed sending forces to Salonika, from which assistance might be given to the Serbs, rather than to Gallipoli. A snag with this suggestion was that Greece was neutral and, after the failure of the Allies at Gallipoli, was even less prepared to join them. The country was divided in its sympathies, with the prime minister, Eleutherios Venizelos, in favour of the Allies and King Constantine, whose queen was a daughter of the Kaiser, pro-German. Nevertheless, on 5 October, the British and French decided that they would each send 75,000 troops to Salonika. This was one of the oddest decisions of the war: fighting was still going on in Gallipoli; it was clear that Serbia was going to be defeated; and there was little point in depositing 150,000 Allied troops to waste their time and catch fever on the Greek–Bulgarian frontier. In addition, Venizelos was no longer prime minister of Greece and King Constantine, quite sensibly, opposed the imposition of Allied forces on Greek territory. The Allied action was a violation of Greek neutrality as flagrant as that of Germany's invasion of Belgium, and Lloyd George's argument that 'there was no comparison between going through Greece and the German passage through Belgium' was untenable.

The final piece in the Balkan jigsaw was put in place when Romania, with its eyes on Hungarian Transylvania, declared war on Austria-Hungary and joined the Allies in August 1916 at a time when it appeared that Russia was winning the war on the Eastern Front. It cannot be said that any of the late entrants to the war in 1915 and 1916 was inspired by lofty motives; all saw an opportunity to acquire territory.

The promises and secret agreements made by the original Entente powers between themselves and with the states they persuaded to come into the war were far-reaching. When they were later revealed, in the first place by the Bolsheviks, they did considerable harm to the claims by the Allied Powers to be fighting a war for purer motives than the Central Powers. The treaties, agreements and understandings concerning the future of the Ottoman Empire proved impossible to reconcile when the war ended. Russia was promised Constantinople and the Straits by both Britain and France, though as these promises were conditional on Russia fighting on till victory was achieved, they had lapsed by 1918. As regards the Ottoman Empire in Asia and the Middle East, the agreements included in the secret Treaty of London of April 1915 were contradicted by promises made to states and factions. The assurances given to the Sherif of Mecca in October 1915 as to the independence of the Arabs were incompatible with both British and French plans for future territorial arrangements and spheres of interest contained in the tripartite (Britain, France and Russia) agreement of October 1916, known as the Sykes–Picot Agreement and the further Tripartite (Britain, France and Italy) Agreement of April 1917, which gave a large region including Adalia and Smyrna to Italy. The Balfour Declaration of 1917, which promised a 'national home for the Jewish people', was clearly contrary to promises given to the Arabs. The question of how the spoils of the Ottoman Empire were to be divided was further complicated by the fact that, as well as the extensive acquisition of Austro-Hungarian territory, Italy had been promised by the Tripartite Agreement or Treaty of London of 1917, an 'equitable' share of the Ottoman Empire in Asia. Even as regards the Far East, treaties and agreements posed problems for the future, with the Russo-Japanese Treaty of July 1916 providing for the extension of Japanese interests to the whole of China.

The imperial and colonial possessions of combatant powers had spread the ripples of a war which had started in the Balkans to Africa and the Far East, while Turkey's entry had brought the war to the Middle East and Central Asia. The involvement of Italy, Bulgaria, Greece and Romania returned the focus to the Balkans where the war had begun and which was in 1918 to play a significant role in its end.

At the end of 1916, the possibility of the power whose entry into the war was to make a significant difference to its outcome, the United States, making the decision to intervene seemed unlikely. There was no pressure on a great economic power secure from external threats to enter the conflict and most of American opinion regarded the war as a European affair, while German immigrants strongly opposed any entry on the Allied side. Europe was the war's epicentre and, if there were those on both sides who favoured new offensives away from the Western and Eastern Fronts to break the costly stalemate, so it remained. Even when, with America's eventual entry, a European war took on more of the character of a global conflict, it was on the battlefields of Europe that the outcome of the war would be decided.

Chapter 6:   Home Fronts and the Test of War

As assumptions that the war would be brief were confounded, governments had to rethink not only their military strategies but also their economic positions and plans, for none had prepared for a long war. The expectation had been that great battles would result in a decisive victory for one side or the other within a matter of months, and there had been a widespread belief that modern industrialised economies would not be able to withstand a war that lasted much longer. As it turned out, the opposite was true: mass societies were able to raise mass armies and to supply them; and, as the gold standard became a fiction, governments had the capacity to print ever more paper money and were able to ignore, at least temporarily, peacetime economics and the comforts of their populations. Combatants relied initially on stockpiles of ammunitions weaponry and supplies; they had not prepared for the shift to a war economy and the new factories and the conversion of peacetime industries that were to be needed. By 1915, it had become apparent that the entire manpower, even a proportion of the womanpower, of the states, and the greater part of their economic capacity, would have to be committed to the war.

The concept of 'total war' is often used to describe the way in which states mobilised their populations and economies for their war efforts, Certainly, if we compare the First World War to the wars of the previous two centuries, it was a war that restricted and directed civilians and saw societies and economies controlled to an unprecedented extent. In Italy certain areas, including Turin, which was quite far from the war front, were declared 'war zones' in which normal industrial bargaining was suspended in the interests of productivity; in France the commander-in-chief had special powers over the areas close to the front; in all the belligerent states the powers of government and the needs of the armed forces meant that the peacetime freedoms of employers, the workforce and consumers were subordinated to the war effort.

Inevitably, the concept of total war fits states whose territories were fought over and/or occupied and those where civilian casualties were high rather better than the United States, in which the few civilians killed were those on ships sunk by the German Navy, or, indeed, Britain, where, again, apart from the many thousands of merchant seamen killed, civilian deaths were limited. Although Zeppelins and Giant Gothas bombed London and some southern towns, and German battlecruisers bombarded east-coast ports, these were intimations of future wars rather than a part of daily life. On the Western Front the battlefield remained relatively discrete and confined to the narrow space between the lines of trenches. On the Eastern Front, where the war was more mobile, civilian casualties were greater, but even there the death rate was due much more to factors such as food shortages and starvation as advancing armies commandeered food supplies and retreating armies scorched the earth than to bullets or shells. Historians have found it difficult enough to arrive at figures for the number of military personnel killed (two estimates are 10 million and 13 million for deaths directly caused by fighting); civilian deaths are a matter of speculation and extrapolation from pre and post war population figures. Estimates for both fighting men and civilians are made more difficult by the impact of the "Spanish flu" epidemic which killed vast numbers towards the end of the war. The destruction by Turkey of a large proportion of its Armenian population is the worst example of civilian carnage by military action but, despite German mistreatment of Belgian civilians and Russian oppression of Jewish minorities in conquered territories, civilian deaths were overwhelmingly the by-product of a remorseless war.

Whether or not we consider the First World War as a 'total war', there can be little doubt that all belligerent states in their efforts to mobilise their resources resorted to economic and social policies that were very different to their peacetime traditions and norms; 'business as usual' turned out not to be an option. Fighting a war and providing the manpower and weaponry with which to fight it while at the same time maintaining the morale of the armed forces and the civilian populations, has been seen as a test of the resilience of the economies and societies of the states involved, their political structures and institutions, and their ethnic and national cohesion.

The Balance of Economic Power and Manpower

The combatant states started from a far from equal position in their ability to pass the test of war. 'Modern' is a vague and relative word, but in the sense it is usually used to describe economies and societies, and their systems of government, some states were clearly more modern in terms of their economic and social structures than others. Britain and Germany, followed by France, were the most industrialised, and their manufacturing capacities gave them the greatest potential to produce the armaments that would be required. Britain had the most sophisticated financial structure and possessed enormous overseas investments. Britain, France and Germany all had well-educated and literate populations as compared to Russia, a state which, although industrialising rapidly in the years before 1914, remained relatively backward and lacked the administrative structure that might have enabled her to mobilise the economy and society effectively. Her problems were compounded by the dislocating social effects of rapid industrialisation. Both Italy and the Austro-Hungarian Empire defy generalisations as their internal variations were so great: much of Austria was industrialised and urbanised, as was northern Italy, but both states had large areas dominated by a backward form of agriculture. Nations do, however, need to feed their populations and here industrialised Britain, which had retained a far smaller rural economy than any other country, was at a potential disadvantage because of its reliance upon agricultural imports, while if Turkey lacked the industrial economy required for a modern state at war, much of its population was used to living at close to subsistence levels.

If the outcome of the war was to be decided on the balance of population size and economic resources, then in late 1914 the advantage lay with the Allies, whose combined population was 262 million (even if we exclude the vast population of the British Empire), as opposed to 135 million for the Central Powers. By 1918, by which time each side had found new allies, the difference had actually grown even though the Allies had lost Russia, their most populous member. In terms of economic strength as measured by national income the balance also favoured the Allies: their combined income in 1914 was 60 per cent greater than that of their opponents. As Niall Ferguson has shown, the difference in economic strength was due to Britain for, 'without Britain, France and Russia had a combined national income approximately 15 per cent smaller than that of Germany and Austria Hungary', while in financial terms Britain, with her stock of overseas capital, again gave the Allies the advantage.[1]

By 1915 as the prospect of a lengthy war dawned, the necessity of giving priority to the war effort and the production of armaments led to the setting-up of command economies and the direction of industry, which in turn involved serious intrusions into the lives and liberties of individuals. Moves from free market economies towards even limited state direction of the economy meant a difficult break with traditions and norms, while the more liberal a society, the more controversial and traumatic was the limitation of individual freedom. In one way, all the states that went to war had, with the exception of Britain, already taken a massive step in increasing the state's power over its citizens by introducing conscription. There had been a campaign by the National Service League to introduce conscription in pre-war Britain, but it had had little success in persuading opinion that such a move was compatible with British tradition. Nearly every other European state had in theory the right to conscript all men of military age, but in practice few did. The Russians, in particular, had, because of exemptions, a much smaller army than their population would have suggested. As the war began, continental countries called up younger and hitherto exempted men, while Britain, still without conscription and with volunteers not yet trained, was soon to be sending divisions from the volunteer Territorial Army and imperial troops to reinforce her expeditionary force in France.

Conscription was not introduced in Britain until the beginning of 1916, but the numbers of those who volunteered were impressive. Few would have seen pre-war Britain as a fertile recruiting ground for a large army for, although the Navy was popular, 'going for a soldier' was considered a last resort for the 'respectable' sections of society. However, the numbers who volunteered once the war had begun were considerable. Kitchener called for 200,000 men in the first month of the war and 300,000 responded; the numbers rose to a peak in September after the retreat from Mons, and by the end of 1915 more than 2.5 million men had joined up and were either fighting in France or in training. As has been demonstrated by a recent study by Catriona Pennell,[2] recruitment testified to the commitment to victory of a United Kingdom convinced of the justice of its cause. These recruits formed an army very different in its social composition to the pre-war regular army; alumni from public schools and university graduates, white-collar workers and the service sector were heavily over-represented, as were miners and Scots.[3]

Whether by conscription or, in Britain's case, volunteering followed by conscription, each state mobilised more and more men for the armed forces as the war continued. Britain mobilised 12.5 per cent of her men, Germany 15.4 per cent, and France 16.9 per cent. Pacifism and conscientious objection has been the subject of disproportionate attention in the context of the numbers of those who refused to fight; many objectors were brave in their refusal, but the numbers were small in most countries. There were limits, however, to how many adult males could usefully be moved into the armed forces, for industrial production had to be increased; those patriotic miners might have been more use in the mines than in the trenches. Each state mobilised an army (and navy) close to its maximum potential size, but 'each arrived at this level of commitment not through careful planning and adjustment, but through 'blind groping in the dark'.[4]

The maxim that, in a modern war, economic strength, productive capacity, supply lines and the ability to maintain the standard of living of populations are as important as the efficiency of armies and the ability of generals and admirals, indeed perhaps more important, has become almost a truism. In a long war there is, indeed, considerable truth in this dictum, though, even then, leadership, the organisation of armies, the ability to exploit weaponry, and morale, make a great difference. For most of the war, the superiority of the German army on the battlefield made up for the relative inferiority of the German economy.

Guns and ammunition were to be as important as numbers of troops, and here Germany excelled, as indeed she had to in view of her disadvantage in the size of population, producing 80,000 gun units[5] a year as compared to Britain's 72,000 and France's 70,000. It was France, however, with the smallest pre-war economy and with much of her industrial heartland occupied by the enemy, which achieved the greatest increase in the proportion of domestic product allocated to munitions, largely by setting up government-run factories – although the attempt to set up a huge, state controlled arsenal at Rouanne in 1916 was a disaster. Russia, despite a remarkable economic surge in the early years of the war, lagged behind in arms production until, after 1917, her output nearly ceased.

The war economies are usually seen as forms of state control or 'War Socialism' but, as existing armaments factories proved incapable of meeting wartime demands, it was to private industry that most states turned in order to increase production. All the combatants moved towards command economies in which governments controlled and directed production and decided what should be produced, but there was little outright nationalisation. Thus, at the very beginning of the war Britain's railways were placed under government control but remained privately owned, with the owners being guaranteed the same level of profits they had made in 1913; the coal mines came under a Coal Controller in 1917 with a similar financial arrangement. Ministries and controllers directed, but with the understanding that these were arrangements for the duration of the war. The profits made by firms led to controversy and demands for curbs on profiteering. Munitions production became politicised and in Britain a supposed shortage of shells caused the 'shells scandal' of May 1915, which resulted in Lloyd George becoming head of a Ministry of Munitions, while the alleged excessive drinking of munitions workers led to new licensing hours, some of which endured until the early twenty-first century.

It is Germany's war economy which has provoked most disagreement amongst historians. According to Jay Winter, Britain and France moved towards an unplanned, but relatively successful, form of state capitalism which put the national interest above that of employers, but Germany adopted a corporatist system which became bogged down by a muddled bureaucracy which, in harness with the army, directed large firms. In 1914 the Prussian War Ministry set up a War Raw Materials Department whose effective head was the industrialist, Walther Rathenau, to control the supply of materials throughout Germany. The production of munitions was co-ordinated by the war ministry in conjunction with a War Committee for German Industry, but it was only in late 1916 that, under the Supreme Command dominated by Hindenburg and Ludendorff, Germany moved decisively towards a militarily controlled command economy. Jay Winter regards these moves as ineffective, and has argued that the German state 'dissolved under the pressure of industrial war'; by putting the needs of the military first, the economy became distorted and civilian needs were neglected.[6] Winter's view is rejected by Ferguson, who argues that 'considering the limited resources with which they had to work, the Germans were significantly better at mobilising their economy for war than the Western powers',[7] while Stone also sees the German economy as performing well: 'the great trusts which ran German industry went over to the production of war goods, the banks which were their own creatures financed this, and the Prussian War Ministry knew how to maintain quality control without getting in the way as its British counterpart did'.[8]

There is, nevertheless, an argument that more autocratic states are capable of making rapid and commanding decisions in response to crises, of which the challenge of war is the greatest, and that the reactions of more democratic states are initially slower and more muddled.[9] Whether Britain and France were inherently more democratic than

Germany can, of course, be debated, but Winter suggests their actions were more empirical and consensual. Just as during the Napoleonic Wars, with which parallels are striking,[10] Britain maintained a competitive market-based system but one in which government did the ordering and firms tendered for contracts, a system which was more flexible than Germany's more state-directed wartime economy.

It is clear that all the states at war found it difficult to balance competing needs, demands and rights: those of the armed forces and industry, the food-producing countryside and the food-consuming towns, and government and the individual. What is perhaps surprising is that most states – Russia is, of course, the great exception - managed to survive through four years of war. It had been widely forecast that complex modern societies would be unable to survive the stress of war, for it was thought that their economies were too dependent on international finance and trade and that any prolonged war would result in financial collapse, but in the event they proved durable.

Countries approached the financing of the war in different ways. A contrast is usually drawn between Britain, which already had a progressive system of income tax, financing the war by covering a substantial proportion of expenditure by taxing current income and profits, while France and Germany did so by borrowing from their citizens. This contrast may have been exaggerated, Germany, on average, financed 13.9 per cent of her expenditure by direct taxation, France 3.7 per cent and Britain 18.2 per cent, while borrowing resulted in national debts growing respectively by factors of 8, 5 and 11. All combatant states suffered from inflation as they allowed money supply to grow rapidly; the gold standard was maintained only in name as gold convertibility was either informally suspended or exports of gold restricted.[11]

What undoubtedly gave Britain a great advantage was her international financial power – she accounted for 44 per cent of total foreign investment in 1914. This meant both that she had assets to sell and a credit rating that enabled her to raise loans on Wall Street and purchase war supplies from the United States. It should not, however, be assumed that Germany was unable to borrow on international markets: Ferguson quotes an estimate that Germany borrowed $35 million of the $2,160 million lent by the USA to combatant states before 1917.

The cost to Britain of its borrowing was considerable. When the seller has an obvious need to sell the price comes down, and when the borrower needs to borrow the price goes up. Further, sales of assets and loans taken out substantially weakened Britain's position to the extent that there was a severe run on the Bank of England's gold reserves early in 1917 and there arose the dangerous prospect of Britain's financial future being in American hands or in the hands of less creditworthy allies to which Britain had lent money borrowed from America. Nevertheless, before the USA entered the war, it was Anglo-American financial relations which underpinned the finances and creditworthiness of the Allies as a whole. It has been suggested that the severity of Britain's financial position in 1917 was exaggerated by John Maynard Keynes, adviser to the British Treasury, who had close to pacifist opinions, as a means of supporting the efforts of Woodrow Wilson to bring about a negotiated peace.[12] With American entry into the war such financing became more certain but at a political price, as Wilson had war aims at variance with those of Britain and France.

State economic management affected many aspects of economic and social life. Labour needed to be directed so that it might be used more efficiently and one ironic result was that, having combed factories for soldiers, a reverse process saw armies being combed for key workers at the very time that the mounting loss of life on the fighting fronts made this difficult. Traditional working practices had to be suspended to make production more efficient, something which trade unions would have fiercely resisted in peacetime, but which, with labour and social democrat parties supporting the war, they grudgingly acceded to. In Britain, 'dilution', the name given to the process of eroding the distinction by which certain jobs could only be done by grades of skilled or semi-skilled workers, caused much dissatisfaction and was only permitted after assurances that it was a temporary wartime measure. New methods of production were also introduced and resulted in larger factories on the lines of what became known as 'Fordism', after Henry Ford, with longer and more efficient production lines and standardised interchangeable parts. The demands of war also dictated what could be produced – guns and, later, tanks instead of motor cars – and which products should have priority – as great an affront to employers as dilution was to trade unionists; war also affected what could be imported. In Germany, industries producing goods deemed non-essential were deprived of materials and labour under the Hindenburg programme.

As regards industrial relations Germany was more successful for most of the war than France and Britain, in part because German trade unions proved either more cooperative or weaker than their counterparts. French trade unions had mainly rallied to the war effort in 1914, but from 1917 a series of strikes began among female workers in the clothing workshops in Paris. More serious were strikes by munition workers; these were met by injunctions from Albert Thomas, the minister of armaments, which fixed a minimum wage but imposed compulsory arbitration procedures. Nevertheless, strikes of railway workers, bank employees and public servants were a feature of the summer of 1917. As they were combined with anti-war demonstrations and were followed by the mutinies after the failure of the Nivelle offensive, they can be seen as part of a widespread war weariness.[13] There was a wave of strikes in Britain in 1917, affecting such vital industries as munitions and engineering. In response the government set up a Commission on Industrial Unrest and combined conciliation with attempts to isolate more extreme workers' leaders.

An emphasis upon the militancy of German trades unions in the last months of the war can obscure the fact that it had fewer strikes than Britain, where the engineers' strike of May 1917 saw a significant victory for the Amalgamated Society of Engineers, while another engineers' strike was in progress in April 1918 during Germany's major offensive. In both Britain and France far more work days were lost due to industrial action than in Germany, where the authorities were empowered to direct male labour from inessential occupations to war work, having gained the assent of the majority in the Reichstag for this. In return, however, significant concessions were made to organised labour, with workers being given the right to organise in war industries in recognition of the need to conciliate trade unions if the war was to be won. As one study has concluded, 'With the exception of Russia, British labour relations were quite simply the worst in the war: neither Germany, nor Italy, nor France suffered as many strikes.'[14] This was in spite of the Labour Party having a minister and two minor office bearers in the Asquith coalition from May 1915 and the support of the main trade union leaders for the war effort. A major reason for this militancy was the erosion of differentials between skilled, semi-skilled and unskilled workers. In all countries the position of skilled workers deteriorated relative to other workers but the British craft unions, well-organised and with proud traditions, put up the greatest resistance.

The Social Impact of the War

If production came to be controlled by the state, so to a lesser degree, for in no country was the state all-powerful, did consumption. That the government should decree what, and how much, he, or his wife, should eat or drink or in general spend money on would have seemed intolerable to a pre-war gentleman or artisan, but, told that patriotism demanded it, the majority acceded. All countries suffered food short- ages, even those which, like Germany, France, Italy and Russia, had been net exporters of food before the war. In Britain, rationing was introduced, public houses closed their doors at inconvenient times and the quality of bread was deliberately lowered to reduce demand. Nonetheless, largely due to the Royal Navy and the merchant navy, as well as to putting more land under the plough, Britain, surprisingly, fared better than other European combatants, even including France and Italy with their large agricultural sectors.

The experience of living through a period where the state had directed the economy and society left its mark; it was to be responsible, whether for good or ill, for the growth of corporatism in the inter- war period. Having become used to a greater role of the state at the expense of the autonomy of the individual and civil society, the way was opened to far greater state interventionism in post-war societies.

The United States was a late entrant to the war, yet it is arguable that no participant in the war saw greater changes in the relations between state and the individual. Like other powers, it had to direct its economy to the war effort, mobilise its manpower and place restrictions on the production and consumption of food. The combination of a state which had traditionally required less from its citizens than any other country in the world and powerful voluntary organisations meant that, lacking the federal bureaucracy to implement the draft, never mind police the Home Front, local and voluntary organisations and pressure groups were relied upon to implement national policies. This had the result that neighbourhood opinion and pressure for social conformity could make Uncle Sam, the figure who substituted for Kitchener in American recruitment and propaganda posters, a more autocratic figure than the original. If a major effect of the war in America was a reluctant increase in the power of the state, this was because govern- mental authority could be seen as fairer and more objective than the alternative of delegation to civil society as represented by voluntary organisations, local government and pressure groups.[15]

War and Society

Although the overall effect of the war was to reduce living standards and individual liberty, some historians, notably Arthur Marwick, whose seminal work, *The Deluge* was published in 1965, found a silver lining, arguing that amongst the war's deleterious consequences there were what they considered to be positive and progressive changes. The stress of war, so the thesis goes, forced governments to appeal to disadvantaged social groups and to erode class and gender differences, and made them address social issues.[16] Contrary arguments are that long-term structural factors were more important in determining the direction of social change than four years of war and that once peace came many wartime innovations, such as the greater number of occupations open to women and improvements in the wages and conditions of sections of working men, were soon reversed. Convention, tradition and the desire of many women to return to pre-war norms meant that by the early 1920s the balance between the sexes in working life was much as it had been in 1914, while a combination of the end of labour shortages and the determination of the unions representing skilled workers to reassert old differentials ensured than wartime changes were ephemeral. Yet, in Britain, Germany, and the successor states to the Austro-Hungarian Empire women gained the vote after the end of the war, and though it is arguable that female suffrage was likely to have come in a few years without the war, the role of women during the war made it a natural development and destroyed much of the opposition to it.

Social change is, however, never easy to measure and only the more obvious aspects are susceptible to proof or disproof by statistical evidence. One effect of war is to make people more mobile, most obviously with respect to those who volunteered or were conscripted into the armed forces, though most of those who experienced 'foreign travel' did not enjoy the experience. Whether within the armed forces, directed as civilians to jobs away from home towns or villages, or self-motivated to find posts in expanding government offices, people who might never have travelled more than a few miles from their birthplace found wider horizons and formed friendships with, had love affairs with and married those they would otherwise never have met. One effect of mass mobility was a wider choice of partners and, certainly during the war and probably after it, some loosening of sexual mores. Another effect was an erosion of provinciality and regional differences. Populations became more homogeneous as developments in popular mass culture were encouraged by mobility and common experiences.

The effect of the war upon class and upon the different social classes varied widely. In the short term aristocrats and landowners found outlets for their traditional warrior role, but the downside was the higher percentage death rate of officers and the consequent economic impact in countries, like Britain, where the state extracted death duties. In the long term, Europe's aristocracies were to find their positions and wealth much diminished. Among those who found their standard of living declining during the war tended to be the hitherto comfortably off, but not rich, members of the middle-middle classes and skilled workers. The former suffered from increased taxation, the decline in the value of currencies, which hit fixed incomes, and the rise in servants' wages. In all combatant countries there was a decline in the number of domestic servants as the war opened up new opportunities for female employment. The salaried middle class did badly In Germany, though not so badly as the equivalent in Austria, where the salary of high bank officials doubled during the war while prices increased five- or six-fold. In all countries, workers in war-related industries did better than those in sectors considered less essential or unessential, but, as we have seen, skilled workers found their trades opened to unskilled workers and, though working-class wages increased slightly, skilled workers found the differentials between them and other workers narrowed and their status undermined.

Before the war, class divisions had been anticipated all over Europe as likely to result in widespread opposition to war, but in the event they did not prove a serious obstacle to wartime cohesion until the war's later stages. Social democratic parties and most trade union leaders rallied to national causes, but this did not mean that industrial relations were harmonious. Industrial disputes punctuated economic life, but were usually about particular grievances, differentials or wage claims in the face of the rising cost of living, rather than motivated by politics or class feeling. Support for nations' wars and the fact that every layer of society had a high percentage of its members serving in the forces may well have been responsible for lessening hostility between social groups. War brings different sections of society into greater contact. The effects of such intimacy were various, although the hierarchy of the army often closely resembled that of civilian life, especially in the case of the British "Kitchener armies", in which whole industrial and commercial units volunteered and went to war – managers as officers, foremen as NCOs and workers as privates. It has been suggested that in some ways the war may have stabilised the pre-war class system in that, 'the military hierarchy both echoed and reinforced the pre-war social order'.[17] In one respect the war may have increased social mobility as the death rate among officers led to a great increase in promotions from the ranks and 'temporary gentlemen' carried their new gentility into the post-war world.

A new and obvious division in all the societies at war was between those in the armed forces and civilians. The soldier returning home on leave is often represented as resentful at finding himself in an alien world where friends and relatives were still enjoying an only slightly more austere peacetime existence and where few had any understanding of the realities of war or the conditions in which men fought. A corporal in the Royal Welsh Fusiliers, on leave just before Passchendaele, came home to find his sister, a munitions worker, on strike for higher wages. He was horrified and said 'We're getting a shilling a day and you're out on strike!'; when he heard that Lloyd George had agreed to the workers' demands he wrote 'when I got back and told the lads what I'd heard and seen – what they had to say about it wasn't repeatable'.[18]

If to some servicemen the society they encountered while on leave seemed distant from the war, the war in fact impacted forcibly on civilian life. On the south-east coast of England or in Paris, the guns of war could be heard, while troop movements were ubiquitous. This was a railway war and the transition from the great railway stations of London, Paris or Berlin to the trenches was bewilderingly rapid. At the end of leave, perhaps after a visit to a variety theatre the night before, the entrance to the trenches was the railway station, where the ambulances awaited the wounded returning from the war. Europe's great stations throbbed to the pulse of the war.

The soldier did not welcome the petty restrictions that 'super-patriots' and puritans placed upon the pleasures he might extract from his short periods of leave. In Britain, it was the heyday of busybodies and purity campaigners like the Bishop of London, 'who embodied the alliance between puritan and patriot'[19] and whose main aim in life seemed to be stopping people doing things they enjoyed, whether drinking or going to the variety theatre; the suspension of cup finals and the closure of the British Museum demonstrates the range of the restrictions the killjoy lobby achieved.

The war revealed the deep patriotism of the British, French and German peoples, evinced in their determination to support the national causes but also 'to do their bit'. In Britain many of the wealthy turned their grand houses into hospitals and convalescent homes; less well-off people took in Belgian refugees. In all the combatant states women volunteered for nursing work, and war charities raised enormous sums. It also brought out less desirable qualities, as hatred of the enemy turned into hatred of expatriate foreigners, many of whom had lived in their adopted countries for years. In 1914 'evidence from all parts of France ... suggests a mentality of fanatical accusations which swept the country; anyone with a suspicious accent, or still more anyone taking photographs or simply carrying a tripod, might well be arrested or brutalised by the crowd'.[20] In London, the once-thriving German community had almost disappeared by the end of the war and there was a conscious eradication of German connections. German war atrocities against Belgian civilians added to hatred of the enemy in Britain and France, and Zeppelin and Gotha bomber raids on London were met with what has been called, 'a unpredictable mixture of sang-froid and blind terror'. One result was an increase in sporadic violence against London's Germans and Austrians.[21]

National Cohesion

When it came to maintaining support for the war, not just in armies, but among civilians, much depended upon the degree of national cohesion. Although a 'nation' can be defined as a people under the same government and inhabiting the same country, our use of the word is inevitably coloured by its other meaning, a people bound together in unity and identity by factors such as ethnicity, language, culture, religion, tradition and history. The word 'state' sits rather more happily on multi-national empires like Austria-Hungary or Imperial Russia. The immediate effect of the war seemed in most states to be a strengthened unity and a healing of differences, but as the war dragged on, states composed of a variety of national groups found it more difficult to maintain cohesion than those which could be best described as nations, especially when fellow national groups were to be found within enemy states. As we have seen, Slav contingents in the Austro-Hungarian armies were sometimes unreliable when facing Russian troops and conversely fought well against Italians. For Russia, its Polish provinces proved to be a weakness for the empire because of the traditional antipathy of the Poles to Russian rule and the ability of the Central Powers to utilise this. Nevertheless, Austria-Hungary, Russia and the Ottoman Empire stood up rather better to the strain of war until 1917–18 than an emphasis upon their national problems might have suggested, while seemingly solid nation states suffered centrifugal pressures, with Bavarian separatism surfacing in Germany in 1918 and the Easter Rising of 1916 demonstrating that the unifying influence of the war had not ended Britain's Irish Question. There were, of course, other factors which determined the ability of states to maintain their war efforts. Unification had given Italy the appearance and institutions of a unified state, but economic and social divisions between north and south were deep, while domestic support for the war was fragile from the beginning, with elite opinion dangerously divided.

Whether the system of government of a country made it more or less able to maintain confidence and support for governments and their handling of the war is debateable. Some have seen Britain and France as essentially more democratic and liberal states and societies than Germany and Austria-Hungary, and the outcome of the war as a 'victory for democracy'. The evidence that it was differing political systems that put George V on the balcony of Buckingham Palace and the Kaiser in exile in Holland is, however, less than overwhelming, and if the outcomes of the offensives of 1918 had been different then so might the positions of the monarchs. Russia certainly collapsed, but whether this was because it was an autocracy or a spectacularly inefficient one is uncertain.

Maintaining Morale

All countries saw efforts to maintain morale and confidence within their armed forces and societies, but the significance of propaganda and censorship has been exaggerated by historians convinced that the will to fight exhibited by civilians and soldiers must have been due to the brainwashing effects of propaganda. This is largely a myth, for governments did not necessarily take the lead in convincing countries of the justice of their causes and, indeed, there was little need for them to do so; public opinion in most countries was convinced that their enemies had been the aggressors and that their governments had had little option but to resist. Public opinion was receptive to messages which confirmed its opinions and there were plenty of voices within civil society prepared to transmit such messages.

The idea that because the demands of war required a population that was not just physically conscripted and directed, but was mentally mobilised as well, governments were able to bring this about has been dismissed by several recent studies which have demonstrated that popular support for the war was so strong that populations were quite prepared to do it themselves. As a study of British children growing up during the war has argued, even the youngest were not passive victims of the war but were mentally part of a society mobilised for war and, indeed, in their play and their enthusiasm for uniformed youth organisations they did much to mobilise themselves.[22]

In Britain the only official propaganda organisation was the secret War Propaganda Agency, whose remit was to promote Britain's cause overseas. For most of the war, the encouragement of patriotic support for the war was left to a hotchpotch of voluntary organisations and to branches of the foreign office and the Directorate of Military Intelligence. The Parliamentary Recruiting Committee produced posters and pamphlets but, with a small budget, confined itself to its stated purpose. Censorship was limited, the press was relatively free for, despite DORA (the Defence of the Realm Act), powers to suppress unwelcome publications were sparingly used. It was only in the summer of 1917 that a semi-official parliamentary organisation, the National War Aims Committee, was set up with the purpose of combating war-weariness and pacifism and, as a study of it has suggested, the fact that it was only 'semi-official' demonstrates an ambivalence of the government towards propaganda and a desire to keep it at arm's length.[23]

In 1914, France and Germany had equivalents to DORA already in place. Old laws, known as 'Anastasie', dating back to 1840 and 1878, enabled the French military authorities to ban any publications which threatened public order, and the ministry of war set up a press bureau to enforce this. Germany had a similar 'state of siege' law which suspended rights to free speech, and instituted a Central Censor's Office, later the War Press Office. To begin with, all the states at war concentrated on censoring reports containing military information, but then went beyond this to ban publications and plays deemed subversive. Niall Ferguson has, however, commented that 'in no continental country was censorship on a totalitarian scale'.[24]

From the beginning of the war, the press became the fuglemen of the patriotic cause. The British press was distinctive both in the range of its newspapers and the wide readership of the most popular and populist ones, and German leaders at the end of the war considered it, and in particular the papers of the Northcliffe group, to have been a highly effective in helping bring about Germany's defeat. The war increased the sales of newspapers considerably, with the *Daily Mail* and *Daily Mirror* both selling more than a million copies in 1916, while the *Berliner Tageblatt* and the French *Le Matin* more than doubled their pre-war circulation.

From the earliest days of modern journalism, generals have, as with Russell's reports from the Crimea, been slow to accept the media as guests on the battlefield. It was no different in 1914; the British Army saw journalists as at best an unwelcome but necessary evil and it was only in November 1915 that accredited war-correspondents were allowed at the front. The French army set up an Information Division, which released information the army wanted the press to report, but later allowed reporting by journalists instead of army officers. In the German instance, the army controlled information fairly tightly via a War Press Office and then, as part of the general centralisation of command in 1917, the War News Service.

Photographs of battlefields were nothing new, having been part of war reporting during the Crimean War, the American Civil War and, more recently, the Boer War, but many newspapers and magazines now had experienced photo-journalists, while changes in technology meant that servicemen and civilians had access to small, roll-film, pocket cameras. Those in authority, however, regarded photography as 'a threat rather than an opportunity' and, apart from the Kaiser – who sent his court photographers to accompany the army – military authorities usually did their best to keep the camera away from the war.[25] Film making was at first regarded by generals and politicians as far from a fit medium to represent warfare as the cinema was regarded as at the low end of popular culture. Unsurprisingly, it was the film production companies rather than the government or the war office which turned cinema into a significant means of informing the public about the war's progress and shaping attitudes. The war office 'did little more than tolerate the activities of the British Topical Committee for Films'. Among films produced by British companies were *Battle of the Somme* (1916). *Battle of Ancre and the advance of the Tanks* (1916) and *The German Retreat and the battle of Arras* (1917). Much the same happened in Germany, where it was also private companies who produced the films like *How Max won the Iron Cross*, though *With our Heroes on the Somme* (1917) was an official record of the battle. Significantly, it was Ludendorff who seems to have recognised the important role film could play in bolstering morale: 'For the war to be concluded successfully, it is absolutely imperative that film be employed with the greatest force in all places where German influence is still possible.'[26]

Governments and the War

Though the power of the state and of government increased markedly, those who had led their countries into war in 1914 did not, on the whole, have good wars. Kings and emperors famously departed in 1917–18, but few chancellors, prime ministers and foreign ministers lasted the course. They found themselves strangled by the very promises they had held out – of a short war and great victories – blamed for defeats and accused of insufficient zeal or inefficiency. In short, they failed, or were thought to have failed, the test of war. They had for the most part not willed the war, and peacetime political life and administration arguably required talents that were not suited to leadership in war. The stalemate that the war appeared to have reached, and the enormous death toll of the battles of 1916 and 1917, led to a loss of confidence in political leadership and the reshaping of governments. In Russia, of course, the entire system of government fell victim to revolution, and in Austria-Hungary there were ominous signs that the creaking Empire might not long outlast the death of the aged Emperor.

In Britain, France and Germany new men emerged who were seen as dynamic leaders who would ruthlessly pursue victory. David Lloyd George replaced Herbert Asquith as British prime minister in December 1916; the fiery Georges Clemenceau became France's fifth prime minister of the war; in Germany, Bethmann Hollweg, who had been chancellor since 1909, was forced out of office in July 1917. However, although he was nominally succeeded by another chancellor, Georg Michaelis, the guiding hands of German policy were henceforth to be the military's in the shape of Hindenburg and Ludendorff.

If societies were shaken by military failures and economic hardships, the normal structures of pre-war government were found wanting, to a greater or lesser degree, in all the states at war. It is significant, however, that changes in government came not from anti-war pressure. For the most part, outright opposition to the war enjoyed little success. In Britain, the main opposition came from middle-class liberals or radical formations such as the Union for Democratic Control, with the majority of the Labour Party not only backing the war effort but joining the coalition. In Germany, the bulk of the SPD gave its support to the war until near the end, while although French socialist and trade unionist discontent mounted, especially after Clemenceau became prime minister, it was never directed at the national cause. It was the perceived failure of governments and leaders to wage war successfully, not the continuance of the war, which, with the great exception of Russia, led to their fall.

Chapter 7:   The Problems of the Offensive

In 1914, Germany, France and Russia had gone to war with plans, all of which had failed. The strategies of the military commands had proved flawed and the technology of warfare had resulted in defence having an overwhelming advantage over offensives, with the latter grinding to a halt once attacking armies had gone beyond their railheads. Given that the war was to continue, military commanders had either to consider new strategies or find ways of making old ones work.

The widening of the war during 1915 brought each side new allies and the possibility of new campaigns and new fronts, but did not alter the fundamental problem of how either side was to obtain victory. The most obvious response to the failure of the offensives of 1914–15 might have been peace initiatives. General peace proposals were ruled out, in large part because of the feeling in all the warring states that the numbers of countrymen killed constituted a sacrifice that would be discredited by anything short of complete victory, but for Germany this left room for von Falkenhayn's hopes that Russia might be detached from the Allies.

A strategic answer for all the powers might have been to cease attacking and go permanently on the defensive, thus allowing the attackers to be worn down by the immense casualties inflicted upon them. Such a policy was more feasible for a power which occupied enemy territory and, indeed, Germany, which held large areas of France and Belgium, was, with the significant exception of Verdun in 1916, to largely employ a defensive strategy on the Western Front from the second battle of Ypres in April 1915 until the spring of 1918. Nevertheless, generals on both sides shared a common military mind-set and, trained to think of breakthroughs and encirclements, saw defence as only a stage towards an offensive. For governments who had to deal with public opinion and maintain morale any overt

115

acceptance of a defensive strategy was equally difficult as it could be seen as timorous and defeatist.

Balance of Power

The Western Front

Germany

How did the balance of power stand? In terms of demographic and economic resources Germany was at a great disadvantage and it can be argued that a major question is why the Allies did not benefit more from this.[1] Germany was committed to a war on two fronts, a considerable hindrance when it came to concentrating its forces, but efficient use of internal railway systems enabled it to move troops between both fronts. Both sides had a weak link: Germany had, since Bismarck's time, been bound to Austria-Hungary, an ally with multiple problems, including a poorly resourced and inefficiently administered army; time and time again, the German army had to come to the aid of Austria-Hungary. Russia, a power with great potential in terms of resources and manpower but an inefficient autocracy unable to utilise them effectively, was the Allies' weak link. British involvement in the war was the potential deciding factor. Her economic and naval strength could prove decisive in a long war, while the size of the British population would enable her, if she chose to do so, to raise a large army. It was, however, by no means certain that she would make such a choice.

It can, thus, be argued that the Allies had the long-term advantage, but that in the first year of the war the German army had proved a superior force to the armies of the Allies, and victory on the battlefield could negate economic or industrial strength or future military potential. The following years were to demonstrate that sanguine expectations that Germany could be worn down greatly underestimated its ability to gear its economy to a long war.

Von Moltke had not proved a capable commander-in-chief, but his replacement, von Falkenhayn, had a cooler head and a firm grasp on both political and military realities. German strategic thinking had begun with the view that a quick victory over France would enable Germany to go on to win a war in the east with Russia. As hopes for that quick victory receded, German generals and politicians tended to divide into 'Easterners' and 'Westerners'. The circumstances of the war against Russia with its more open warfare seemed, especially after the much celebrated victory at Tannenberg, to offer the opportunity for campaigns that would involve decisive battles, and von Hindenburg and Ludendorff and their supporters argued consistently for great sweeping offensives on the Eastern Front. The Western Front offered only a protracted attempt to wear down and exhaust the French and British, but, it could be argued, it was the only battlefield where total victory could be achieved. Von Falkenhayn was too realistic to be either an 'Easterner' or a 'Westerner'. He knew that great victories were more likely in the east and was prepared to support operations there for tactical reasons, but he was pessimistic as to Germany's ability to win a war against the three great powers of France, Russia and Britain with only Austria-Hungary and Turkey as major allies. Rather than victory, he told the Kaiser, Germany's best hope was not to lose the war, and the way forward was not to defeat Russia but to maul her, then convince her that a separate peace was in her interests and that the old friendship between the two conservative monarchies should be resumed. He played a clever game in placating Hindenburg and Ludendorff by ordering offensives in the East, but at the same time thwarting their ambitions for massive sweeping advances. His blind spot was that he despised his Austro-Hungarian allies and never cooperated with them, keeping Conrad in ignorance of major initiatives; the Austro-Hungarians had their weaknesses, but they were the only firm ally Germany had.

Hew Strachan sees Falkenhayn as, throughout 1915, considering the Western Front as 'the decisive theatre of the war', and David Stevenson argues that he saw Britain as the main enemy, expecting, even at the high tide of Germany's advance in the east in September 1915, that 'the decisive campaign of the war would come later and in the West'.[2] In contrast, Norman Stone has argued that, 'Falkenhayn, like Churchill, knew that the west offered only stalemate, and he was quite right.' Perhaps the answer is that Falkenhayn was genuinely fighting a war on two fronts, saw that the gains were to be made on the east in 1915, but saw them as a means towards impelling Russia to a separate peace, while he was always alert to opportunities in the west, an approach which can be considered as either pragmatism or vacillation.

France

The French were not in a position to choose where to fight for it was clear that, as Germany occupied a swathe of her territory, her main effort would be made on her own and Belgian soil. They did have the resources to divert some of their forces from the Western Front to the Balkans and the Dardanelles, moves which could be seen as, at once, supportive of their Russian ally and markers of French interests in any final peace settlement. Even these minor subtractions from the forces that could be thrown against the German invader aroused the opposition of Joffre, who was bent upon organising large-scale offensives and was calling upon Britain to send more troops to take part in them. There was little the French could do to directly support their Russian ally, except to provide financial assistance and supplies and point to the possibility that their troops in Salonika might be of assistance in the future, but they could and did align offensives on the Western Front with times when the Russians were hard-pressed.

Britain

Of the combatants, Britain was the only power with the luxury of being able to ponder what sort of war she should fight and where to fight it. Having rather stumbled into the war, Britain had no war plan. It had vague war aims: victory for the Allies and a strong position for Britain vis-á-vis both her allies and her enemies at the end of the war. After the Pact of London in September 1914 there were rather more definite aims for inheriting parts of the Ottoman Empire. Britain had a naval and economic strategy, but, apart from the decision to demonstrate support for her allies by sending the BEF to France, the British government had, early in the war, no considered military strategy and certainly not one which involved a large British army fighting year after year in France and Belgium.

The traditional policy of Britain at war was to use economic muscle to provide support to continental allies and use maritime power to command the seas and blockade enemy ports. In keeping with this, the Asquith government was determined that Britain's main efforts would revolve around her navy and her economy. In 1914, the Royal Navy began to impose a blockade, and British bankers and manufacturers to supply British allies with money and munitions. These 'business as usual', or Britain's usual way at war, policies were to continue and be effective but were to be accompanied, incrementally, by the recruitment of a large army, and then the deployment of that army in France and Belgium, a result that came about via an empirical process rather than resulting from a conscious decision.

It was not surprising that in Britain there arose a major division between 'Westerners' and 'Easterners' which was far more important than the eponymous division between German strategists. On one side were those who believed that the only way to victory was by persevering with attrition on the Western Front and close cooperation with the French, despite the enormous loss of men and little sign of progress; on the other were those who sought another way of winning the war, one more in keeping with British strengths and interests. Churchill, when planning the attempt to use the navy to break through the Dardanelles had asked: 'Are there not other alternatives than sending our armies to chew barbed wire in Flanders? Further cannot the power of Navy be brought to bear upon the enemy?', while Lloyd George at the War Council meeting January 1915 argued for pulling out of France and Belgium and launching operations in Syria against Turkey and in Salonika against Austria-Hungary: 'Was it not possible to get at the enemy from some other direction and to strike a blow that would end the war once and for all? Are we really bound to hand over the ordering of our troops to France as if we were her vassal?'

Even when the decision was made to raise a large volunteer army, it was by no means certain that it would be committed to cooperation with the French or, indeed, to the Western Front in the near future. Kitchener, convinced that the war would last for years, thought a larger army necessary so that Britain would be in a strong position to protect its interests at the war's end, but did not favour committing it to debilitating battles until the third year of the war when the continental powers would have worn themselves out. In a sense, Kitchener's strategy was one of 'attrition', but what he meant by this was allowing the German army to suffer great losses while launching offensives, something the Germans declined to do on the Western Front during 1915. A number of factors worked against this strategy. The failure of the Gallipoli campaign, reverses in Mesopotamia and the redundancy of the Anglo-French force at Salonika discredited the view that an alternative to the Western Front existed, while the very presence of the BEF in France worked against Kitchener's policy of holding an expanded British army in reserve for, once it was fighting alongside the French, there was an ineluctable pressure for the army in France to be reinforced. A further factor was the success of the Central Powers against Russia in the course of 1915, which raised fears that Russia might be driven to make a separate peace, and led to calls for British efforts in France to take the pressure off the Russians. Gradually the Kitchener policy of attrition, or rather the interpretation of it, changed. There was talk of 'active defence', a term that was then discarded in favour of 'co-ordinated offensives', which were agreed at the inter-allied conference at Chantilly in

December 1915. The replacement of Sir John French by Douglas Haig, with Sir William Robertson as his chief-of-staff, played a major part in the change of strategy and by June 1916 they had 'succeeded in blurring in the minds of the War Committee the distinction between a breakthrough battle and a policy of intensifying attrition'.[3] British strategy thus fell in line with that of Joffre, who believed that attacking on the Western Front was essential, for otherwise, 'our troops will little by little lose their physical and moral qualities'.[4] The old obsession with *elan* tended to override attrition and led to demands for attempts at breakthrough.

The Eastern Front

The course of the war in 1915 was to demonstrate that the Central Powers, thanks to the ability of the German army, had the advantage on the Eastern Front and were able to withstand the French and the British efforts in the west. Things did not look that way in the early months of 1915 when Austria-Hungary faced a military crisis as Russian forces penetrated deeply into the Carpathians and the Austro-Hungarian retreated, leaving the great fortress of Przemyśl and its garrison of 120,000, isolated. The fortress held out and became a symbol of Austro-Hungarian resistance, but such symbols are dangerous because they assume an importance beyond their military significance; Conrad wasted some 100,000 of his troops trying to relieve it. Further north, the German armies under Hindenburg were winning the 'Winter battle in Masuria' and von Falkenhayn was having to rein back the *Oberost* (commander-in-chief on Eastern Front), who pressed for ambitious offensives at the very time the Austro-Hungarian position was worsening – Russian forces were threatening the great plain of Hungary and Przemyśl was taken by the Russians. At this point Falkenhayn set in motion a great offensive. Taking troops from the Western Front, he formed a joint Austro-German army, commanded by the very capable German general, August von Mackensen, thus sidelining not only Conrad but Hindenburg and Ludendorff too. The Central Powers attacked through Galicia, shattering the Russian lines at Gorlice-Tarnów and pushing the Russians out of the territory they had taken, before driving them out of Poland and Lithuania. During the 'great retreat' the Russians suffered losses of some 1.4 million men, more than half of whom were taken prisoner. Falkenhayn now turned his attention to the Balkans. German and Austro-Hungarian armies, supported by Bulgaria, which declared war on Serbia in October, overran Serbia and its tiny ally Montenegro. Soon, the Serbian Army had been routed and had to evacuate its country and retreat across the mountains to the Albanian coast. Britain and France could do little but transport the remainder of the Serbian army to Salonika, where British and French troops also arrived, too late to do anything to help the Serbs. Russia now had no longer a Balkan ally of any weight.

Meanwhile, Austria-Hungary had acquired a new enemy, Italy, and had to fight on a new front. In theory, Italy's entry into the war should have been a great blow to the Central Powers and of enormous benefit to the Entente. Both alliances had alternatively great hopes and fears of an Italian intervention. Italy appeared to be nearly a great power and as a national state seemed to have advantages over multi-ethnic Austria-Hungary, while it had on paper a formidable army. Events were, however, to demonstrate the weaknesses of Italy as a state and a society, weaknesses which were exemplified in its army. The Italian offensive foundered because the geography of the Austro-Italian border favoured the defending Austro-Hungarians but also because fighting the Italians brought out the best in the Austro-Hungarian armies, uniting Germans and Slavs against a common enemy. In four battles on the River Isonzo the Italians made little progress and suffered over 200,000 casualties. The record of the Eastern Front in 1915 was overwhelmingly in favour of the Central Powers.

Western Front Offensives

In contrast to the offensives and retreats to the East, the Western Front remained comparatively immobile. Largely preoccupied with dealing with Russia, von Falkenhayn was content after April that German forces should stand on the defensive. The first British offensive of 1915, at Neuve Chapelle in March, saw an attempt by General Sir Douglas Haig to advance on a broad front. Preceded by a bombardment by artillery, which took the Germans by surprise, infantry advanced and gains were made, but the problems that were to doom many attempts at a breakthrough manifested themselves: the Germans had a defence in depth that enabled them to fall back to another line of trenches; poor communication systems combined with an inflexible British command system held up the advance; and the ability of defenders to bring up reserves enabled the gap in the German lines to be plugged.

Neuve Chapelle was significant, John Keegan, has written, 'because it anticipated in miniature both the character and the course of the spring offensive in Artois, to which it was a preliminary, as well as its renewal in Artois and Champagne in the autumn'.[5] Almost immediately, however, the British army ensconced around Ypres, important to the British and Germans alike for respectively control of the Channel coast and its adjacency to the German supply lines, found itself under attack. Departing for the only time in 1915 from his defensive policy in the West, von Falkenhayn decided to order a limited attack on the Ypres salient and to try out the new weapon of poison gas. The confusion caused in the British ranks by the use of this ghastly weapon might have allowed a German breakthrough if reserves had been available, but von Falkenhayn had not been prepared to move troops from the east and the British line was held by the Dorset Regiment. The salient was dinted but not broken. French and British attacks in May on the strong German positions on Vimy and Aubers Ridges to the south of Ypres both failed, with the attack on Aubers Ridge costing 9,500 British casualties.

By the time of the British and French offensives in Artois and Champagne in the autumn, British forces, increased by the transfer of territorial regiments to France and the first divisions of Kitchener's new volunteer army, had taken over responsibility for more of the Allied line and now manned the stretch from Ypres to the Somme. The offensives were designed to penetrate the German line where it bulged in an extended and seemingly vulnerable salient towards Paris. Artois, where the British attack was to take place, was on its northern edge and Champagne on its west. Both offensives failed to make headway. An Anglo-French attack on the German-held town of Loos saw the first and rather bungled British use of gas; the town was taken but the reserve divisions which were supposed to follow and consolidate success had been kept too far back to do their job effectively. The French attack in Champagne enjoyed greater initial success and this time reserves followed up promptly to exploit a breakthrough but, as was becoming a pattern, the Germans were able to move up reinforcements by train, and advancing troops found themselves crossing land full of shell-holes made by their own artillery.

The failure at Loos had an important repercussion in that it led to the removal of Sir John French as the British commander-in-chief in December. Sir Douglas Haig had asked Sir John to release two reserve divisions before the battle and French had refused, an episode which led to the replacement of French, already the object of criticism by some of his subordinates, by Haig, who, 'sinuous in his relationships with the great',[6] used his influence with King George V to secure French's recall. There were attacks on French in parliament, but the real damage was done, 'by astute hatchet-work behind the scenes'.[7] British strategy was now to be directed by the duo of Haig and his chief-of-staff, Sir William Robertson, both committed to offensives on the Western Front and both impatient with interference by civilian government.

The problems French and British commanders faced were considerable, for both military technology and the geography of the Western Front made successful offensives extraordinarily difficult. The artillery available for an offensive provided an enormous amount of firepower, but was relatively immobile, and the physical devastation artillery was able to inflict on enemy positions was counter-productive when it came making a breakthrough beyond the enemy's lines. Control of battles was impeded by the lack of communication between commanders at the rear and attacking units as buried telephone lines became severed. Even when breakthroughs were made, the defence could be quickly reinforced, especially if railway communications were adequate. Allied commanders, committed to offensives, had an almost impossible task as they were faced with a German army adopting the tactic of elastic defence in depth.

The next three years were to see constant experimentation and the testing of new weapons and tactics as both sides attempted to find the tactical solutions which would produce a war-winning strategy. Yet, in practice, from the winter of 1914–15 until the spring of 1918 the powers at war adopted a style of combat which David Stevenson has seen as characterised by 'escalation and stalemate, both sides applying rising levels of violence but failing to terminate the impasse'. The most common term used to describe the approach to war that was, although adopted pragmatically, rationalised as the planned erosion of one's opponent's strength, primarily by killing more of his troops than he managed to kill of yours, was 'attrition'. Indeed, the term accurately describes the war that is indelibly lodged in the European memory.

A strategy eschewing great, ambitious offensives might well have been the most sensible course, but generals on both sides found it difficult to content themselves with modest ambitions. This was more understandable in the circumstances of the war in eastern Europe. There, great breakthroughs and encirclements still seemed possible; defenders, especially the Russians, often lacked the railways which, by speedily bringing up reinforcements, could limit the ground gained. Hindenburg, Supreme Commander in the East, and his chief-of-staff, Ludendorff, encouraged by their victory at Tannenberg and the winter battle of Masuria, still thought in terms of great encirclements and had to be held back by von Falkenhayn who considered, rightly, that their plans were far too ambitious. Von Mackensen and his chief-of-staff Hans von Seeckt had the more modest aims of breakthrough rather than encirclement and they, not Hindenburg and Ludendorff were, Hew Strachan considers, 'the most successful double act in the German army in the First World War'.[8]

In December 1915, an inter-Allied conference met at Chantilly. The powers conferring could not look back on the past year with equanimity for it had seen a series of reverses on both fronts. All the Allies agreed to mount offensives in the coming year and to coordinate and time them so as to prevent the Central Powers transferring reserves between theatres. There was pressure upon Britain, rapidly becoming the dominant partner on the Western Front as Kitchener's new armies began to arrive, to take a greater role, and agreement was reached for joint offensives in 1916 on the centre of the front. Sir Douglas Haig argued for an offensive by the British in Flanders to be accompanied by a French offensive further south, much the same plan as that of the previous autumn, but reluctantly agreed to an attack along the line of the River Somme. What the coming offensives hoped to achieve was becoming clear. Although some generals still dreamed of encirclements, and most hoped for breakthroughs, a strategy of attrition had become the more common aim and success or failure was becoming measurable. On 31 March 1916, the General Staff suggested to Kitchener that if permanent casualties could be inflicted on the Germans at a rate of 150,000 men a month the enemy would be forced to sue for peace after another ten months or so. Attrition had become a cold-blooded matter of a body count.

Chapter 8: 1916, The Killing Fields

1916 was the year on which the reputation of the war turned, both for contemporaries and posterity. It has been called 'the year of battles'. Not only was the great sea battle of the war, Jutland, fought then, but for France and Britain respectively Verdun and the Somme stand out as the two land battles that are most prominent in the national memory of the Great War. Jutland, though its outcome was contested, was a British victory in that it confirmed the Royal Navy's supremacy, but neither Verdun nor the Somme are remembered as victories in any sense. Rather, they have most firmly lodged themselves in memory because of the huge numbers of those killed for what laymen, as opposed to generals then and some military historians later, have seen as negligible advantages. This may well be a western-centric view of 1916 and one which disregards the last throw of Tsarist Russia in the shape of the Brusilov advance in the summer, but, nevertheless, these battles symbolise the way in which the mounting death toll on the Western Front destroyed views of the war as a glorious or brave encounter and last hopes that it would soon be over, even if it did not diminish the determination of both sides to achieve eventual victory.

Trench Warfare

Stalemate became ever more firmly established through 1915. The most arresting physical evidence was the 475-mile line of earthworks that made up the Western Front, but trenches also stretched along the Isonzo River, protected British and French forces in Salonika, and marked the line between Russia and the Central Powers in Poland.

Life in the trenches has, with justice, been portrayed as peculiarly hideous: mud, rats, trench foot, frostbite and, out in 'No man's land', bodies unretrieved after encounters and left to rot. Yet trenches saved lives, and, Hew Strachan has trenchantly argued that 'To speak of the horror of the trenches is to substitute hyperbole for common sense: the war would have been far more horrific if there had been no trenches. They protected flesh and blood from the worst effects of the fire-power revolution of the late nineteenth century'.[1] Men were relatively safe in trenches; it was when they were ordered to leave their shelter and attack that they were likely to get killed or wounded.

Throughout the history of warfare, whenever large numbers of soldiers were massed together in crowded conditions, disease accounted for more deaths than were due to combat, and it might have been expected that the conditions of trench warfare would have seen this repeated, but on the Western Front, though not in other theatres, inoculations, antiseptics and field medical treatment meant that disease was not a major killer.

One further development, again mainly on the Western Front, was that far more of the wounded survived than in previous wars, despite the fact that the developers of weaponry had become so ingenious in finding new ways to kill. Military medical staff were perhaps more successful than the generals in adapting to the challenge of modern war. As a recent study of the treatment of the British wounded has shown, it was not just the new weapons – poison gas, flame-throwers and high explosive shells – that presented the challenge; even the bullets had changed – 'the neat round holes made by rounded ammunition' were no more and 'instead the cylindro-conical bullet fired by the new powerful weaponry hit fast and hard, went deep and took bits of dirty uniform and airborne soil particles with it'. Modern hospitals well behind the front had the disadvantage that too many wounded men failed to survive the journey from the battlefield. An answer was found in bringing surgeons and nurses as close to the battles as possible. It was more important that surgical treatment was available quickly than that operations took place in a tent rather than a purpose-built hospital, and casualty clearing stations intended to provide little but a dressing, became, in practice, field hospitals.[2] The numbers of wounded were large, around 450,000 in the case of the French and over 420,000 for both the British and the Germans, but, due to improved medical treatment, a substantial proportion of those wounded – 55.5 per cent in the British case – were able to enjoy the, perhaps dubious, benefit of returning to service.[3] This also affected the numbers of casualties it was necessary to inflict upon the enemy if a policy of attrition was to be followed and, in part, explains why combatants were able maintain the size of armies.

What killed and wounded troops in huge numbers were offensives, for the combination of defensive firepower, trenches and dug-outs, barbed wire and the ability to quickly supply reinforcements and munitions by rail disadvantaged the attacker on the Western Front. To win a war without offensives seemed impossible, yet, considering the strength of defence, how could the Allies hope to kill 150,000 or more of the enemy a month without losing more men than the enemy? This was the problem Allied generals were faced with and which they had discussed in December 1915 when they made their plans for offensives in 1916. One answer was greater coordination of Allied efforts. The communications between German forces on the Eastern and Western Fronts were good, enabling the Germans to switch troops to where they were needed, but if Russian and Anglo French, and perhaps Italian, offensives were simultaneous, then this should not be possible. Equally, if an ally was in difficulties, then an offensive elsewhere might result in German forces having to be moved. A Russian offensive in the early summer was, therefore, planned to relieve pressure upon Italy, hard pressed by Austro-German armies, and was to be synchronised with an Anglo French offensive on the Western Front.

The strength of Allied forces had grown considerably. Russia, which had lost large numbers of men as casualties or prisoners after Gorlice-Tarnów, had managed to conscript new armies and would have two million men in the field army by the spring, and they would be better equipped with artillery, rifles and munitions, thanks to greater production by Russian industry. Even Italy had succeeded in raising its number of battalions and artillery pieces. France, though handicapped by the fact that a large percentage of its male population of military age had already been conscripted, had formed 25 new infantry divisions, and industrial expansion had provided more artillery and munitions. Most importantly, Kitchener's six new armies were now available and Britain had now 70 divisions under arms, a ten-fold expansion since 1914.[4]

Verdun

Before Allied plans for offensives had been translated into action, however, the Germans struck for the first time in nearly a year when they, also thinking in terms of attrition, launched their attack on the fortified town of Verdun. Exactly why von Falkenhayn made what proved to be a major error in turning his attention away from eastern Europe, where German forces had been so successful, to the

Western Front, where he had put German forces on the defensive for nearly a year, has been much debated. It has been put down to a basic pessimism as to Germany's chances of winning a long war and his identification of Britain as the major obstacle to an eventual German victory. If attacking Verdun seems an odd way of forcing Britain into submission, his previous attempts to break the British lines at Ypres seem to have convinced him that an attack on Britain's main ally might succeed in forcing it out of the war. In a document known as the 'Christmas Memorial', supposedly sent to the Kaiser on Christmas Day 1915, in which he outlined his plans for the coming year, he twinned an offensive in France with a plea for unrestricted submarine warfare in order to weaken Britain. If the British part of the Western Front was too strong to attack, then the blow must fall on Britain's ally.[5]

Von Falkenhayn claimed after the war that his plan was not to take Verdun, but to inflict enormous casualties on the French: the Germans would use their superiority in artillery and, having first taken the fortresses on the high ground east and west of the River Meuse would bombard the town causing maximum casualties and impelling the French to commit more and more men to its defence and to counter-attacks, thus becoming sucked into a battle of attrition. If this was indeed the plan, and John Keegan largely agrees that it was,[6] it backfired: if 162,440 French soldiers died in its defence, then 143,000 Germans were killed in its attack. It may well be, however, that as, Strachan suggests, Falkenhayn's claim that he had limited objectives was a later and spurious excuse, for his army advanced 'as fast and as far as it could' and he really aimed at a breakthrough.[7] Yet, Falkenhayn had only allowed himself nine divisions for the assault, hardly sufficient for a major breakthrough. Military historians remain divided as to his purpose.

On 21 February, 'some 1,220 guns, half of them mortars or heavy artillery pieces, fired 2 million shells in eight hours along an eight-mile front before the infantry rose to attack'.[8] At first, all went well for the Germans and in three days they advanced several miles and took the great fort of Douaumont on the east bank of the Meuse. They did not take the west bank, however, and this made them subject to fire on their flank. In strictly military terms, Verdun was not crucial to the defence of France, nor a good place to mount a desperate resistance, for it became a death trap. GQG (Grand Quartier Général), the French high command, initially favoured withdrawal, but the longer the battle went on – and it did so for many months – and the greater the number of casualties, the more important it became symbolically.

Falkenhayn did succeed in luring the French into committing more and more men and taking great casualties, but found himself dragged into an attrition contest as, from the Kaiser down, pressure on him to take Verdun increased, while Joffre, under similar pressure from prime minister Briand, appointed General Philippe Pétain as commander. Pétain, an artillery expert, coordinated the gunfire of the defence, which held up the German attack, and gave priority to the maintenance of supplies and the rotation of French units to the garrison, which depended on keeping open a single road from Bar-le-Duc. Because of the numbers killed in ensuring that lines of lorries got through to Verdun, the road became known as the 'Sacred Way'. 'Three quarters of the divisions of the French army fought at one time at Verdun during 1916, forty three were committed once, twenty three twice, and seven three times or more', and on their arrival at the front, they entered a world which with its noise, smells and confusion rivalled 'Dante's description of Hell'.[9]

As German forces assaulted the forts on the west bank of the Meuse, their casualties grew, while French losses were even greater, though this did not perturb Pétain unduly. Casualties became greater still when Pétain was replaced as commander by General Nivelle, who mounted a number of suicidal counter-attacks. Verdun became the 'meat grinder' costing three million casualties, French and German. On 25 June the Germans made a great effort, but they had not the troops to prevail and Nivelle now mounted better-planned counterstrokes. But, by this time Falkenhayn had other matters on his mind and after a final attack on 11 July, the Germans went on the defensive. The battle continued, but as a diminuendo after Falkenhayn's dismissal in August, and during the autumn the French recovered the ground they had lost. However, Verdun had not been a victory for either side. The morale of the German troops had been hit badly, but the French had suffered more; French soldiers ceased to trust their generals and the morale of their army never really recovered. Norman Stone has seen Verdun as 'France's last moment as a great power'.

The Eastern Front

At the critical moment in June, when von Falkenhayn was conducting his last serious attempt to take Verdun, he was forced to move three divisions to the east. He had switched his attention from east to west in February at a time when German and Austrian positions seemed secure and the Russians demoralised. Events in March had appeared to bear out this confident analysis, for under pressure to do something to assist the French, as they had promised at the Chantilly conference, the northern Russian armies launched an offensive in March in White Russia near Lake Naroch. It was a complete disaster. The Russian prospects seemed good, the armies had been expanded and Russian industry had successfully increased its production of weapons and ammunition, but, although they had a numerical superiority of two to one, their attack came to an abrupt end after they had suffered 100,000 casualties. The failed offensive illustrated all the defects of the Russian army: favouritism and mutual antipathy amongst the *Stavka* (Russian High Command) at the top, shortage of competent middle-ranking officers, poor relations between officers and men, and lack of cooperation between artillery and infantry. The major authority on the Eastern Front has called Lake Naroch one of the decisive battles of the war as its result, 'condemned most of the Russian army to passivity'.[10]

But, even given that the Eastern Front seemed secure when von Falkenhayn attacked Verdun in February, was he right to move from the position he had taken up in late 1914 of defending in the west and concentrating on the Eastern Front? The east was, after all, where victories were to be won and where, a year and more later, complete victory was won, and where he had hoped, prematurely, that peace might be made with Russia. His judgement may have been influenced by his poor relations with Hindenburg and Ludendorff and also with Conrad von Hötzendorf. His dislike of the last, and of the Austrians in general, may have blinded him to the very real possibility of knocking Italy out of the war with all the unforeseeable, but possibly momentous, consequences that might have followed. In mid May, while the struggle for Verdun was at its height, the Austro-Hungarians attacked from the Trentino and had soon overrun the Asiago plateau; it looked as though they might succeed in the aim of cutting off the whole Italian army on the Isonzo. This offensive eventually petered out, as offensives were wont to do, but full support from the Germans could well have produced a decisive victory. Rarely, however, have two allies distrusted each other so much and, just as Falkenhayn had told Conrad nothing about his intention of attacking Verdun, Conrad had not informed Falkenhayn about his plans to attack the Italians. Germany was in the bizarre position of not being at war with Italy, although Italy was allied to France and Britain, but, if this complication had been set aside, German forces could almost certainly have made a difference.

The great surprise of the early summer of 1916 was what had come to seem a contradiction in terms, a successful Russian offensive.

Hard-pressed by the Austro-Hungarians, General Luigi Cadorna, the Italian commander-in-chief, and King Victor Emmanuel appealed to the Russians to once more contribute to the Allies' cause; they were backed by Joffre, who needed to divert German forces from Verdun. General Mikhail Alekseyev, now the real commander of Russian forces as the Tsar had replaced Grand Duke Nicholas as supreme commander, worried that the Germans were ready to renew operations against Russia, promised Joffre that he would deliver a new attack. After the debacle at Lake Naroch the commanders of the Russian northern army and central army groups facing the Germans were not prepared to take the offensive, but Alexei Brusilov, recently appointed as commander of the south-west group facing the Austro-Hungarians, was eager to do so and he had a new strategy. The main problems facing generals on all fronts were that a breakthrough seemed only viable by means of an extended bombardment followed by a concentrated attack on a limited front, but time and again such thrusts through enemy lines had foundered because of the ability of defenders to bring up reserves. Brusilov's answer was, that, after a short artillery bombardment, there should be an attack on a broad front and in several places at once, so that reserves would be bewildered and disrupted and the breakthrough broad enough to prevent attacks on its flanks.

Accordingly, Brusilov's attack on 4 June against Austro-Hungarians in the southern sector of the front began with a four hour bombardment followed by attacks in four places along a 300-mile front, though with the main blows at the northern end. The Austrian reserves that would have been able to plug one gap were confused and incapable of plugging four and by the end of the day the Austrian 4th Army on the north of the front was retreating in disarray, while to the south the 7th Army was also in muddled retreat. Brusilov had advanced 60 miles along the front and had taken 350,000 prisoners, an achievement that other Allied, never mind Russian, generals would have given their eye teeth to emulate.

At the beginning of July, Brusilov's advance was supported by an offensive north of the Pripet marshes by General Alexei Evert's army. Being opposed by German troops, rather than Austrian, this soon petered out, but Brusilov continued to be successful against the Austrians. That his offensive, the most successful on any front since the war began, eventually came to a halt was due to his inability, because of the lack of railways and the poor state of the roads behind him, to bring up supplies and reserves. He pushed forward too far with an exhausted, poorly supplied army suffering in the summer heat. Austrian troops were moved up from the Italian front and Germans from the northern side of the Eastern Front and from France; they brought an end to the best effort from the Russians in the course of the war.

Brusilov's offensive was of course made easier by von Falkenhayn's decision to go west and attack Verdun and his failure to support Conrad against the Italians. He had taken German units away from the east and failed to stiffen Austro-Hungarian armies facing the Russians. Nevertheless, and especially because of the lack of support he received from other Russian commanders, Brusilov's offensive stands out from the otherwise inchoate and unprofessional campaigning of Russia's armies. His fault was not to realise when it was time to halt and consolidate. The Russian advance petered out, but before it had done so, the Russian success had encouraged the cautious but land-hungry Romanians to join the Allies at the end of August.

Romania had vacillated, not only hesitant to join in the war, but undecided as to which side to join if it did. Enticed by the prospect of gaining Hungarian Transylvania, promised Allied support from Salonika, and convinced, after Brusilov's offensive, that the Allies were winning, the Romanian government came off the fence, with disastrous consequences. The Romanian offensive against Hungary was a fiasco, the promised Allied support from Salonika was pre-empted by the Bulgarians who took the Allies by surprise and defeated the refugee Serbian army, and Romania soon found itself attacked by the Turks as well. Then came the Germans, commanded by von Falkenhayn, given the job as partial compensation for his recent dismissal as commander-in-chief. The Romanian capital, Bucharest, was taken in December. Romania's late and self-interested entry into the war did nothing to assist the Allied cause. Russia, which had at first committed only three divisions to Romania's assistance, was forced to commit major forces to save her from total collapse and found itself fighting on an extended front, while the occupation of two-thirds of the country provided Germany with the Black Sea port of Constanza and new resources, oil from the Ploesti oilfields and grain from Romania's fertile plains.

The Somme

The Brusilov offensive did detach some German units from Verdun, but the German siege continued to bleed the French army and this gave an urgency to French demands that the much enlarged British

Army fulfil the agreement made at Chantilly and cooperate with the French in launching an offensive. The French were originally to have to have committed the most troops to the proposed offensive and Haig's preference was for his forces to attack in Flanders, the British part of the line since 1914 and an area important to Britain as adjacent to Channel ports, but in the event, the date, time and place of the summer offensive were decided by the French. Haig's position in relation to Joffre was complex: he was clear that he was, '*not under* General Joffre's orders, but that would make no difference, as my intention was to carry out General Joffre's wishes on strategical matters, as if they were orders'.[11] The French army had been severely weakened and the BEF must come to its aid.

The Somme seems to have been chosen as the area for the attack for no better reason than that the long line of trenches controlled by the British and those by the French met around Amiens, which bestrode the River Somme. There was no great strategic reason for an offensive on the Somme and some reason to doubt its suitability. It was probably the strongest German position on the front, for the Germans had positioned themselves on ridges and had had time to dig deep into the chalky soil to create deep dug-outs impervious to artillery fire, and to establish a network of machine-gun posts.

There was some confusion amongst the British command as to what, in addition to taking pressure off the French, the offensive was meant to achieve. Was the goal to be attrition and 'the killing of the maximum number of Germans at the least loss to ourselves', as General Sir Henry Rawlinson, in charge of the troops ready for the fray, planned, or was it to be a breakthrough, which Haig, the commander-in-chief, favoured? Haig feared that a 'wearing out' battle, or *bataille d'usure* as the French called it, would cost as many British as German losses; also, he clung to the view that once the enemy line was breached the cavalry could advance.

Both generals, however, were overoptimistic as to what a preliminary bombardment could achieve. British industry had supplied guns and shells in enormous numbers and the intention was for field guns to deal with the enemy's barbed wire, while the heavy guns destroyed the German artillery and obliterated trenches and strong points. In theory, a creeping barrage from the field guns would have emptied the German trenches before the British infantry advanced. It did not work out like this: the artillery fire was not accurate; contemporary battlefield communications meant that the artillery and infantry could not coordinate their action; sloppy manufacturing meant that a high number of shells did not explode; the wire was not cut; and the barrage was lifted when the infantry was still ploughing across no man's land.

The result was carnage: 20,000 British dead and 37,000 other casualties on 1 July, the day the assault was mounted. The dead and wounded belonged to what was potentially the finest British army ever raised; one which went into battle with high morale and insufficient training. What added a numbing dimension to the general horror of so many deaths was that so many of the dead came from the same parts of Britain and Ireland, even from particular towns and villages from which they had been recruited by territorial regiments or volunteered for Kitchener's army. The telegrams announcing the death of a father or son could arrive at many doors in the same street or at the manor house and cottage doors in the same village. The Ulster Division, first into the fray, was particularly hard hit, as were the 'Pals' divisions who had often come, not just from the one town, as with the Sheffield and the Accrington Divisions, but from the same workplace. Edith Storey from Sheffield remembered how 'several of the boys I went to Sunday School with had joined the Sheffield Pals. We'd grown up together and they'd all joined up as a crowd ... Dad came in and said he had something very sad to tell me. They'd all been killed on the Somme.'[12] The Northumberland Fusiliers had 2,440 men killed, 70 from one small mining village.[13] Far off, in sparsely populated Newfoundland, the dreaded telegrams would arrive, for the Royal Newfoundland Regiment had been virtually wiped out, losing 684 of its 758 men. The British had advanced a mile over a three-mile front. The French had done rather better with their four divisions, all that could be spared from Verdun, and reached most of their first-day objectives at the cost of 7,000 casualties.

Haig went into the Somme with what David Stevenson has described as an 'an attritional model of a "wearing-out fight" that was the unavoidable precondition for a decisive result',[14] but the means became the end when the hope of a decisive victory disappeared. Unlike the battles of previous wars, but like Verdun, the Somme was not won or lost in a day or so, but dragged on for months. After some piecemeal attacks there was a better-planned attack, instigated by Rawlinson, on 15 July in the southern sector astride the Somme during which South African and Australian troops made a substantial breakthrough, but this came to little when the cavalry failed to take advantage of it. Haig persisted in arguing that the enemy was being worn down, but, although German losses increased due to orders not to give ground and the launching of counter-attacks, Allied casualty rates continued to be higher than those of the Germans. John Keegan has summed up the quandary of those launching offensives:

> The simple truth of 1914–18 trench warfare is that the massing of large numbers of soldiers unprotected by anything but cloth uniforms, however they were trained, however equipped, against large masses of other soldiers, protected by earthworks and barbed wire and provided with rapid fire weapons, was bound to result in very heavy casualties among the attackers.[15]

John Terraine, whose *Douglas Haig, the Educated Soldier* (1963) sought to rescue Haig from the mixed derision and hatred of the popular opinion of posterity, claimed that what appeared a callous and obstinate perseverance with offensives that cost so many lives was a necessary learning experience for his subject and other British generals. The experience gained resulted in the strategy and tactics of modern warfare being refined and produced the highly professional and victorious British army of 1918. Certainly, the 'Donkey' caricature of the generals, and Haig in particular, needed correction; few military commanders in history had been faced with the need for such a radical change in their professional skills, for the technology of warfare had far outpaced and made redundant much of the theory and practice instilled at pre-war staff colleges. The realistic appraisal by Terraine and other military historians, such as Corelli Barnett, Brian Bond, and Gary Sheffield, emphasises the limited room for manoeuvre Haig and other generals had. Nevertheless, though British commanders did learn and adapt, their learning curve involved enormous casualties, and, as Niall Ferguson has argued, when it came to attrition and the 'net body count', the German army had the better record, killing or capturing, month after month, on the Western Front more Allied soldiers than they themselves lost.[16]

Haig wrote of the Somme in his diary, that, 'the casualties could not be considered severe in view of the numbers engaged and the length of the front attacked',[17] and argued that the battle had relieved Verdun and worn the Germans down. It did take pressure off the French at Verdun, where Falkenhayn went on the defensive, but whether the Germans were more 'worn down' than the British is debateable, as is whether the casualties were justified or unavoidable. Terraine argued that, 'within the terms of reference of the 1914–18 war, the battle of the Somme was an unquestionable Allied victory' and that the essence of the victory was not the negligible gain of land, but the cost to the enemy of taking that land from him'.[18] Yet, if casualties are the 'cost', the Somme was at best a draw, with British official figures reading, British casualties 419,654, French 204,253 and German 680,00; however, the German estimate of their loss was 450,000, which Ferguson argues is the 'more likely figure',[19] while Stevenson also concludes that 'the defenders sustained fewer casualties than the attackers'.[20]

The fighting on the Somme dragged on until the autumn. Rawlinson disapproved of Haig's continued attempts at a break-through, but the basic fault of the British command tradition was unquestioning obedience and he did not demur. In mid-September, however, an intimation of future warfare and a development which would eventually change the balance between defence and attack made its appearance, in the shape of the tank. Thirty-six British tanks advanced at Flers and these 'land dreadnoughts', moving across the battlefield like lumbering monsters, terrified the German infantry and enabled the British to take some 3,500 yards of territory. Flers was a local victory, although it was an insignificant area of land on the Somme front. Many of the tanks soon broke down and some were destroyed by artillery fire, while, as usual, the Germans were able to fill the gaps made in their defences. This new weapon, strangely neglected by the German army,[21] but not by the French, who quickly realised its potential, was to become more effective during 1917 and 1918. In the longer run, tanks were to enable warfare to become open once more as they replaced cavalry as the forward thrust of armies and enabled the great advances and encirclements to which the generals of the First World War aspired.

The very small gains that the Allies had made at such great cost, some seven miles of territory for hundreds of thousands of lives, when the Somme offensive was finally called off on 19 November, is put into perspective by the much greater amount of ground the German army gave up voluntarily a few months afterwards when it withdrew to the shorter and more easily defended 'Hindenburg Line'. The British soldiers who died at the Somme have been called 'an army of innocents', a phrase similar to the 'massacre of the innocents' that Germans had used to describe the loss of their fresh and eager volunteers at the first battle of Ypres in 1914. John Keegan's verdict was that, 'The Somme marked the end of an age of vital optimism in British life that has never been recovered' and it can be applied more widely to Europe as a whole, as with Norman Stone's view that 'in 1916 the world of nineteenth-century Europe died'. Verdun had severely strained the French army and destroyed public morale, and German confidence was badly shaken by military setbacks and the effects of the British blockade. The battles of the year shattered the spirit of sacrifice in the national cause and confidence in victory in all the combatant countries. That spirit was not, however, to be replaced by a search for peace, but by a more ruthless and determined prosecution of the war.

Home Front

In none of the countries at war did 1916 end with confidence and optimism. After the great offensives, the balance between the Allies and the Central Powers looked little altered, victory was postponed, the death toll continued to mount, and, particularly in Germany, where the winter of 1916–17 was dubbed the 'turnip winter', economic hardship was becoming evident.

From the viewpoint of the early twenty-first century, it is difficult to see why calls for an end to a war which had come to no decisive result and destroyed so many lives were not more vocal, but within each of the states the conviction held that the war was just and had been forced upon the nation by the enemy; it was reinforced by the bleeding. No major combatant power had, as yet, given up the expectation of ultimate success. The European generation which had found itself at war gritted its teeth and continued to fight and support its nation's struggles. This resolution, and the toughness, resilience and patriotism which made it possible, has been hard for later generations to comprehend. Posterity, a century later, continues to wonder why soldiers kept on fighting and civilians kept on supporting a war which had brought advantage to no side.

If there was as yet little sign of any of the main combatants losing the will to continue, the dashing of hopes as offensives failed and stalemate continued did affect public confidence in governments and generals and created divisions between civilian ministers and army high commands. In general, there were demands for a more dynamic and more ruthless prosecution of the war.

In Britain, this was made evident in the last month of the year when Asquith was replaced as prime minister by Lloyd George. The Liberal government had given way to a coalition in 1915, though Asquith had remained prime minister, but his position had weakened during 1916, in large part because the government was blamed for lack of progress towards victory in the war. The Somme offensive and the battle of Jutland had not been defeats, but nor had they been the obvious or overwhelming victories that had been hoped for. The Western Front had hardly moved since late 1914 and in the Middle East the war had gone badly; Major-General Sir Charles Vere Ferrers Townshend's expeditionary force, advancing upon Baghdad, had been cut off and forced to fall back upon Kut, where it was surrounded by Turkish forces and obliged to surrender in April. The government's position was also made more difficult by divisions in the ranks of the coalition, not just between Liberals and Unionists, but increasingly between Asquithians and those Liberals close to Lloyd George, while the backwash from the Easter Rising in Dublin and the government's handling of it brought further animosity between Unionists and moderate Home Rulers, together with some backbench Liberal MPs. Lloyd George, who, as minister for munitions, had built a reputation for decisiveness, had succeeded Lord Kitchener as Secretary for War when that icon of leadership died at sea in June. The replacement of Asquith came about as the result of a confused coup by an odd alliance of Unionists, newspaper proprietors and Lloyd George, which demanded a small inner council or 'War Committee' to streamline government. This began a struggle which ended with Asquith resigning and the King unwillingly sending for Lloyd George. The new prime minister had probably not meant to displace Asquith; it is likely that his real aim had been to diminish the influence of Haig and Robertson for he had no confidence in the military high command, not an opinion which was shared by the Unionist leaders or the King. Britain, it turned out, had found its Cromwell, the man who could deliver the 'knock-out blow', and the Lloyd George government would remain in office for the rest of the war and beyond. He was not, however, powerful enough to get rid of Haig, who would also retain his position until the war's end.

Chapter 9: 1917, Germany's Victory in the East

That states which had gone to war with promises of a swift victory were able, after years of war, to reject peace initiatives, call up new generations to form new armies, and remodel their economies, despite the enormous loss of soldiers' lives and the hardships and food shortages that their civilian populations suffered, continues to puzzle posterity as it puzzled those contemporaries who opposed the war's continuance. Few significant figures demurred at the time; Lord Lansdowne, a Conservative minister who suggested to the British cabinet in a paper of 13 November 1916 that a friendly ear be given to any offers of peace or mediation that might bring the war to an end, was an honourable but solitary exception.

Support for the War

How did monarchs, politicians and generals, whose promises had proved empty and whose policies and strategies had had such bloody consequences, manage to maintain the broad support of societies for a determined effort to fight on to victory? Compulsion, censorship and propaganda may have played a part, but, as David Stevenson has written,

> The First World War cannot be understood without acknowledging the widespread and continuing acceptance that it was a just, even noble cause. Every belligerent relied on a combination of state compulsion with patriotic support from society, even if the

139

former was relatively more important in the eastern European countries than in the western European ones. Between them these forces not only created an initial political truce in 1914 but also maintained domestic cohesion when the conflict intensified with a corresponding increase in its demands.[1]

This widespread acceptance of the necessity and justice of the war goes a long way to explain not just the solidity of domestic support, but why soldiers continued to obey orders and to fight fiercely. That they did so has puzzled those whose views of soldiers' opinions have been influenced by the 'War Poets' and Henri Barbusse's novel, *Le Feu* (*Under Fire*) and by post-war recollections such as Robert Graves's *Goodbye To All That* or Erich Maria Remarque's *All Quiet on the Western Front*. These powerful literary works have embedded vivid and horrific images of the war and a depiction of disillusionment and bitter anger as the common reaction of soldiers, but great literature does not necessarily express general opinion, and other sources suggest such reactions were far from typical.

If not all soldiers became disillusioned, neither of course did all continue to fight with determination and the Russian Army had a high rate of desertion, as did the Italian. Men also surrendered and, although defeats often made surrender unavoidable and men isolated from their units and surrounded may have had little other option, the numbers of men surrendering was an indication of the morale of different armies; again, the Russian and Italian Armies displayed high losses because of surrender. As with domestic cohesion, the degree of national unity in combatant states was a major factor in the maintenance of morale in armies. Confidence or lack of confidence in commanders and officers was a further factor in determining men's motivation; soldiers in states which were cohesive national entities, such as Germany, Britain and France, did not have to be forced to fight, but they did need to be well led, in addition to being adequately fed and quartered. They also, of course, had to be prepared to kill, and if the threat of being killed was a spur to killing the enemy, there is no great evidence to suggest most soldiers were reluctant killers. Another factor was loyalty, not just to country, but to regiments even to platoons and to friends. Loyalty to 'pals' or comrades has been seen as a sacred bond and the letting down of one's comrade's as an unforgivable crime, while the death of a pal and the desire to avenge him was a strong inducement to fight on.

Political Struggle

The West

A general determination to persevere, especially in Britain, Germany and France, was, however, accompanied by declining faith in the ability of governments and generals to deliver victory and a search for a dynamic leadership that could. A growing division between civilian governments and army commanders was a common development. It would have been surprising if the governments who had gone to war in 1914 had remained intact as victory remained elusive or that, after many setbacks, the military commanders who had led their nations' armies in that year had still remained in command at the beginning of 1917. The developments apparent in 1916–17 pointed, however, not just to changes in personnel but to structural changes, for the pressures of war tested the ability and efficiency not just of governments or individual commanders, but of all the institutions and systems of government of the belligerent states, while defeats, failed offensives, mounting casualties and food shortages led to a search for heroes and scapegoats. The replacement of the Liberal government which had led Britain to war by a coalition, though one still led by the same prime minister, Asquith, in May 1915 could be seen as an almost inevitable and necessary broadening of the British government, but the new Lloyd George-led coalition marked a drastic reordering of government and politics, even if it did not resolve deep divisions between the new prime minister and the army commanders. In France the government of René Viviani had been at odds with Joffre, whose position was even stronger than Haig's and Robertson's as he had constitutionally endorsed powers as commander-in-chief within the war zone. The new French prime minister, Aristide Briand, had managed to replace him with Nivelle in December 1916, though he balanced his powers by appointing a minister for war with increased authority. French and British changes in government did not resolve tensions between generals and politicians, but the essence of control by civilian government was retained and, in Britain's case, strengthened.

In Germany, however, the demotion of von Falkenhayn, cosmetically disguised though it was by his appointment to lead the campaign against Romania, marked a decisive shift in the control of the wartime state. The military in Imperial Germany had always exercised considerable influence over policy but this had come from their direct association with and close links to the monarch, while chancellors and ministers had also answered directly to the Kaiser.

Von Falkenhayn, who had owed his position to Kaiser Wilhelm, had fought the war with one eye on a future peace. His natural ally should have been Bethmann Hollweg, who shared his pessimistic view that Germany could not win a war in which Britain was an enemy, but they disliked each other. Both depended ultimately on the Kaiser's support, and both were replaced in 1916 and 1917 after the Kaiser withdrew that support. Though he failed to realise it, Kaiser Wilhelm's own position depended on the preservation of his prerogatives and the continuation of a system in which the military came under the control of the monarch and the ministers he appointed. In 1914, he had dismissed Moltke and replaced him with Falkenhayn, with whom he had a cordial relationship, but Falkenhayn's hold on office had weakened with the failure to take Verdun, the setback of the Brusilov offensive, his evident inability to cooperate with the Austro-Hungarian high command and the antipathy between him and Hindenburg and Ludendorff. His dismissal in August 1916 had above all been due to the last factor, for Hindenburg and Ludendorff were seen by the German public as the victors of Tannenberg, and as such the only generals capable of winning the war. Despite feeling threatened by Ludendorff, increasingly the dominant figure of the two, the Kaiser gave in and appointed Hindenburg Chief of the General Staff and Ludendorff First Quartermaster General. There was sense in this, for command of the Central Powers' forces on the Eastern Front had become inchoate, with Falkenhayn and Conrad not communicating and Ludendorff refusing to send divisions to where his commander-in-chief directed, but the new regime marked changes, not only in military strategy, but to the nature of Germany's war and its system of government.

The decline of the Kaiser's influence was of great significance. Germany had never been the autocracy that the western powers and the Kaiser himself proclaimed it to be. Though Wilhelm II had considerable powers under the constitution – when he chose to exercise them – he usually held the ring between the civilian ministers he appointed and the military, and all needed at least the acquiescence of the Reichstag. Remove the Kaiser's influence and what was left was the army command in the shape of General Erich Ludendorff, who has been seen as becoming an unacknowledged military dictator, but also the political parties which he had to cooperate with. The Kaiser had been the linchpin, not always a very adequate one, but the linchpin all the same.

New radical leaders had thus emerged, charged with task of winning the war by ruthless methods. Their room for manoeuvre was limited by this primary remit because a negotiated peace was not an option that public opinions were prepared to accept. The leaders who had led their countries to war had imagined that they had had the capacity to end the war they had started if and when circumstances justified it. Now they had gone, and total war and the sacrifices made had opened a Pandora's box of hatred of the enemy that was so embedded in popular feeling that to end the war with a compromise was not possible for Britain, Germany or France so long as there was the possibility of complete victory. Such victory still seemed possible; as the French prime minister declared, 'for us the word peace is sacrilege'.

The East

Other combatants were in a different situation as the support of domestic opinion was far less solid. Russia, Italy and Austria-Hungary were far less able to withstand the test of a long war, in large part because they had severe domestic problems at its beginning and in none of them did the mass of the population exhibit the unity of Britain, France and Germany. Russia, though surprisingly few in the west foresaw this, was about to succumb to revolution, while in Italy there had never been a consensus for war and it is surprising that, even with considerable economic support from Britain and France, it remained in the war to the end despite defeats and the high casualties its armies suffered. As regards Austria-Hungary, the surprise is that despite its manifold problems, which had inspired forecasts of its demise as a state long before the war, it held together for so long. However, the Emperor Karl I, who had succeeded to the throne on Franz Josef's death, was already looking for a way out of the war.

On Bethmann Hollweg's prodding, Germany did propose peace negotiations on 12 December 1916, but this was a hollow initiative as the army insisted on terms that would have been tantamount to an Allied acceptance of German victory. This was followed by an invitation from Woodrow Wilson on 18 December to all the belligerents to set out their terms, but differences were irreconcilable. It became clear that the Entente powers had no interest in a peace along the lines favoured by the President of the USA, and the Germans failed to make concrete proposals. States which still thought total victory possible were not prepared to settle for anything else. Germany might still win, its new leaders considered, by further efforts in mobilising its citizens for war, increasing the output of war materials by further moves towards a command economy, and by unconditional submarine warfare. In France, hopes that stimulation of the economy in combination with Nivelle's promises that new tactics would win great battles led to continued hopes of victory, while in Britain, Lloyd George pledged that a firm and efficient control of the war would enable Britain to deliver a 'knock-out blow'.

Germany's problem had always been the difficulty of fighting a war on two fronts. The hopes for a rapid victory in the west had faded and, with Britain now a formidable military force, seemed further off than ever. Could Germany win in the east? Had the decision to make the Western Front the priority been an error, as 'Easterners' amongst the German command had long argued? The opposing argument was that, even if victories in the east were possible, British involvement in the war meant that the conflict could continue for years, while Britain amassed larger armies, prevented supplies reaching Germany by its control of the seas, and secured its own supplies from across the Atlantic. The road to a German victory, declared Admiral Henning von Holtzendorff, chief of the naval staff, was unrestricted U-boat warfare which would cut Britain's shipping by half and starve its population. It might, of course, bring America into the war, but this was a risk worth taking. The U-boat campaign was to fail (see Chapter 10), but, in the meantime, there could be no victory in the west. The new high command in Germany reinforced the policy of defence in France and Belgium by withdrawing in February and March 1917 via Operation Alberich to more easily defended positions along the shorter *Siegfriedstellung* or, as the British called it, the Hindenburg Line.

At a second inter-Allied conference in November 1916, the military chiefs had, as David Stevenson has commented, 'concluded from their 1916 experiences that they should try more of the same', a number of synchronised offensives with the main effort in the west supported by Russian and Italian attacks.[2] In the event, the Italians were unenthusiastic and they and the Russians declared they could not be ready until May, but the French and British went ahead with plans for a co-ordinated offensive in which a British attack near Arras was to be followed by a major French onslaught against the Chemin des Dames north of the Aisne, almost a mirror image of the September 1915 offensive. Lloyd George was far from happy with the Chantilly plans as he had little confidence in the capability of British generals on the Western Front and was constantly itching to try other options, such as operations in the Middle East or Salonika to put pressure on Turkey or sending troops to assist the Italians, rather than continuing a war of attrition in France with its high casualty rates, but a confident Haig had his way.

Western Front Offensives

General Nivelle, now in charge of French forces on the Western Front, had concluded that the correct use of artillery could overcome the advantages of defence over an attacking army. Instead of pounding defenders for hours and giving them warning of an impending attack, the creeping barrage would only precede advancing infantry by some sixty yards, thus keeping defenders in their dug-outs and trenches until the attackers were almost upon them. Instead of waves of massed infantry, dispersed-order tactics would see small groups of men dashing forward and taking cover when they could, while other units gave them covering fire. His initial plans for an offensive were confounded by the German withdrawal from the very areas in which he had chosen and where he had had carefully mapped out German gun positions, but he remained determined to go ahead. Nivelle was now formally in command of the British as well as the French forces for Lloyd George, rather impressed by him and definitely hostile to his own commander-in-chief, had placed Haig under the command of his French counterpart for the duration of the campaign. Nivelle was actually junior in rank to the British commander-in-chief, who was now a field marshal; this was a humiliation Haig was never to forgive. Nivelle's plan was to achieve a decisive breakthrough in the Champagne area while the British pinned the down German reserves in Arras.

   The British, more accurately a British Empire, force (and, indeed the major role played throughout the war by the Dominion and the Indian Empire troops is too often underestimated[3]) launched their attack at Arras on 9 April and met with success. The artillery bombardment was more intense and more accurately directed than that which had preceded the advance at the Somme and the infantry, which enjoyed a considerable numerical advantage (18 divisions against 7), was able to conceal its first moves by using tunnels prepared by sappers.[4] The Germans had positioned their reserves too far back and had a relatively weak front line which was pinned down by the British bombardment with the result that Canadian troops were able to storm and take Vimy Ridge, long a target for the British commanders as not only did it overlook Ypres, but stood between the Allies and the German railways in the Douai plain. The success of the Canadian divisions was, Keegan wrote, sensational:

   In a single bound the awful, bare broken slopes of Vimy Ridge, on which the French had bled to death in thousands in 1915, was taken, the summit gained and, down the precipitous eastern reverse slope, the whole Douai plain, crammed with German artillery and reserves, laid open to victors' gaze'.[5]

There seemed little to stop a major advance, but the usual pattern followed: an inflexible plan demanded a pause, momentum was lost, the Germans brought up reserves by rail and an unproductive battle dragged on, bringing 150,000 casualties by 17 May and no further territorial gain.

Nivelle's offensive at Chemin des Dames began on 16 April. The Germans were ready for it, partly because of espionage and partly because Nivelle had broadcast his battle plan too widely. Senegalese troops were good soldiers and Nivelle had placed this regiment in the centre of his attack, but they were not best suited to advance through a snow storm. Nevertheless, the French troops were initially confident and advanced in waves across a broad front, but then the German reserves, held back out of reach of the artillery barrage, sprang into action and machine guns hidden in shell holes and caves mowed down the French infantry, who had to toil up a steep slope – the Chemin des Dames Ridge was 600 feet high. The Senegalese broke and fled, but Moroccan troops were among the few units to reach their objective. The French brought in their light Schneider tanks, but they foundered under artillery fire and against trenches which served as anti-tank ditches. None the less, Nivelle, who had promised to suspend the attack if things went badly, persevered and after two weeks had taken most of the ridge, though at a cost of 130,000 killed or wounded.

Coming after Verdun, this was too much for many French soldiers, who refused to advance again into what had become a death trap. Nivelle was replaced by the far more cautious Pétain, who halted operations, but the French army was nevertheless faced with mutiny. Whether this was a revolt with a political dimension has been debated by historians;[6] some 40,000 troops appear to have been involved, but it seems probable that most were simply demoralised and fearful of being ordered back into what had become a charnel house, while lack of leave, poor food and ghastly living conditions, even at so-called rest camps, exacerbated discontent. It was not aimed at the junior or middle-ranking officers who were even more at risk of death than their men. French soldiers, though demoralised, were still prepared to fight for their country, but they no longer had faith in their generals and their plans for great offensives.

Petain was sensible and retrieved the immediate problem by improving conditions as regards leave and supplies for the troops.

Mutiny incurred the death penalty, but Pétain was relatively merciful and of 40,000 who had refused to obey orders only 45 men who were identified as leaders were shot, while no new great offensives were mounted and actions were limited to small, well-organised operations with limited aims. Nevertheless, the French army was never the same again and henceforth it was the British who had to do most of the fighting on the Western Front.

Meanwhile the allies were losing one of their partners and acquiring a new, if not entirely sympathetic, one, the former giving new opportunities to Germany and the latter promising reinforcement to Britain and France.

The End of Russian Involvement

Although it is an old saw that Russia should never be underestimated, Germany may well have overestimated Russia's military strength in the years immediately before 1914. Fear of the Russian steamroller and an appreciation of the dangers in getting bogged down like Napoleon in Russia's great land mass, together with a belief that Russia's rapid industrialisation, the extension of her railways, and the recovery of her army after its defeat in the Russo-Japanese War had made her an increasingly formidable adversary, all led to the German High Command's decision to favour the Schlieffen Plan. If Germany had waited for Russia to declare war and then fought a defensive war against both her and France, if she joined in, then Germany might have had the strength to triumph, provided, crucially, that Britain did not come to France's aid. As the invasion of Belgium would have been unnecessary with a German defensive strategy, Britain might well have abstained. A victory was, arguably, available in the east, and indeed was delivered in 1918. What the Germans and the Allies had not taken account of, largely because they had thought in terms of a short war, was the degree to which Russia was vulnerable to the strains of a war of attrition: her administrative structure, essential to a successful mobilisation of the economy and society, was inadequate, while the incompetence and corruption of the army, which was given the task of administering the military zone (which included Petrograd and a large part of the Empire), made the preceding civilian administration look efficient. In terms of the production of war materials, Russia did surprisingly well, but as Norman Stone has written, 'What was not adequate was the organisation that more modern countries could show as regards transport, finance, national unity'. The army had had its victories, particularly during the Brusilov offensive, but the casualty figures had been enormous and the insane decision to make the Tsar assume personal command meant that the very focus of national loyalty, but a man with no military training or experience, would be associated with any defeats and with the shortages and deprivations of the people. Britain and France had not been worn down by attrition, nor had Germany, but Russia had been.

Few would challenge the view that the Russian economy had been dislocated and its society demoralised by three years of war. Corruption was widespread; the transport system was unable to satisfy the demands of the army and the civilian economy, which resulted in insufficient trains to take grain to cities crowded with refugees; and the army's administration of the greater part of the Empire was carried out with astonishing ineptitude. Whether this was bound to lead to revolution is, however, debatable. Much depended upon the army. Michael Florinsky, who had served as a Tsarist artillery officer, painted a depressing picture in his study, published after the war, of widespread disaffection in the ranks and hostility toward officers which led to a flurry of mutinies in late 1916.[7] Though the French army was able, under Pétain's careful handling, to survive the mutinies after the failure of Nivelle's offensive, it was much weakened. Historians have not agreed whether the initial refusals of Russian front line troops to obey orders in late 1916 was likewise a broadly apolitical manifestation of despair exacerbated by poor food, brutal discipline, and abysmal conditions, or whether the vast number of desertions pointed to an army of the verge of disintegration. Certainly, political unrest began among troops stationed at the rear, rather than at the front, but in much of the army there was an internal war between officers and men that was not found in the other Allied or the German armies.

Yet, early in 1917, Russian generals were, in Norman Stone's words, 'full of fight'. They shared the confidence of the other Entente powers that in men and guns the Allies were superior on every front and, moreover, generals, ministers and the Tsar himself could see Russia as on the verge of accomplishing what their nineteenth-century predecessors had dreamed of: domination of the Balkans, the end of the Habsburg Empire, control of Constantinople and the Black Sea Straits, and the hope of expansion further east with gains in central Asia and Persia. None of this was, of course, to come about, for Tsarist Russia was on the brink of revolution.

On 8 March or, by the Russian calendar, 23 February, a demonstration by housewives against the rising price of bread in St Petersburg, or Petrograd, as anti-German feeling had insisted it be renamed, was badly handled by an inadequate police force. The army had to be called out and, after a number of demonstrators had been shot, the troops, largely disaffected conscripts stationed in Petrograd, refused to open fire at the crowds. A poorly organised system for supplying the most basic and essential food item and allowing it to be monopolised by speculators led to the breakdown of authority and within days soldiers were electing councils or 'soviets'. The inadequacy of the regime's machinery for repression of disorder raises the question as to whether Tsarist Russia collapsed because it was an autocracy or because it was a weak and inefficient autocracy, but collapse it did and with bewildering speed.

Tsar Nicholas ordered the chief of the Petrograd Military District to march into the capital and restore order but by this time disorder was turning into revolution and soldiers began fraternising with the revolutionaries. General Alekseyev, temporary commander-in-chief of the army, called off further military preparations, considering that this would assist liberal constitutionalists in the Duma, the Russian parliament, to form a government, and thus stave off the worse result of yielding power to the Petrograd Soviet. Many of the generals now decided that the Tsar had to abdicate, and he did so on 2 March (the 15th by the old calendar). The Duma set up a provisional government and then declared a republic. The Russian state and society, which had seemed, between the Revolution of 1905 and the outbreak of war, to be moving towards a more liberal political and economic structure, had been unable to withstand the strain of war.

Some in the West nurtured hopes that the new regime would lead Russia in a new liberal-democratic direction and continue to be a useful military ally, but the revolution had solved none of Russia's basic problems, nor had it stimulated the will to continue the war. Alexander Kerensky, the new head of government, wished for an end to the war, but believed that Russia should continue fighting alongside its Allies until a general peace could be negotiated. Kerensky appointed Brusilov commander-in-chief, and he initiated an offensive against the Austro-Hungarians in late June. It began well, with the Russians taking territory, but troops in the rear refused to advance to follow up the success and a counter-attack by the Central Powers pushed the Russians out of Habsburg territory altogether, while the Germans drove on towards Riga. The Kerensky offensive fizzled out amidst mutiny and desertion; the Allies could expect no further support from Russia.

Russia was not to drop out of the war until December, when, after the Bolshevik coup, an armistice was concluded at Brest-Litovsk to be followed by a peace treaty signed there in March 1918. Nevertheless, there was little fighting on the Eastern Front after the failure of the Kerensky Offensive. The Entente had lost a partner. As Bernard Waites has put it:

> over time, the triple Entente was like a see-saw pivoting on France, but while British land power rose, Russia's declined. Only for a relatively brief period in mid 1916 when Brusilov's offensive was smashing through the Austrians in Galicia and the Kitchener armies were engaged on the Somme, did both ends of the see-saw pull their full weight.[8]

The most important result of Russia's defection was that Germany had won the war in the east and had no longer to fight a war on two fronts.

Italy

For a while, it looked as if another Allied partner might see its government overthrown by revolution. The Italian army had suffered nearly three times as many casualties as the Austrians in the many battles of the Isonzo for very small gains of territory, and in the eleventh battle, from August to September 1917, the Italians lost 100,000 men. The Austrians had fought well, especially when under the command of the Croatian general, Svetozar Boroević, but were exhausted and, with the end of the war in the East, German divisions were available. Under German command, a new offensive was launched by a combined German–Austrian force led by General Otto von Below. This was one of the most successful military operations of the war. It involved the use of new and radical tactics already used in the German counter-attack at Cambrai and against the Russians at Riga: the utilisation of technological advances in gunnery which enabled hurricane bombardment to neutralise rather than obliterate the enemy's defences and 'box' bombardments to protect advancing infantry and prevent the bringing up of the enemy's reserves; and the development of storm-troops, specially trained and powerfully armed units, whose job was to infiltrate and disrupt enemy lines. Such tactics, along with the ingenuity and daring of Alpine and other mountain divisions who scaled commanding heights and transported guns and ammunition over them, resulted in the massive defeat of the Italians at Caporetto. One junior officer who particularly distinguished himself was an Oberleutnant Rommel who scaled Mount Matajur and, with two other officers and a few riflemen, forced 43 officers and 1,500 men of the Salerno Brigade to surrender.[9] By 2 December, when the Caporetto offensive was finally halted, the Germans had advanced 80 miles and captured 250,000 prisoners.

The Italian commander-in-chief, General Luigi Cadorna, attributed his defeat not to his own incompetence but to the poor morale and mutinous and socialist tendencies of his troops; he referred to the retreat at Caporetto as a 'military strike'. He had a point, but much of the blame for the large numbers of deserters even before Caporetto lay with the harsh discipline administered in the Italian army. There was a huge cultural and mental gap between officers and men, especially the peasants of the south who had been conscripted into an army and a war they little understood, and officers reacted brutally. At least 750 men were executed for desertion or insubordination and 'Cadorna re-introduced the Roman practice of decimation – the killing of every tenth man – for units which failed to perform well in battle'.[10] There seemed clear parallels between Italy and Russia: thousands of deserters roaming the country, an army close to mutiny, and food shortages caused by much of the land in the south, where tenants had been conscripted, lying uncultivated. Long before Caporetto there had been violent protests led by women in Milan and Turin against bread shortages and against the war. The combination of social and industrial unrest in the cities and a disgruntled and demoralised army could have been fatal, but Italy did not follow Russia into revolution. Cadorna was dismissed, the scale of the defeat made the war now seem a defensive one in protection of the nation, a war council introduced rationing, and the British and French sent troops and with the Italians set up a Supreme War Council to coordinate Allied efforts. Ludendorff, who had other plans, reined in the Austrians and insisted that there should be no more large Italian offensives without OHL's consent, while during December he moved the German divisions to the Western Front. It was clear, however, that the Allies could not expect too much from the Italian army and with French forces, still recovering from the summer's mutinies, Allied strength had been weakened and the onus on the British army increased.

The Entry of the United States

The one positive development for the Allies in a bleak year was that as Russia departed from the war the United States had come into it, not, as might have been expected, because of the sinking of neutral ships by German submarines, for although unconditional U-boat warfare had angered US opinion and weakened the pro-German lobby in

America, Woodrow Wilson, who had been re-elected on a policy of keeping America out of the war, was still reluctant to enter it. What helped finally to persuade him to declare war was the bizarre episode of the Zimmermann telegram.

German policy since the very beginning of the war had, either out of over-confidence or the desperation born of deep pessimism, been marked by outrageous risk-taking, but to imagine that Mexico could be persuaded to attack her formidable neighbour, the USA, in the interest of reversing the result of the Alamo and retrieving Texas, New Mexico and Arizona, was madness, while for the German foreign minister to set out this proposal in a telegram to the German Ambassador in Washington was carelessness on a grand scale. It is far from rare for a power to eavesdrop on friends and even allies, and British Intelligence was keeping a close watch upon opinion in the USA and upon communications between Berlin and Washington. Zimmermann had sent the message to his Washington ambassador for him to forward to the German minister in Mexico City offering the Mexican government an alliance. It had been sent by three different routes, via Sweden, by a German receiving station on Long Island, and by a secure line made available to the German government to facilitate peace overtures. The British had cracked the code used for the message and the deciphered document landed on the desk of the head of Naval Intelligence, Rear Admiral William Reginald Hall, in Room 40 of the Admiralty. Hall made sure that the American government and press were informed of its contents, but, rather than admit to snooping routinely on cable traffic to the USA, pretended that the telegram had been intercepted in Mexico City.[11] Once the American press had published the story, the anti-war lobby in America lost much of its influence.

Even without the Zimmermann telegram, it is probable that the USA would eventually have come into the war. The Germans had made a conscious decision to risk acquiring a new enemy, convinced that U-boat warfare would assist them to win the war before any US intervention could be effective, not as unreasonable an assumption as many have considered it. The discovery of the telegram, at the least, precipitated the American declaration of war on 6 April 1917, and may have made it certain.

Passchendaele

The immediate consequence of the Russian Revolution for the remaining Allies was that the position of the Central Powers was immensely strengthened. Plans for synchronised offensives were largely redundant, although the Italians did launch their promised attack, which led to the tenth and eleventh battles of the Isonzo, in May and August and then to the major defeat at Caporetto, after which little could be expected from them. The French were still recovering after the failure of the Nivelle offensive and the subsequent mutinies, though Pétain organised surprise offensives with limited ambitions at Verdun and Chemin les Dames, which enjoyed modest success. By now the British and French were not even synchronised with each other, Petain planning to make gains in Alsace, while Haig, as ever, was preoccupied with Flanders. It would take many months before American forces could be present in Europe in any strength and only the British still had the resources and will to launch a new offensive. Haig, having attacked at Arras in May–June, and now no longer having to defer to the French, was determined on a further and major attack in Flanders.

Many soldiers in the British army must have wondered why, year after year, their generals kept them fighting in and around Ypres for the sake of modest gains of land, which had, by the summer of 1917, been turned, by previous battles and at the cost of so many lives, into a wasteland. The British had been fighting there since the autumn 1914, when the 'race to the sea' had seemingly stranded the BEF in a permanent Hell. No wonder that, soldiers referred to Wipers, published the 'Wipers Times' with its gallows humour, and gave inappropriate London names to the wrecked villages or battered farmhouses, which were the backdrop to their tenuous daily lives. There were, of course, strategic reasons for the British generals' fixation, though none for the obsession with defending the Ypres salient, upon which the Germans had been able to rain down shells from the commanding heights of the ridges above. If, however, the Messines, Menin and Passchendaele ridges could be taken, a key German railway would be vulnerable. Moreover, Ypres was close to the Channel ports and, while the ridges were attacked, Haig's plan was for a second force to advance along the coast and in combination with landings from the sea take Zeebrugge and Ostend, where light U-boats had their pens and German destroyers were harboured. April had seen the worst months for losses of merchant ships at the hands of U-boats and Jellicoe was worried that if their Flanders bases were not destroyed, Britain could be starved out by Christmas. To clear the coast would be a major achievement and could even open up the opportunity of pressing on so as to push the Germans back to the Dutch border.

There were other, not strictly strategic or tactical reasons for the Flanders offensives of the summer and autumn of 1917. The entry of the USA into the war was a mixed blessing from the viewpoint of the British and, indeed the French, governments. American troops might well assist in the defeat of Germany, but Woodrow Wilson's ideas for a peace settlement were far from compatible with those of the existing Allies. Norman Stone has argued that the general aim of the Flanders offensive was 'to win the war and impose a British peace before President Wilson could muddy the waters'. Worries over French morale and capability argued for a demonstration of British determination, as did hopes of keeping the Russians fighting. What were the other options to a Flanders offensive? Lloyd George had no confidence in Haig's plan, but the alternatives he toyed with were not attractive: an offensive from Salonika, now Greece had declared war on the Central Powers, assistance to Italy, or a Middle Eastern campaign. Essentially, he sought to defeat Germany's allies, the Austrians. Turks and Bulgarians, while conserving British strength and putting Britain in an advantageous position before any peace negotiations, but he had weakened his influence by his support for Nivelle and had to allow Haig's plans to be implemented, though he subsequently distanced himself from them when they failed.

A major difficulty was the terrain: 'the whole area was known as the Low Countries for a very good reason: it had been rescued from the sea, the water table was close to the surface, and if it were churned up by shell, there would be mud, if there were rain, it would be morass'.[12] Preparations for the initial stage, the taking of Messines Ridge had been well-made, with hundreds of miners tunnelling under the German positions and laying powerful mines. As the mines were set off on 7 June there was a great artillery bombardment, and the Germans, too dazed to respond, withdrew before the attacking infantry made up of Australian, New Zealand, Irish and Ulster divisions. Haig had considerably improved his position and now commanded the southern wing of the Flanders Front, but the Germans now knew that a major offensive was coming and set about improving their defences. They had time to do so, for the next British attack did not begin until 31 July, by which time a complex defensive forward defence system of pillboxes, sheltering heavy machine guns, backed by a second line of defence sheltering reserves, and then by a third defensive position had been constructed by the Germans.

Third Ypres, or Passchendaele as the battle is better known because Passchendaele Ridge was a primary target, was in many ways a more ghastly and demoralising battle for the British army than the Somme.

By the time it stuttered to a finish in mid-November, the British had suffered 275,000 casualties of whom 70,000 were dead. Like many of Haig's battles, it started off well enough. There was the usual initial artillery bombardment, which lasted fifteen days during which over 4 million shells were fired, and this gave the Germans plenty of warning of the attack to come though it failed to destroy the German guns positioned behind the ridge. Assault troops of General Herbert Plumer's 2nd Army, accompanied by tanks, made fair progress up the ridges, but then came the rain and then the mud.

It rained heavily and almost ceaselessly throughout August, and, as years of constant shelling had destroyed the field drainage system, mud with the consistency of porridge built up thickly; it bogged down and even sank the artillery and tanks; infantry had to squelch through it; mules sent to tow guns were sucked down with their burdens; and it not only accompanied and hastened the deaths of soldiers, but often caused them as wounded soldiers taking shelter in shell-holes drowned as they failed to clamber up the slippery sides. These were not conditions in which to make sweeping advances, though Haig ordered Hubert Gough, an impetuous cavalry officer commanding the 5th Army to try, with disastrous results. Haig then transferred command for the next effort to the prudent and experienced General Plummer, who, as the land dried out in September, achieved some success with limited operations (Menin Road, Polygon Wood and Broodseinde), but in October the rain returned and further attacks were expensive failures. At this point Haig, military historians are agreed, should have stopped, but he pushed on. The ANZAC corps got close to the ruins of the village of Passchendaele on the highest point of the ground east of Ypres on 12 October, but, caught in front and flank by machine gun fire, had to retreat to where they had started. Then, as Keegan puts it, 'Having consigned the 11 ANZAC corps to a pointless sacrifice, Haig then turned to the Canadians'. Reluctantly obeying his commander's orders to advance, the Canadian, General Sir Arthur Currie, ordered his man forward on 26 October. By 10 November they had captured the ruined village of Passchendaele at the cost of 15,634 casualties.

Passchendaele may well have been the most pointless battle of the war. It was certainly expensive in terms of dead and wounded, though the defenders' losses were as great or greater than the attackers, the Germans having made the mistake of seeking to counter-attack and regain ground throughout much of the long battle. The costly battle achieved little and Keegan's comment that the point of Passchendaele 'defies explanation' seems apposite. Coming after the

Somme, it did much to disillusion educated British opinion and to establish the view of Haig as unimaginative, stubborn and wasteful of the lives of soldiers.

The battle of Cambrai which began three weeks later was also ultimately unsuccessful in that the British attack was repulsed, but it did display a more sophisticated response to the problems of offence than had been seen at Passchendaele. There was intelligent preparation and a sophisticated co-ordination between artillery and infantry, while, above all, it demonstrated how effective tanks could be on hard ground, for the battlefield was composed of dry chalk on which they did not get bogged down. This was the first major tank attack of the war and saw the employment of 476 tanks, mostly the new Mark IV model. The plan of battle owed nothing to Haig but was devised by General Julian Byng in conjunction with Brigadier-General Hugh Elles, commander of the Tank Corps, and Brigadier-General Henry Hugh Tudor of the 9th Scottish Division. Three hundred tanks were to launch the offensive and were to be followed by infantry and supported by 1,000 artillery pieces. Initially all went well: the short creeping artillery barrage was followed by the advance of columns of tanks followed closely by infantry and the attackers made a rapid advance of as much as four miles as German troops, taken by surprise, fell back. Prematurely, bells rang out in London to announce a victory, but the attack faltered, a number of tanks were destroyed, and the Germans managed to plug the gaps in their lines with reserves. They then launched a massive counter-attack with 20 divisions and, using storm-troop tactics, regained most of the land they had lost.

The bungling of Passchendaele had obscured the fact that the British army was making progress along a learning curve and Cambrai demonstrated that, both in terms of the development of new tactics and the adoption of new technology, weaponry, and tactics, some British generals were receptive to new ideas; however, the German counter-attack showed that the German army had equally made radical changes to its methods.

Prospects for the Next Year

Few on the Allied side in a conflict in which the death toll continued to mount foresaw an early end to the conflict. The British forces on the Western Front had suffered some 800,000 casualties in the course of 1917 and, despite the relative recovery of the French after the mutinies, it was apparent that British forces would now have to take the main role in future battles. Where were men to maintain the army's numbers to come from when Sir Auckland Geddes, the Director of National Service, was declaring that no more could be drafted if economic strength was to be maintained? It looked, so the War Cabinet declared in late November, as if the war would last until 1919 – and many felt that this was optimistic.

One factor in favour of the Allies was that the failure of Germany's unrestricted submarine warfare was becoming evident. If it had succeeded, as it had appeared in April that it would, Britain would have been forced to sue for peace, but by autumn the convoys were getting through, transatlantic links were intact and Britain, France and Italy were getting essential supplies. Shipping lanes were also open to American troopships, and within months American troops would be in France.

Most importantly, the Royal Navy's blockade was remorselessly squeezing the German economy. Britain's economic and financial strength and control of the seas had, from the beginning, given the Allies an advantage in a long war, but had been offset by the ability of the German army. Whether those advantages would prevail against a German regime whose economy was deteriorating whose civilian population was suffering food shortages, but which was determined on military victory and whose army was vitalised by its success in the East, was far from certain.

If the Allies were much weakened by the loss of their Russian partner and the problems of the French and Italian armies, the German high command could not be sanguine about the state of its own allies. Austria-Hungary was an increasingly ineffective power. Despite being in a relatively strong strategic position after the Russian collapse, the empire faced major internal problems. The monarchy was a major unifying force in the multi-ethnic Habsburg Empire and the death of 86-year-old Emperor Franz Josef in November 1916 weakened the loyalties of Empire's diverse peoples. Although Austro-Hungarian armies had fought well against the Italians, the German army had time and again been forced to come to the rescue of its ally. By 1917 the Austro-Hungarian army was well on the way to becoming merely part of the German army, under the command of OHL and stiffened by German officers, even in the middle ranks, a process that was not welcomed in Vienna, where the Germans were often referred to as the 'secret enemy'. Austria was particularly hard-hit by food shortages and inflation: by 1916 the cost of living had gone up by 236 per cent since the start of the war, a development which demoralised the hitherto prosperous upper-middle sections of society whose support was so important to the government. Strains between the Empire's nationalities were increasing: the Czechs had never been enthusiastic for a war against fellow Slavs, and tensions between Magyars and Austrians worsened as the war continued. No wonder that the new Emperor, Karl I, fearing that his inheritance was about to disappear, had two mutually dependent aims: to try to negotiate a new federal constitution more suited to the ethnic structure of the Empire, and to bring an end to the war. It was, however, late in the day for both aims to have much chance of success: Hungary was bound to resist any weakening of its privileged position and by 1917 Austria-Hungary was able to exercise only a limited independence from its dominant German partner. Karl went behind the back of his ally by conducting secret peace negotiations with Britain, but, so long as Hindenburg and Ludendorff were in charge of Germany's fortunes, the only acceptable peace for Germany was a 'German peace'.

The Ottoman Empire

Germany also had problems with its Turkish ally, while those in Britain who were most horrified by waste and deadlock of the Western Front had long been attracted to the idea that operations against the Ottoman Empire provided not only a strategic alternative but a tremendous opportunity to expand the British Empire. In the autumn of 1917, as the Western Front seemed more deadlocked than ever, both Britain and Germany turned their attention to the Middle East. The British cabinet had watched in horror as Passchendaele seemed to become a replay of the Somme, and Lloyd George was increasingly frustrated by the failure of his attempts to prevail over Haig and find an arena other than France in which to bring British military force to bear. It was perhaps as well that his plans to reinforce the Italians came to little, but, like Churchill in 1915, his mind turned to the possibility that Turkey was a weak link in the Alliance of the Central Powers. Although Haig continued to be determined that nothing should interfere with the supreme importance of the war in France and Flanders, Robertson who, as Chief of the General Staff, had responsibilities for Britain's imperial position, was more sympathetic to a strengthening of British forces in the Middle East. The result was a British offensive by the Egyptian Expeditionary Force (EEF) under the command of General Sir Edmund Allenby. On 31 October, this force of seven infantry and three cavalry divisions, which outnumbered the Turkish enemy by two to one, began the third battle of Gaza. This was no open conflict with armies ranging widely across the desert: the theatre of fighting was a narrow strip between the Mediterranean and the desert and, if casualties were lower than in the battles in France, they were high enough: British losses were 18,000 as compared to a Turkish figure of 25,000. The Turks were pushed back and on 9 December Allenby entered Jerusalem.

The Germans were already on their way to assist their ally and the Middle East was to become an important, if secondary, theatre of the war. Germany had placed great hopes in the Ottoman Empire which had not been fulfilled and on the eve of the Russian Revolution it had seemed as if the Tsarist Empire was on the brink of achieving its traditional territorial aims at the expense of the Turks. In the Caucasus, Turkish forces had had the worst of it, losing eastern Anatolia and being pushed back to Trabzon on the Black Sea coast in 1916. Neither had the expectations aroused by the Allied defeat at Gallipoli and British surrender at Kut, that the Turks could threaten the British Empire, been realised. The withdrawal of Turkish troops from Mesopotamia to assist in the Caucasus had led to the loss of Baghdad to the British in March 1917. Germany's answer to Turkish weakness was not dissimilar to its response to the failings of Austria-Hungary; the German army needed to take command; von Falkenhayn and some 18,000 German and Austrian troops were despatched to the Middle East.

Chapter 10:   The War at Sea

It was the strength of the German position gained in the first year of the war, and the ability and adaptability of the German army that, contrary to all the wisdom of pre-war staff colleges, enabled the German army to remain on the defensive on the Western Front from 1914 to the spring of 1918 and it was, similarly, the strength of the Royal Navy that allowed it to adopt the essentially defensive policy of containing the German High Seas Fleet. By the beginning of 1916 the war at sea had come to resemble that on land in that it, too, was characterised by stalemate. The great decisive sea battles that had been expected in view of Germany's pre-war naval challenge to Britain had not taken place and the German High Seas Fleet had only rarely left its ports, while the Royal Navy's Grand Fleet had only occasionally ventured forth from Rosyth and Scapa Flow. The flurry of naval activity in the early months of the war, which had seen German battlecruisers and cruisers loose on the oceans, had come to an end with battle of the Falkland Islands, while the engagements at Heligoland Bight and Dogger Bank had not involved the main battle fleets. The High Seas Fleet only left port on another five occasions during 1915.

A major reason for stalemate at sea was that capital ships were just too expensive to build and too valuable to lose. They were immensely powerful, but also vulnerable; a shell in the right place or a torpedo from a submarine could destroy a ship which had taken years to build. No wonder admirals were cautious and sometimes missed the chance of victory because of the consequences of defeat. Admiral Jellicoe, commander of the Grand Fleet, was acutely aware of his responsibility and of the unpredictability of the outcome of any great naval battle and made it clear that he would not risk losing his capital ships in order to destroy the enemy's.

The building of a powerful fleet of battleships and battlecruisers by Germany had been an expensive expression of Germany's desire for world-power status and an attempt to put pressure on Britain to come to terms with Germany. The money spent on the German Navy might have been better spent on the army, for Germany's fiscal resources had been insufficient to maintain its large army and to outbuild Britain in the building of dreadnoughts. German admirals thus found themselves in possession of a powerful High Seas Fleet that was nevertheless inferior to the British Grand Fleet. German policy was, therefore, to 'keep the fleet in being' as a risk to the Royal Navy and as a potential bargaining counter at any peace negotiations. The Kaiser's orders in August 1914 were for the fleet to stay in port and not challenge the Royal Navy, and the High Seas Fleet's instructions were to damage the British fleet by mining, submarines and, when opportunity allowed, attacks on its ships, but to avoid a major engagement; the fleet commander at the beginning of the war, Admiral von Ingenohl was told not to risk action unless victory was probable.

The options open to the German admirals were limited by Germany's short North Sea coastline and the difficulties of their capital ships reaching the Atlantic. The Channel was effectively denied to them, while if the High Seas Fleet sought to pass between Britain and Norway in order to reach the open ocean, it was almost certain to be detected by British cruisers who would warn the Grand Fleet at its bases at Rosyth and Scapa Flow. Von Tirpitz's brain child was bottled up. The strategy adopted was a naval form of attrition. By taking opportunities that offered the chance of sinking British ships without risking its main force, the German fleet might eventually achieve parity with the Royal Navy. Such an ambition was not realised and by the time the long-expected great sea battle was fought, the Germans had actually fallen further behind in terms of the number of capital ships.

The stalemate did not represent a draw but, rather worked to the advantage of the British. Only the Germans stood to gain from a full-scale encounter and the Royal Navy's success in containing the German fleet was a positive achievement. Jellicoe could not have won the war in an afternoon, but as Churchill wrote, he could have lost it in the same period of time. To be in possession of a powerful weapon that has taken many years to create and used up considerable resources in its building, and then not to be able to use it, is, in itself, a sort of defeat, while the stalemate that kept capital ships in port did not prevent the Royal Navy maintaining an effective blockade of

German and neutral ports, a distant blockade enforced in the Atlantic rather than the close blockade the German navy had expected.

Jutland

With both navies nervous about the dangers of losing ships and tentative in the engagements that had taken place, a major encounter was by no means certain and, as one historian has put it, 'It may seem surprising that an encounter between the battlefleets took place at all'.[1] Jutland can be viewed as an almost accidental battle with the two fleets stumbling across each other. It would, probably, not have occurred but for a change in the German command, which put the more aggressive Admiral Reinhard Scheer in charge of the High Seas Fleet in February 1916. Senior German naval officers had been chafing at the passive policies they had been ordered to follow, while the army was taking the leading role in the war, and Scheer, though not seeking a great sea battle, began sorties with capital ships, in the hope of tempting a portion of the Royal Navy into a position in which it could be destroyed. At the end of May he took the whole of his fleet into the North Sea and steamed northwards to the entrance to the Baltic, a move which led by a chapter of accidents to the battle of Jutland, or, as the Germans came to call it, the battle of the 'victory of the Skaggerrak'.

A great advantage the Royal Navy had over its adversaries, in the First as in the Second World War, was the ability to listen into and decode German naval communications. Room 40 in the Admiralty Old Building in London was able to read Scheer's signals and by the time the German fleet had left Heligoland Bight not only were Beatty's battlecruisers heading south from Rosyth, but Jellicoe's battleships had left Scapa Flow and were not far behind them. The superior Grand Fleet was proceeding at speed towards the Jutland coast, where Scheer's High Seas Fleet was steaming northwards, unaware of its danger.

The balance of strength was in numerical terms very much in the Royal Navy's favour: 28 dreadnoughts, nine battlecruisers, eight armoured cruisers, 26 light cruisers, 78 destroyers, a sea-plane carrier and a minesweeper to von Scheer's 16 dreadnoughts, six pre-dreadnought battleships, five battlecruisers, 11 light cruisers and 61 destroyers. In terms of fighting efficiency, however, the Germans had the edge. Their ships were designed for the North Sea and not for the control of a world-wide empire; they were better armoured and had more watertight bulkheads, while on the evidence of the battle of Dogger Bank, German gunnery was more accurate.

The Germans had also learned from Dogger Bank and the damage inflicted on both British and German battlecruisers. The battlecruiser, was in some ways an unsuccessful hybrid. It was largely the brainchild of Fisher, who, though his name is forever associated with the dreadnought battleship, believed that a ship which combined the gun-power of the battleship and the speed of the cruiser would revolutionise naval warfare. What the combination left out was, of course, armour, as the need for speed meant less armour plating, but Fisher believed that speed itself would enable the battlecruiser to escape being hit, and the German navy followed the British example by building battlecruisers. Dogger Bank should have revealed to both sides the vulnerability of these ships, but it was only the Germans who decided to increase the armour plating on theirs, even at the cost of reduced speed, and to keep magazines and cordite charges well away from gun-turrets, despite the consequent reduced rate of firing.

As with the war on land, advances in communications had gone far enough to facilitate the bringing of forces into battle, while not solving the problems of communicating during battle. Both the British and German fleets had embraced radio systems which enabled ships to communicate over long distances and vastly improved the ability of reconnaissance as scouting ships could immediately report back to fleet flagships. The downside was that a ship which broke radio silence could be immediately detected, while one side could listen in to the others' communications and, though elaborate codes were supposed to prevent this, the British had by good fortune acquired German code-books so that the experts in Room 40 were able to decrypt German messages. When it came to battle, however, communication remained a problem for both navies: wireless telegraphy transmitted messages in Morse code, which took time to be decoded, and flag signalling remained the method of inter-ship communication. However, a simplified system of manoeuvre which made fewer signals necessary gave some advantage to the German fleet.[2]

Room 40's decrypting of Scheer's signals had give the Royal Navy a great opportunity, but it was compromised by Jellicoe becoming convinced that Scheer had not left port – his wireless call sign was still transmitting from harbour, but on going to sea he had changed it. Jellicoe consequently slowed his rate of knots and a gap opened up between his dreadnoughts and the battlecruisers of Beatty's fleet steaming ahead of them. The first clash came when Beatty sighted von Hipper's reconnaissance squadron and both fleets turned south, Hipper hoping to draw Beatty on to the guns of Scheer's ships which had been following him. In this phase of the battle the

Germans got far the better of it. The 5th battle squadron of the latest dreadnoughts, which had been sent to reinforce Beatty's battlecruisers, lagged behind due to signalling error and in the exchange between British and German battlecruisers the *Indefatigable* was blown up, the *Queen Mary* was sunk, and Beatty's flagship, *Lion* dropped out of line after receiving a direct hit on a gun turret: 'What's wrong with our bloody ships today?', asked Beatty.

By late afternoon, British cruisers reported that the High Seas Fleet was ahead and Beatty ordered his fleet to turn around; now the situation was reversed and Beatty was trying to draw the main German fleet towards Jellicoe's dreadnoughts. The fast battleships of the 5th battle squadron had now caught up with Beatty and inflicted heavy damage with their 15-inch guns on the following German ships, including the *Seydlitz* – hit again, as at Dogger Bank – as both fleets steamed northwards. At around 6 o'clock, Scheer, hitherto unaware that the Grand Fleet was ahead of him, came under fire from Jellicoe's battleships. A third British battlecruiser, the *Invincible* was lost in what now became a confused mêlée as visibility decreased. Jellicoe, though ill-informed by Beatty as to exactly where the High Sea Fleet was, managed to position his warships in line ahead and to 'cross the enemy's T', thus becoming able to fire on Scheer's ships as they presented a soft target in line abreast. The British gunnery may not have been as accurate as the German, but the light was fading and Jellicoe's fleet had more guns; the German ships suffered 27 hits. There the battle might have ended as Scheer turned away and headed for home, leaving his battlecruisers and cruisers to cover his retreat. Jellicoe could have, and several said later that he should have, pressed home his advantage, but conscious of the threat to his ships from torpedoes, he also turned away. Fierce and confused fighting continued throughout the night between ships covering Scheer's escape and the British cruisers and destroyers that followed them, but the German fleet made it back home.

The great and much anticipated sea battle was over, but who had won? Fourteen British ships had been sunk and 11 German ships, though in terms of tonnage, the British loss was 110,000 tons as opposed to a German loss of 62,000. The loss of men (6,094 British and 2,251 Germans) can seem quite small when compared to figures for the great battles on shore, but with few exceptions 'loss' meant dead, as opposed to dead, wounded or captured. The 'score' enabled Germany to claim a victory, but, although it is incorrect to say that the High Seas Fleet never emerged from harbour again, it never did so in numbers that could have challenged the Grand Fleet. Tirpitz had provided Germany with a Neptune's sword, but it had proved to be blunt.

The significance of Jutland has long been debated and British public opinion at the time was understandably disappointed that instead of the clear victory it had expected the outcome of the battle could be contested. Why had it not been a clear victory, the press asked, and whose fault was it that the High Seas Fleet was not at the bottom of the sea? Jellicoe, cautious, professional and impatient with journalists, was not the popular figure with the press or the public that he was with the officers and men who served under him. Beatty was the popular hero, another Nelson or a dashing and fearless cavalier of the seas with the battlecruisers as his cavalry and, for much of the press, if things had gone wrong at Jutland, it could not have been his fault – indeed he had almost won the battle and Jellicoe had thrown victory away. As Robert K. Massie, a forthright champion of Jellicoe, has commented, 'The fact is that if any British admiral had been "defeated at Jutland", it was Beatty who led ten capital ships into action against Hipper's five and suffered the loss of two with heavy damage to others', but, for the press, Beatty could not become a scapegoat; he 'had brilliantly delivered Scheer's vessels into the jaws of the Grand Fleet only to see the opportunity to annihilate them thrown away'.[3] Beatty played a devious role in orchestrating criticism of Jellicoe while privately congratulating him on his victory, and his wife joined in a campaign in support of her husband, rather similar to that of Lady Haig's in support of hers, to the denigration of Jellicoe. As a result, Jellicoe was denied immediate promotion to Admiral of the Fleet.

A clear victory, perhaps the annihilation of the High Seas Fleet, would, undoubtedly have had advantages: it would have dealt a heavy blow to German morale; any danger of an invasion of Britain would have disappeared; the Baltic could have been opened up to the Royal Navy, enabling a tightening of the blockade and perhaps making possible a supply route to Russia; and without a surface fleet to protect their ports German U-boats would have found it difficult to operate. The consequences of defeat would have, however, been disastrous. The Grand Fleet was more important to Britain than was the High Seas Fleet to Germany and this, above all, justifies the verdict that Jellicoe's caution was justified. He was indeed 'the man, who could have lost the war in an afternoon' and he didn't.

Blockade and the Submarine Threat

Britain's containment of the High Seas Fleet was a strategic victory. The German navy was confined to waters close to its harbours, and was not able to challenge the 'distance blockade', which the Royal Navy was able to impose not only on German ports and shipping but on those of neutrals as well. Maritime supremacy was once again serving Britain well, as it had done in previous wars. The blockade, an instrument of economic warfare, was working: though it was a slow means of starving Germany of imports, it was beginning to bite. Conversely, German expectations that Britain, a country highly dependent upon agricultural imports, would itself suffer severely from economic warfare were confounded by the failure of the German navy to prevent supplies of food and raw materials arriving from across the Atlantic and by Britain's ability to put more land under the plough and increase wheat production. It was in this context that, after Jutland, Germany began to consider unrestricted submarine warfare.

Submarines had not figured greatly in the thinking of naval strategists before the war. Their potential was only gradually being realised for they were in an early stage of development and existing models were small, fragile and had a short range. The Royal Navy, thanks to Jackie Fisher, one of the few senior admirals in the world to foresee that these new craft could play an important role, had 55, while the Germans, the last major power to develop submarines, had 28, though these, largely due to Germany's late start, were larger and more strongly built.

By 1914, both naval commands had come to the conclusion that submarines could play a useful, if limited, role in naval warfare. The main use foreseen for them was sinking warships, and the first months of the war proved that they could indeed do so. In September 1914, four British cruisers were sunk by German *unterseeboote*, or U-boats as the British came to call them, which caused considerable alarm in the Admiralty. However, the fear of Jellicoe that submarines might prove a real threat to the Grand Fleet was misplaced and no dreadnought was sunk by a submarine in the course of the war. In fact, warships were not vulnerable to submarines so long as they took the precautions of steering a zigzag course and maintaining speed, for submarines had to submerge to attack and submerged they could do little more than 10 knots. At such a speed a submarine could not keep up with warships of her own navy and co-ordinate attacks with them, while to attack an enemy warship a submarine had to lie in wait and was usually faced with the difficult target of the prow of the warship.

Jellicoe was more prophetic when he argued that submarines might be used for commerce raiding and might even attack merchant shipping while submerged, a concept that horrified contemporaries.

The laws of war at sea demanded that a surface raider had to instruct an intercepted vessel to heave to and allow its crew to abandon ship before sinking it, and the submarine was expected to behave in the same way. However, voices in the German navy were soon demanding tougher action and the abandonment of these 'cruiser rules'. For the first months of the war U-boat commanders stuck to the law but it put them at a considerable disadvantage, for, while surface raiders had guns large enough to deal with an armed merchantman, submarines had not and were vulnerable to retaliation when surfaced. It is, therefore, not surprising that by February 1915 only one British merchant ship had fallen victim to a U-boat as opposed to 14 that had been sunk by mines and 51 by surface raiders. However, as Fisher had predicted, the Germans then moved over to unrestricted warfare: the Kaiser announced that the North Sea was a war zone and all merchant ships were liable to be sunk without warning. The policy was denounced as barbaric by the British, but it had some justification as they themselves had declared the North Sea a military area and started to use Q-ships, which sailed under a neutral flag but then opened fire on the surfaced U-boats.

Unrestricted submarine warfare was, like so many of German stratagems, from the declaration of war on Russia onwards, a calculated risk. The blockade was hurting and posed a long-term threat to the German economy, though as yet not one which seriously hindered the war effort, and the destruction of allied and neutral shipping by U-boats could, it was hoped, not just loosen the noose that prevented imports to Germany, but turn the tables by cutting off transatlantic supplies to Britain. It was, however, bound to anger neutral, and particularly American, opinion and was, again like other German moves, a triumph of military thinking over diplomatic considerations. There was by no means a consensus on the policy and it led to a division of opinion both within the German navy and between the navy and the German government. The Chancellor, Bethmann Hollweg, and the foreign ministry were opposed to it, but the press, stirred up by sections of the navy, campaigned in favour.

Bethmann's forebodings were soon justified when a British passenger ship, the *Lusitania*, was sunk off the Irish coast on 7 May 1915. She had been carrying over a hundred Americans and, even though President Woodrow Wilson remained determined to keep the United States out of the war, he sent Germany a strongly worded note demanding an end to the use of submarines against unarmed merchantmen. British propagandists in America made the maximum use of the sinking: they were handed a gift in the shape of a medallion struck in Germany to celebrate the sinking, which they circulated copies of.

Bethmann Hollweg and others were opposed to a policy they believed would be counter-productive if it brought the USA into the war, and the outcry in America enabled him to gain the support of the Kaiser, who rarely maintained a settled opinion for long. The German navy was forced to suspend U-boat warfare. However, after Jutland, Scheer, who had become convinced that submarines were the navy's best chance of winning the war at sea, campaigned for its renewal. Those in the navy pressing for the resumption of the U-boat campaign received valuable support when Hindenburg and Ludendorff replaced von Falkenhayn as commanders of the army and sidelined not only Bethmann Hollweg but the Kaiser, taking for themselves the position of the real rulers of Germany. Whereas Bethmann Hollweg had always looked towards some sort of peace settlement, albeit one favourable to Germany, and had never entirely subordinated diplomatic aims to military expediency, Ludendorff, the dominant figure in the new regime, thought only of total victory. The ruthless nature of submarine attacks on merchant shipping tuned in with his general approach to warfare, and he enthusiastically supported a memorandum written by von Holtzendorff, chief of the naval staff, which argued that a return to unrestricted use of U-boats could bring the war to a speedy conclusion.

The failure of the tentative peace initiatives of December 1916 strengthened the hand of those who favoured an offensive that it was claimed could win the war, and in January 1917, faced with a demand from both the army and navy, the Kaiser changed his mind again and declared the resumption of unrestricted submarine warfare necessary. This was not Bethmann Hollweg's finest hour; rather than resign, he announced in the Reichstag a decision to which he was totally opposed. He was in a weak position, however, for there was little opposition to the reckless policy, even among businessmen who should have known better. An exception was Max Warburg who wrote in January 1917: 'If we end up at war with America, we will face an enemy with such moral, financial and economic strength that we will have nothing more to hope for from the future.'[4] Just over two months after the decision to renew unrestricted U-boat warfare, the United States declared war.

Like a reckless gambler who tries to recoup after previous bad bets, Germany, under what was increasingly a military regime, took an enormous risk, the extent of which they had not properly considered. The German Admiralty underestimated how much tonnage they would need to sink in order to force Britain into submission and the number of U-boats they would need to do it, while Ludendorff had failed to realise how quickly the economic consequences for Germany of an American entry into the war would make themselves felt. The notion that the British would be hit so hard that they would have to sue for peace was also erroneous and, by a combination of rationing tonnage, and then introducing convoys, Britain was able to continue fighting.

Britain's survival was, nevertheless, a near thing. Germany planned to sink 600,000 tons of Allied shipping a month, an amount, it was estimated, that would starve Britain into submission within six months and would also deprive France and Italy of the British coal they needed for their industries. In April 1917, U-boats sank more than 850,000 tons. The U-boats that undertook the campaign were very different from their predecessors of 1914 and could range further, though only the latest 'U-cruisers' could go as far as the east coast of America. Even before the new ruthless attack had begun, the shipping magnate Lord Runciman had warned that a complete breakdown of shipping was imminent and, by April, Britain's wheat stocks were dangerously depleted.[5] There was near-panic at the Admiralty, which admitted its helplessness in the face of the U-boat menace, and so confident was the German Admiralty that it placed no further orders for U-boats until June.

Why then did the U-boat campaign fail? It can be argued that it was bound to fail as the German navy did not have sufficient U-boats for the task, underestimated the number they might lose, did not give sufficient priority to building more, and ordered too many different types from different yards, thus forfeiting the benefits of mass production. The total force at the beginning of the final campaign was around 100; between January 1917 and January 1918 some 87 were built and 78 were lost.

It did not, however, look that way in April 1917. Counter measures were ineffective; sweeps by destroyers were a total failure though mine-laying was more successful. New anti-submarine technology developed by the British made only a marginal difference: wireless detection methods improved but still depended upon the U-boat captain breaking radio silence; U-boats had to be found before depth charges could be useful; and the hydrophone was only able to find a U-boat if it was within a few hundred yards. Protection of shipping by organising merchant ships into convoys protected by destroyer escorts, essentially a revival of a stratagem used during the Napoleonic Wars, made a more significant difference. The Admiralty did not think convoys would work, and some of their major objections make sense at first sight: a collection of ships makes an easier target than a single ship; convoys would have to keep to the speed of the slowest ship; another, that merchant navy captains would not be capable of maintaining the position of their ships in station, rather under-estimated the seamanship of the merchant navy. It was probably the mindset that admirals shared with generals, favouring the offensive and the seeking out of the enemy rather than protecting merchant ships, that lay behind these objections. In fact, distances on the high seas are so great that even 20 ships together were only marginally less difficult for a U-boat to find than a single ship, while merchant navy captains found little difficulty in maintaining positions and speed. The splendid story that it was Lloyd George, who, after taking advice from a naval commander, knocked the admirals' heads together and insisted on convoys, was largely the prime minister's own invention. It was probably Maurice Hankey, Secretary to the Committee of Imperial Defence, who pressed hardest for their adoption, though senior admirals had come to favour the idea, and the prime minister eventually threw his weight behind it. First Sea Lord Jellicoe was slow to appreciate the importance of convoys and cautious when it came to initiating them without what he considered sufficient escorts. What Lloyd George, rather unfairly, thought was his unwarranted delay over convoys was a factor in his dismissal in December. The first convoy sailed on 10 May; by June, there were eight every eight days. 'In August to October 1917 the loss rate among convoyed ships was 0.58 per cent compared with a non-convoyed rate of 7.37 per cent'.[6]

U-boat commanders had a difficult task even when they had found their target. It could be likened to grouse shooting from underwater; the torpedo tubes were at the prow and stern and had to be fired at right angles to the merchantman target, which was going at high speed and was likely to change direction. After one or two shots the subma-rine's position would probably have been given away by the wake of the torpedoes fired and most U-boats carried only eight to twelve torpedoes, while the destroyers protecting convoys had increased the number of depth charges they were equipped with to 30 or more by 1918.[7]

Attention has tended to concentrate on Atlantic convoys from the USA or Argentina or Brazil, which carried most of Britain's trade. Ninety per cent of vessels sailing the Atlantic were convoyed by 1918. However, convoys were also essential to the protection of shipping in the Mediterranean and British home waters. The shallow Mediterranean was well-suited to submarines and as the Austro-Hungarian navy was in control of the Adriatic, its and German submarines, plus four German

U-boats stationed at Constantinople, were able to inflict great damage on convoys between Egypt and Gibraltar supplying Italy with coal and armaments. Convoys in the North Sea, whether emerging from the Atlantic or on short haul, were particularly vulnerable to U-boats based in German ports or in Flanders, which inflicted even greater losses than those in the Mediterranean.

Offensive efforts to stem U-boat activity included the Royal Navy's raid on the U-boat pens at Zeebrugge and Ostend and attempts to block the entrance to the Adriatic with a 45-mile-long barrage, but it was essentially the convoy system, which gradually and unspectacularly improved in efficiency while the numbers and experience of destroyer escorts increased, that defeated the U-boats. The entry of America into the war on 6 April may have added the capital ships of the second-largest navy in the world to Allied sea-power, but with the High Seas Fleet rarely venturing out of harbour, what made a significant difference was the availability of US destroyers for Atlantic convoy duty. In the Mediterranean, 14 Japanese destroyers were invaluable as escorts for troopships. Aircraft were used to patrol narrow waters, and 685 planes and 103 airships were dedicated to this purpose, but proved more useful as convoy escorts. By 1918, it had become evident that the menace of unrestricted submarine warfare had been contained. In 1917–18, 175 U-boats were commissioned and 177 sunk or lost in other ways, while at the same time, the numbers of sinkings per U-boat declined steadily, with loss rates in Atlantic convoys almost halving between October 1917 and October 1918.[8]

As Hew Strachan argues, the attempt to bring Britain to its knees by sinking Allied and neutral shipping backfired on Germany. It actually strengthened the blockade as the Americans had no reservations in enforcing it on neutrals and this cut the flow of imports entering Germany from adjacent neutral states, while shipping losses forced the Allies to co-ordinate their controls on purchasing, thus squeezing the Central Powers out of world markets. 'Both indirectly and directly, the German decision to adopt unrestricted U-boat war tightened the economic stranglehold in which it was gripped.'[9]

The unrestricted U-boat campaign was always likely to lead to American intervention in the war, a risk that the German government had factored in, gambling on the fact that, if it led to the collapse of the British economy, victory could be achieved before the USA declared war or, at least, before its forces could make a difference to the war in Europe. Had the U-boat campaign been successful, as it threatened to be in April, the risk might have been justified and, even after it had begun, American intervention was far from certain – it was the Zimmermann telegram that brought America into the war (see Chapter 9, pp. 151–2).

Time was all important to German policy in 1917, the U-boat campaign had to succeed in bringing Britain to its knees within six months or it had failed. Failure or success was not determined by the tonnage of ships or the number of U-boats sunk but by the fact that British shipyards were able to build more merchant ships than were being destroyed and by the survival rate of the merchant ships that were the U-boats intended prey: 'Sinking submarines was a bonus, not a necessity', Robert Massie has concluded, 'What mattered was that merchant ships survive and deliver their cargoes. If they could do that – because the U-boats had been avoided or forced to keep out of the way – it did not matter how many U-boats were sent to the bottom.'[10] It was convoys and the Royal Navy's ability to protect them that resulted in the failure of unrestricted U-boat warfare. At sea as on land, it was defence that was crucial.

Time was equally important when it came to America's entry into the war. It did not make an immediate military difference for, as the Germans had foreseen, it took months for the USA to assemble an army of any real strength and transport it to Europe, and German plans were for victory in 1917. It did, however, make a greater difference than Germany's rulers had expected in terms of economic and financial support for the Allies at a time when the creditworthiness of Britain and France was threatened by the collapse of Russia, to which both powers had extended loans that now looked unlikely to be repaid. The combination of Britain's ability to keep the sea lanes open and her consolidated financial credit meant that Germany's position on the Western Front was no stronger at the end of 1917 than at the beginning.

Chapter 11:   The Final Struggle

At the beginning of 1918 the military advantage seemed to lie with the Central Powers and there was little expectation in Britain, France or Italy of an early end to the war. The position of the Allied powers had, indeed, deteriorated during the previous year and it has been described as 'more difficult than at any time since spring 1916'.[1] German forces still occupied a great swathe of French and Belgian territory won in 1914, the Italian army had been routed, and in central and eastern Europe, Germany, Austria-Hungary and Bulgaria were triumphant as the new Bolshevik government in Russia sued for peace. On the credit side, America had come into the war, but the United States had had a tiny army and, though it was being expanded rapidly, it was inexperienced, while getting US troops on to European battlefields would take time. Negotiations between Germany and Russia for the peace treaty that would be signed in March at Brest-Litovsk were already under way and provided a somewhat bizarre spectacle as revolutionaries, along with an ex-Tsarist admiral and a 'delegate of the peasantry', sat down with Habsburg princes and Junkers and posed for the cameras – for this, according to Norman Stone, was the first diplomatic treaty ever to be filmed.[2]

Germany had won the war in the East. Romania had been defeated and forced to sign the Treaty of Bucharest on 27 February, losing great expanses of its territory to Austria-Hungary and Bulgaria, and transferring control of much of its economy to Germany. The disintegration of the Russian Empire was already under way in Poland and the Baltic states and, by signing the peace treaty on 3 March, the Bolsheviks gave up Poland, Lithuania, the Baltic provinces and Transcaucasia. Neither side viewed the treaty as a permanent settlement. The Bolsheviks, encouraged by a wave of strikes and the setting up of workers' and soldiers' councils in Vienna, were confident that an international revolution was imminent and would negate Brest-Litovsk, while the Germans considered that Russia would soon fall apart and be replaced by disparate national states.

The German Spring Offensive

In the meantime, Germany could now consolidate her control of East and Central Europe or move divisions to the Western Front. This was the great choice OHL or, in practice, Ludendorff had to make. The Allies had failed time and again with offensives on the Western Front and since the Germans had, early in 1917, withdrawn to the shorter and more easily defended Hindenburg Line and progressively refined their methods of defence in depth, operations in the west seemed to have been abandoned for the time being. Ludendorff was, in fact, planning a massive attack on the Western Front, which was designed to be a knock-out blow. Why, in the circumstances of what seemed a strong military position, did the German High Command gamble everything on a great offensive, which might have brought victory, but involved an enormous risk?

One answer lies in the psychology of German leaders, together with their long-term assessment of Germany's position as a great power. Hindenburg and Ludendorff were, with Ludendorff increasingly the dominant partner, now effectively in charge of German policy, exercising direct control in military matters and a negative control over foreign policy by vetoing policies of which they disapproved. They seem to have believed that Germany must either triumph or go under; there was no middle way. This outlook can be seen as characteristic of German leaders since the beginning of the war and underlies the risk-taking nature of so many German decisions. Just as it is arguable that Germany went to war in 1914, not in a mood of confidence, but one of pessimism, believing that an encircled nation was gradually getting weaker and her enemies stronger, that the implementation of Schlieffen Plan, which resulted in Britain's entry into the war, was worth the risk, and that, similarly, unrestricted submarine warfare was worth the probable consequence of American entry, so the spring offensive was a desperate throw to win victory before ineluctable long-term forces brought defeat.

There was, however, much sense in Ludendorff's decision and in his diagnosis in November 1917 that: 'our general situation requires that we should strike at the earliest moment, if possible at the end of February or the beginning of March before the Americans can throw strong forces into the scale. We must beat the British.'[3] What were the alternatives? They were to sit tight behind the Hindenburg Line and remodel east-central Europe to Germany's advantage, or to initiate peace proposals.

The disadvantages of embedding a defensive posture in the west were fourfold: the balance between the offensive and the defensive had been shifting and it was no longer axiomatic, due to new weaponry and tactics, that more attackers than defenders were killed; a permanently defensive posture was bad for the morale of armies and for that of civilians as food shortages hit the German and Austro-Hungarian populations hard; although OHL had a poor opinion of the efficiency of the US army it realised that by late 1918 or 1919 America, which planned a force of nearly 3 million men, would have large and expanding forces in Europe; and the deteriorating state of the war economy pointed to a choice between an attempt at outright victory in the immediate future and eventual economic collapse.

The Hindenburg programme had been successful in increasing the production of war materials but at the expense of agriculture and the domestic infrastructure. The German economy was declining rapidly as the British blockade tightened and the army's voracious appetite for men starved agriculture and industry of workers. Early in 1918, there was plenty of artillery, munitions and other supplies for the army and, in addition, divisions could be moved from east to west, thus putting a temporary end to manpower problems. However, the army's strength was a wasting asset, which could not be maintained if the economy which supported it declined. It could be seen as now or never for a last great push for victory and for a superior military machine to counteract Germany's desperate long-term position.

The deadlock on the Western Front that had prevailed since 1914 was not just a matter of a balance between opposing armies, for the forces that Britain and France and Germany could assemble were determined by wider factors: Germany's need to fight a war on two fronts and the relative economic strength of the two sides. If revolution in Russia had removed the former German disadvantage, the economic balance which, largely due to Britain, had always been in the Allies' favour, was moving remorselessly against Germany. The position of the combatant powers at the beginning of 1918 can be seen as a classic test of the relative importance in modern warfare of the strength of the economies of the belligerents and the effectiveness of their armies on the battlefield. There can be little doubt that the German army had proved itself in over three years of continuous fighting to be the superior fighting force, but, though popular support for the war remained steady, the continued erosion of living standards and a diet that was insufficient to maintain health was testing the consensus that had been created in 1914.

The other option was to put out feelers for a negotiated peace. A peace settlement which accepted German and Austrian territorial gains in Eastern Europe might have been acceptable to the governments of Britain and France, but Germany's military leaders and some industrialists were determined on gains in France and Belgium, war aims which had been extant since Bethmann Hollweg's September Memorandum of 1914, however much Bethmann Hollweg himself may have later regretted the straitjacket those hastily assembled war aims placed on diplomatic initiatives. Richard von Kühlmann, foreign minister, whose appointment had been opposed by Hindenburg, argued that the war could not be resolved by military means and that, although the war had to be continued, it should be done with an eye to the most advantageous peace settlement possible. To this end, he let the British know in September 1917 that Germany might give up its claims on Belgium in return for a free hand in the east, but Ludendorff saw that he was soon dismissed. Alsace-Lorraine was another sticking point, with Lloyd George insisting that its return to France was a British war aim, but it was, above all, the determination of the German military and heavy industrialists to hang on to at least part of Belgium, and in particular Liege, in order to protect the Ruhr, that ruled out any chance of serious negotiations. Alone among the senior German generals, von Falkenhayn had realised early in the war that Germany could not hope to achieve a peace with major annexations in the West, but the German high command both failed to realise this and overruled any sensible negotiations, as with the proposal for a peace based on the pre-war status quo suggested by America's Colonel Edward M. House in December 1916 and Pope Benedict's offer of mediation in July 1917.

Essentially, the German high command, rather than seeing war and diplomacy as twin and mutually supportive ways of pursuing the nation's interests, had abandoned diplomacy This had become ever more evident from late in 1916, when real power had passed to Hindenburg and Ludendorff. Though Hindenburg was the heroic figure who commanded loyalty, it was Ludendorff who gave the new regime its ethos. A member of the military meritocracy, rather than aristocracy, he had championed a mass army, something which the more traditional military elite opposed. 'We must become the people in arms again' he had said in 1912, harking back to Prussia's wars.[4] The Kaiser was still on the throne, civilian chancellors and ministers still exercised nominal power, though Kühlmann was replaced by an admiral, and Ludendorff made no move to become chancellor, but monarchical conservatism had been replaced by radical military nationalism and OHL determined policy, largely by the power of veto, demanding the army's ultimate right to direct the nation's policies.

The question of whether to make the British or the French the main target for the spring offensive was much debated within OHL; Operation Michael, named after the Archangel, the plan eventually decided upon by Ludendorff, was a compromise in that it was aimed at the point where British and French lines met near St Quentin, just beyond the old Somme battlefields. It came at a time when, after Passchendaele, the morale of the British army was at its lowest point during the whole war and it was almost a million men under strength, while the French army was still weakened after the mutinies of the previous year. Ludendorff's official designation as quartermaster was apposite; he had great ability for organisation and deployment. He brought up 750,000 men and 6,000 guns, and when the offensive began on 21 March German divisions outnumbered Allied divisions by 200 to 189.

Attacking at the most vulnerable point on the Allied lines – from near Arras in the north to La Fere further south, the Germans enjoyed immediate success against General Gough's 5th Army, which defended the longest sector with the fewest troops. Gough had the reputation of being an 'unlucky general' and certainly his luck was out this time for, facing a superior force, the defence was handicapped by a dense fog. Following a five-hour bombardment in which tear gas shells were used at the same time as phosgene, forcing the British gun crews to tear off their masks, the German infantry were protected by their artillery as they assembled. Then the storm-troopers advanced, not in lines or columns, but in groups, staying close to a creeping barrage in front of them. The British communications broke down, Gough lost control, and substantial gaps appeared in the British lines of defence which the Germans poured through. Although General Byng's 3rd Army held on at Arras, the Allies were overwhelmed and retreated, and with German troops infiltrating behind pockets of resistance the retreat became a disorganised scramble. The British suffered around 17,000 casualties and 21,000 were taken prisoner during the day's fighting.[5] By 24 March, Byng's 3rd Army as well as Gough's 5th had been forced back and German forces were across the Somme and progressing northwards, while French attempts to assist the British were driven back. The German army's attack was remorseless and in a week British and French forces were pushed back 40 miles on a 50-mile front. It seemed as if Ludendorff's plan to separate the Allied armies, roll back the British towards the Channel and then defeat the French might succeed. Haig was initially sanguine but, when he learned that the 5th Army had been driven back over the Somme, he began to fear that the British and French forces would be divided. He knew that he and Pétain had different priorities, the first concern of the French being the defence of the Champagne and then Paris, while that of the British was the Channel ports.

The Allied defences stiffened as French reserve divisions and some of the British reserve from Flanders were brought up by rail, lorries and red British buses, and Ludendorff, realising that he was not making a breakthrough, suspended the offensive on 4 April. There was only a brief pause, for five days later two German armies attacked again: Operation Georgette was initiated, sweeping across the Lys River, intending to take Dunkirk and Calais. The Germans pushed through a weakly held section of the front manned by British and Portuguese[6] divisions and attacked the vulnerable British-held Ypres salient. Here the Germans had another victory as their forces advanced over that familiar battlefield, taking the Messines Ridge captured by the British in the previous year and pushing the British back to the gates of Ypres. The Germans now threatened Dunkirk, essential to the BEF for the supply of men and material and, further south attempted to surround Ypres. It was at this stage that Haig, insouciant in the first days of the German offensive, issued his famous, 'With our backs to the wall' order calling on his troops to fight to the last man.

There were, inevitably, calls for Haig's replacement as British commander-in-chief, something which Lloyd George had long wished for. The War Cabinet discussed the matter on 8 April but, concluding there was no obvious replacement, left Haig in command. Haig had, however, already taken pre-emptive action. He had, at a hastily summoned meeting of Allied leaders and generals at Doullens on 26 March agreed to put himself under the command of Foch, now replacing the more defensively minded Pétain as the driving force of the French army. Whether this was a purely altruistic move or an act of self-preservation by a man sensing danger to his position is debatable. Haig's champion, John Terraine, has seen it as a crucial and selfless act that led to a unified command being able to stem the German offensive and then move on to victory.[7] Norman Stone has seen Haig as 'doing what he should have done before',[8] while others have seen the act of a man in a panic, who believed the BEF was in a desperate position.[9]

The crisis inevitably reignited another 'battle', the long-running struggle between British military commanders and Lloyd George.

For a number of senior military officers and sections of the press which supported them, a major military defeat must, necessarily not be the fault of Haig or other senior generals, but had to be due to the government and in particular Lloyd George. In fact, the prime minister had energetically responded to the crisis and more than 22,000 men were rushed across the Channel in weeks, while the government scraped the barrel to find more soldiers. The claim by Major-General Frederick Maurice that the government had withheld necessary troops from the Western Front aroused a furore in press and parliament from which Lloyd George, largely blameless, extricated himself, with a slight departure from the 'actualité', in the ensuing debate in parliament.[10]

By the end of April, however, both of Ludendorff's first offensives had failed, for Operation Georgette, ran into some of the same problems as Michael and, despite gains of territory, failed to reach crucial targets. His careful preparations and the German army's use of new methods of attack had briefly achieved in the spring offensive what generals on both sides had been seeking since 1914, a major breakthrough and a return to mobile warfare, while, if German losses were heavy, totalling 348,000 by the end of April as opposed to 332,000 for the Allies, 212,000 Allied troops had been taken prisoner. In the end, however, his offensive ran into the same basic problem that had hindered previous offensives, the difficulty of feeding and supplying troops once they had pushed beyond the railheads. The German army was a railway army and lacked sufficient lorries, while those it had were often denied rubber tyres because of the blockade and had to make do with metal; it also lacked horses. In addition, the artillery found great difficulties in hauling guns over territory, such as that near the Somme, which had been devastated by past battles, hence artillery and infantry became separated.

Ludendorff himself had responsibility for the situation the Germans now found themselves in. Like most commanders during the war he found it difficult to know when to stop, and pressed on when it would have been wiser to consolidate. Impatient with lack of progress, he allowed close-order attacks which, unlike the infiltration tactics so successful in March, resulted in German casualties eventually exceeding Allied losses. He was not the determined emotionless figure he appeared to be; Stevenson argues that 'His constant telephone calls to his subordinates and his rapid changes of direction testified to his nervousness and uncertainty of purpose.'[11] He overruled other German commanders, like Prince Rudolf of Bavaria, and, rather than pursue a firm strategy, he followed up success rather than concentrating on decisive sectors. After the initial successes in March, he ordered that, instead of rolling up the British north-westwards, the German armies should 'splay out', with the result that its strength and momentum was dissipated.

There followed a pause until May, when the German army attacked in Champagne. Germany was now presented with a mini replica of the 'two fronts' problem: was it best to try and finish off the British so that the French might give up or *vice versa*? German troops were by now becoming disillusioned with promises of victory. A senior officer believed 'the infantry were more or less fought out'[12] and the best troops had been used up in Operation Michael. Nevertheless, the army had been rested and reprovisioned and, while there was a shortage of experienced troops, the German 7th Army was able to muster 37 divisions for a new attack made up almost entirely of men who had taken part in the offensives of March and April, and the Hindenburg Programme was still cranking out the necessary guns and munitions. In May a third offensive (Operations Blucher and Gneisenau) was launched. While Operations Michael and Georgette had been aimed at the British and their links to the Channel ports, Ludendorff now turned his attention to the French. The new offensive, which began on 27 May, was aimed at the French interior and at Paris, though its main purpose was to divert French reserves from Flanders. The assault began in Champagne where the Germans, with a huge predominance in artillery, attacked across the old battlefield of Chemin des Dames, advancing to within 56 miles of Paris, forcing the evacuation of its suburbs and taking 50,000 prisoners. The French defence was not helped by French commanders' reluctance to adopt 'defence in depth' as it involved conceding more French soil. The German advance opened up the possibility of a German victory over France and the British government was so rattled that it began to consider whether the BEF might have to be withdrawn from France. This had previously been unthinkable and was still unmentionable, so a secret 'X Committee', consisting of Lloyd George, the new CIGS, General Sir Henry Wilson, the Secretary of State for War, Lord Milner and Sir Maurice Hankey, Secretary to the War Cabinet, had to be set up. Its preliminary view was against a general retreat unless the situation worsened and, as French resistance stiffened and the French army began to counter-attack, the crisis passed. X Committee, however, continued in being and 'became the instrument by which Lloyd George was able to take greater control of the strategy of British forces on the Western Front'.[13]

The second stage of the German offensive began on 9 June with intention of exploiting and extending the gains made in May.

After it had advanced some six miles it seemed well on the way to accomplishing these limited objectives. Again, however, Ludendorff did not know when to stop. He reacted to the success and speed of his advance by ordering his troops to continue to advance and spread out to left and right to widen the gap in the Allied defences. German objectives multiplied – Rheims, the Marne and Paris. Stevenson sums up the German commander's error: 'Once again Ludendorff was succumbing to mission creep, exploiting success while losing sight of his larger goals, and this time irretrievably.'[14] He was also faced with more co-ordinated opposition now that Foch was in overall command of the Allied armies. The Allies were able to bring up reserves and, far ahead of their rail-heads, the Germans were increasingly fighting with light weapons, while the French were able to bring up heavy artillery. At this stage American forces played their first significant role, assisting in the successful defence along the Marne at Chateau Thierry and, on 2 June, a Franco-American counter-attack held the Marne line. The first major setback to the Germans came on 9 June, when their assault on Montdidier, to the north of the developing battle and close to the Somme, failed, largely because the French had, at long last, learned the techniques of defensive warfare. Not only was Operation Gneisenau faltering, Ludendorff's advance had created vulnerable salients which were difficult to defend. Time was running out for a swift victory as American reinforcements continued to arrive. On 11 June a French counter-attack commanded by General Charles Mangin assaulted the over-stretched Germans on three sides of their Champagne salient and Ludendorff abandoned Operation Gneisenau.

On 24 June, Kühlmann made a speech to the Reichstag in which he said that the war could not be won by military means alone. Hindenburg's and Ludendorff's response was to threaten to resign unless the foreign minister did. No support for Kühlmann was forthcoming from the chancellor, Count Georg von Hertling, and he was replaced. His intervention was, however, significant in that it publicly aired the choice that Germany faced. For the moment, it still had a choice. To have initiated peace negotiations in June, when the German Empire's territorial conquests were at their widest and when its army still appeared a formidable force, would not have delivered the sort of peace treaty which the German high command and many political and industrial elements desired, but could well have resulted in a far better peace settlement than another five months of fighting was to obtain. Ferguson argues that the proponents of a 'German Peace', which meant a peace with annexations, including at least part of Belgium, 'fatally underestimated the advantages Germany would have been able to retain, if, in agreeing to restore Belgium, she had been able to secure a negotiated end to the war before her own collapse'.[15] Had Bethmann Hollweg still been in office, and the chancellorship and the Kaiser's authority still been intact, things might have been different, but what has been seen as a 'silent (i.e. unstated) military dictatorship'[16] had emerged; civilians' and even the monarch's views were sidelined. It was to Germany's disadvantage that opposition to the military's determination to cling to the hope of total victory signalled by Kühlmann and by increased dissatisfaction among the SPD members, did not become more vociferous until after it became clear that the war was lost.

Germany's Final Offensive

Time was running out for the Germans by the early summer. Germany had always suffered a disadvantage in terms of the inferiority of its financial position, numbers of population, and even its economy compared to those of the Allies combined, but had been able to make up for this by its possession of an army superior in almost every aspect – generals, junior officers and NCOS, and tactics. This superiority had been demonstrated by the grimmest of all tests, its ability to consistently kill, wound or take prisoner more of its opponents than could the Allies. Even in the spring of 1918, when German casualties mounted, the numbers remained almost equal.[17] Nevertheless, the failure of the spring offensive had demonstrated weaknesses and lowered morale, while the army could ill-afford the high casualties; neither, of course, could the French or the British, but the Allies could look forward to large numbers of American reinforcements. Just as important were ominous signs of economic collapse as the blockade tightened and the Hindenburg Programme debilitated all production but that of armaments, while civilian living standards continued to plummet. The military High Command, nevertheless, reaffirmed its commitment to a military victory and annexations at a conference at Spa on 2–3 July and the fifth German offensive of the year, Operation Friedensturm (or Peace Storm), began on 15 July. It can be seen as Ludendorff's last attempt at a decisive victory before inexorable forces made one impossible.

One intention of the operation was, as with the April–May campaigns, to force the Allies to draw reserves away from Flanders, as Ludenforff was still intent on rolling back the British and taking the Channel ports, but another was to deal with the problem of the large, vulnerable salient in Champagne that the operations of April–May against the French had left in the Germans' position. The wisest military choice would have been to withdraw to better defensive positions on the Hindenburg Line, but Ludendorff refused to give up hard-won territory and decided to attack on the Marne with the objective of taking Rheims, and the final scheme was for a two-pronged offensive on the Marne and in Champagne. After this he intended to revert to his main aim, a renewal of the attack on the British in Flanders.

German armies struck west and east, from the Marne and in Champagne, but this time they lost the element of surprise and the French were awaiting the attack, had reserves at their rear, and had mastered the techniques of defence in depth and counter-battery fire. Despite having a superiority in divisions, the German advance was halted on 17 July. Then came a massive counterstroke by eighteen French divisions under the command of Mangin; troops advanced, along with 300 light Renault tanks, behind a creeping artillery barrage. Ludendorff, who had optimistically begun removing artillery for his planned attack in Flanders was forced to order a fighting retreat and, a sure sign of declining morale, 50,000 Germans were taken prisoner by the end of the operation.

The Turning Point

Foch, sensibly, suspended the attack, but maintained pressure in Chemin des Dames. On 24 July, at a meeting of Allied commanders, he declared that the war had reached a turning point and that the Allies now had the advantage and should keep it. The failure of 'Peace Storm' had, indeed, changed the balance between the two sides, but Ludendorff rejected advice to withdraw and fall back as far as the Meuse and Antwerp, and the German position began to deteriorate rapidly.

The BEF now demonstrated with an offensive at Amiens which began on 8 August that it had learned from experience and developed into what has been called 'the most deadly army in the world... a huge modern mechanised army that had truly grasped the art of war as far as it existed'.[18] The essence of the new British approach was the 'All arms battle', the coordination of infantry, artillery, machine guns, tanks and aeroplanes. Amiens began with the limited aim of pushing the Germans back, but General Rawlinson's 4th Army gained complete surprise. Making maximum use of new weaponry and raining down gas and high explosive shells in the German rear to disrupt any counter-attacks, and with Rawlinson abandoning his previous 'bite and hold' tactics, the British advanced some seven miles on a ten-mile front, taking 50,000 prisoners.

Amiens has been called the 'Black Day' for the German army and was a major victory for the British army. Again, this must be qualified as British Empire army – there were major roles played by Australian and Canadian divisions. Even critics of Haig acknowledge the quality of his generalship at this stage of the war. Rather than seeking one point at which to aim at a breakthrough, he ordered massive offensive blows along the whole front, thus enabling Rawlinson's 4th Army to make its advance. The victory owed much to the artillery, which adopted the German system of neutralising counter-fire, rather simply aiming to destroy the enemy's defences, and did so with an accuracy which benefited from making the full use of technical advances. The British army was also now becoming superior in firepower to the Germans, who had neglected to develop the tank, while the British were able to muster 552 Mark V and Whippet tanks for their attack and were also superior in air-power and had more heavy guns and more Lewis guns per battalion. Amiens was followed by a wave of British successes at Arras, Bapaume and Mont Kemmel, while the French took the entire German salient in Champagne.

The Central Powers' position was now visibly crumbling. Not only had the Allies gained the initiative on the Western Front, but the state of Austria-Hungary had become parlous. For the empire the choice was clear, to stick close to Germany, even at the price of coming under German control, in the hope that Germany would still win the war, or to make a separate peace with the Allies before the empire fell apart. These alternatives were, respectively, favoured by the foreign minister, Count Ottokar von Czernin, and Emperor Karl I, who was secretly sending out peace feelers as he struggled to save his inheritance. Karl eventually secured the foreign minister's dismissal but not before Czernin had secured agreement to a new offensive against Italy. This was launched in June, but, though the Germans' welcomed this as a support for their Western Front attacks, no German divisions were allocated to it and the Austrians had only a bare superiority in men over the Italians, who now had the aid of three British and French divisions and a two-fold advantage in aircraft, mortars and artillery. The result was a crushing Austro-Hungarian defeat, for although the army managed to cross the River Piave, British bombers destroyed their pontoon bridges and they were driven back, suffering enormous losses. Germany could expect no more assistance from its main ally. Karl was intent on preserving his throne by a separate peace, the Slav populations of the Empire had lost their residual loyalty, and the

Hungarians were concerned with their own salvation. Vienna was on the verge of revolution and even the German Austrians began to see their future in union with Germany rather than under Habsburg rule.

Germany's other main ally, Turkey, was also nearing collapse. The campaign in the Caucasus had greatly weakened the Turkish army, a weakness exacerbated by the chronic inefficiency of the government, which failed to deliver adequate numbers of new recruits. Dismayed by their failure to gain any benefit from the Treaty of Bucharest, Turkish hopes were, nevertheless, raised by the collapse of Russia and they doubled their efforts in the Caucasus, taking Trabzon and Erzurum in February and March, while Brest-Litovsk promised them the return of territory lost previously to the Russians. Concentration on the Caucasus resulted, however, in the neglect of the defences of the southern part of the Ottoman Empire, where the revolt of the Sherif of Mecca, Hussein, which had begun in 1916, had seen an Arab army fighting under the direction of T.E. Lawrence. The Arabs had done little more than draw Turkish reinforcements away from the main battlefronts, and it was a largely Indian Empire army that had conquered Mesopotamia, taking Baghdad in March 1917. In Palestine it was a British force that proved the main threat to the Turks, who had been forced to evacuate from their defensive Gaza line, and General Allenby had taken Jerusalem in December 1917. The fall of Baghdad alerted the Germans to the danger of a Turkish collapse in the Middle East and they were concerned enough to despatch Falkenhayn with 18,000 German and Austrian troops to stiffen Turkish resistance. The scene was set for a confrontation between Allenby and Falkenhayn. When the battle of Gaza began on 27 October 1917 the British mounted the heaviest artillery bombardment of the war outside Europe, but what gave the campaign its special character was the effectiveness of cavalry, both British and Australian. Allenby advanced northwards and made a breakthrough in September at Megiddo in northern Palestine which led to the virtual collapse of Turkish resistance. Falkenhayn, who had retreated north of Jerusalem, was recalled to Germany early in 1918.

The End

As Germany's Allies were weakening, British, French and American forces pushed on in France and Flanders towards German territory. In Lloyd George and Clemenceau, Britain and France now had leaders determined on total victory, and a largely harmonious command structure for their armies. Foch, in overall command, still occasionally squabbled with Haig, while the American commander, General John J. Pershing, resolutely refused to put his army under any command but his own, but the scent of victory resolved differences.

On 12 September, Pershing appeared to justify his disdain for the cautious tactics of the British and French by clearing the St Michel salient the Germans had continued to hold near Verdun, but a further attack in the Argonne showed that ignoring the hard-earned lessons of 1916 and 1917 did not pay, when the Americans ran into formidable German resistance and the attack had to be halted. After Amiens, however, the British emphasised their new mastery of offensive warfare by breaking through the Hindenburg line at Cambrai. Carefully planned though it was, the battle lasted from 29 September till 9 October; it was not an easy victory but it was decisive one. A huge assault force attacked nine miles of the strongly fortified German positions, and a feature of the battle was the crossing of the St Quentin canal with its steep-sloping banks. Canadian divisions of the British 1st Army managed to get artillery across and used it to repel counter-attacks. Although the initial attack was more successful than the follow-up, which slowed up amidst heavy fighting, the end result was the penetration of the formidable Hindenburg Line and its reserve positions.

For the German army, a tipping point had been reached. Its soldiers, their morale low, ceased to fight effectively and began to surrender in ever-larger numbers. At this point, the Allied forces in Salonika, who had languished in what the Germans derided as a large prisoner-of-war camp, at last proved useful and moved forward against the Bulgarians. Germany's ally collapsed and a war which had begun over a Balkan incident was hastened to its end by the failure of a Balkan power to reverse the results of the Second Balkan War, when the Bulgarians asked for an armistice on 28 September. Earlier in the war, Bethmann Hollweg had said of Ludendorff that he was, 'only great at a time of success. If things go badly he loses his nerve'.[19] He was now proved correct, for Ludendorff gave wild orders and railed against other generals, the socialists, the Kaiser and even Hindenburg and alternated between bluster and declaring that the war must be ended.

Yet, was the German situation as bad as Ludendorff and most historians have concluded? Niall Ferguson has argued otherwise:

...it is now clear that the exhausted and ill Ludendorff was overreacting. Just as Germany's war had begun with a nervous breakdown (Moltke's) at the top, so it ended with one: Ludendorff's. A tired and sick man after the failure of his offensives, Ludendorff jumped to the conclusion that the army would collapse if he did not secure an armistice; it seems more likely that his desire for an armistice was what made it collapse. Haig believed that the German army was capable of retiring to its own frontiers and holding that line.[20]

Ferguson is surely correct in saying that German army was not yet finished as a fighting force, that it could have fallen back to Germany's frontiers and there fought on, perhaps with determination once it was defending the fatherland, and that this might well have resulted in a better peace settlement for Germany. The army's failure to maintain the will to fight began at the top and then spread to the middle and lower ranks, while the political crisis followed on the army's. How long Germany could have held out for in such a scenario is, of course, another matter, but Haig's opinion was that German army was capable of retiring and holding the line. Nevertheless, the high command convened a conference at Spa on 29 September attended by Kaiser Wilhelm, the chancellor, von Hertling, and the foreign secretary, Paul von Hintze, to advise them that Germany must now seek peace terms. Ludendorff demanded an immediate armistice on the basis of the Fourteen Points of Woodrow Wilson's proposals put forward in December. These proposals were a highly idealistic concoction of calls for democracy, national self-determination for 'peoples', and an abnegation of secret diplomacy, almost as unwelcome to Britain, France and Italy, with war aims which diverged from most of them, as to Germany. Clemenceau expostulated, 'Fourteen points, it's a bit much. The Good Lord had only ten.' To seek peace on the basis of the Fourteen Points was certainly a mistake and Ludendorff had probably never read them. In any case, to seek an armistice and then proceed to peace negotiations was to weaken further an already weak position. Implicitly, any acceptance of Wilson's points as the basis for peace negotiations threatened the structure of German government, for, although the position of the Kaiser was not mentioned in Wilson's proposals, it could be assumed that 'more democracy' questioned his constitutional position and the whole political system of imperial Germany. The decision to seek an armistice was Germany's and not that of Germany and her allies. It shattered the remnants of the German-led coalition. The Turks signed an armistice on 30 October and Austria on 3 November. That Hungary did not secure one until 13 November was symbolic of the collapse of Austria-Hungary, for the Empire had disintegrated into chaos and revolutions.

Prince Max von Baden, who became chancellor of Germany on 1 October, realised how foolish requesting an armistice was: 'a request for an armistice makes any peace initiative impossible'. His policy was to continue the war while negotiating. At the same time, he introduced a number of constitutional reforms and included representatives of the centre and left parties in his cabinet, hoping to satisfy at least one of Wilson's points. Indeed, Wilson's notes of 14 and 23 October emphasised that he would only deal with a democratic Germany. As the heir to a throne himself, Prince Max was also concerned to safe-guard the Kaiser's position.

It was all too late. Once word got out that the high command was in search of an armistice, the will of both the army and the civilian population to continue the struggle was destroyed. If Ludendorff had thought an armistice might bring a temporary respite in which the army could reorganise, he was soon proved wrong. An armistice, it was soon clear, would mean the end of the German army as a major military force.

Ludendorff, still in his position until he was forced to resign on 28 October, became increasingly erratic, changing his mind on an armistice when the probable terms became apparent and advocating *Endkampf* or some great final battle, in which, even if Germany was defeated, military honour would be preserved. Max von Baden and his government had their own more rational concept of Endkampf as a last battle fought by a more representative government with broad popular support. Neither were feasible, for by late October army morale had further deteriorated, and the navy had mutinied rather than put to sea for its own Endkampf, while with councils of work-ers and soldiers being formed, peace became more urgent as there seemed a threat of revolution.

The Kaiser's position became critical. Nothing about the last weeks of Germany at war is more bizarre than the way he was forced to abdicate, not by the politicians – for most of the cabinet shrank from this – but by senior military figures, the very men who might have been expected to protect the monarchy until the end. Tirpitz, Ludendorff and many other senior officers had moved to a position where their loyalty had become attached to the nation and state rather than the crown and, indeed, one historian has written that, 'It would be more accurate to say that their loyalty was attached, not to the national state, but to the armed forces which they claimed embodied and were synonymous with it.'[21] For some, Wilhelm could, selflessly, provide one last service to the army: he could lead a 'Death Ride' and charge the enemy at the head of a cavalcade of high-ranking officers and thus meet a glorious and patriotic end. Wilhelm declined. Max von Baden hoped to preserve the throne if not the Kaiser or the Crown

Prince, but on 7 November the SPD leaders, fearing that as revolution spread they would lose control of the workers to the Independent Socialists (USPD) and more extreme leftists, told the chancellor that not only must the Kaiser go but the constitution had to be fully democratised. On 9 November, Prince Max announced that Wilhelm had abdicated and himself stepped down, handing the chancellorship over to Friedrich Ebert, who headed a socialist administration. By 10 November, Wilhelm was on his way to Holland and exile.

Fighting continued throughout October and early November while the terms of an armistice were argued over, giving a particular piquancy to the deaths of soldiers who died when a ceasefire was imminent. Even unrestricted U-boat warfare continued, claiming a notable victim when the British passenger liner, *Leinster*, was sunk. Nevertheless, Germany had by now no option but to accept whatever terms were on offer. It was clear that the Allies were determined that the Armistice would have to bring the war to a definite end and mark their victory. As regards the Western Front, the conditions were simple enough: the German army would make an orderly withdrawal from occupied territory and also from the right and left banks of the Rhine. All other major questions were left to be decided at a future peace conference, but it was clear that Germany was to face a punitive settlement.

Did the Armistice that Germany, now a republic, agreed to on 11 November mark a clear Allied victory? The fact that the Allies took the Rhine ensured that the Germans would not be able to continue the war, but victory would have been more clearly evident if, instead of German troops marching back in good order, Allied troops had paraded down Unter den Linden. The speed of their success had taken Allied commanders by surprise, for most had considered that the German army could hold out until 1919. Some French generals, including Mangin, were against an armistice and favoured invading Germany to emphasise outright victory, but Haig, fearing that the British army would have to take the brunt of a continued war, argued, 'But why expend more British lives – and for what?'[22] For Niall Ferguson the reason there was not a 'true Allied victory' with the Allies penetrating deep into Germany was because 'Haig, Foch and Petain doubted their armies had the strength to do it.'[23]

Whether the German army would have been able to mount a defence of Germany had the Allies refused an armistice is, however, doubtful, as much because of the state of the economy and the internal disarray of Germany as because of the weakened morale of German soldiers. Famously, the sight of the army marching back from foreign soil, gave rise to the 'stab in the back' legend that the army had been undefeated in the field and been betrayed by unrest and the threat of revolution at home. Yet, it was the failure of nerve by Ludendorff and the High Command, their refusal to countenance peace negotiations in the early summer, and the premature decision to request an armistice, which had set in motion the process which ended in the Armistice marking a complete Allied victory.

Chapter 12:   The Peace That did not Bring an End to War

The Armistice was more than a cease-fire, for its terms, together with her internal crisis, made it virtually impossible for Germany to restart the war. Germany's military leaders had prevented peace negotiations while Germany was still in a relatively strong position and then, in panic, had precipitately requested an armistice, the very action that destroyed the fighting spirit of their armies. Germany could not expect a generous peace settlement, and the loss of Alsace-Lorraine seemed inevitable; but President Wilson's notes in October gave some hope that a peace on the basis of his Fourteen Points might not be excessively punitive.

What were the Allies to do with their victory? Other than the pursuit of that goal, the war aims of Britain and France had been developed in the course of the war and were a mixture of the self-interested and the punitive, though the former, whether openly acclaimed or secret, were camouflaged by lofty verbiage about a war for civilization, while Italy and minor allies like Romania had entered the war largely in the hope of territorial gain. Like their enemies, both the remaining Entente powers had found it necessary, while fighting a war which called for mass participation and great sacrifices from their populations, to emphasise the virtues and nobility of their causes and the peculiar wickedness and barbarity of their opponents. This made for some contradictions when it came to the peace settlement for, if the Central Powers and particularly Germany were peculiarly wicked and culpable, then any settlement should be punitive, but, if the victorious powers were so virtuous, then a settlement should create a better, more peaceful world that reflected this virtue.

That victory for the Allies came after Russia's revolutions and withdrawal from the war, after the United States had entered it, and after the disintegration of Austria-Hungary, made a great difference to Allied aims. If the war had ended with a victory early in 1917 for the Allies as they were then constituted, the map of Europe that resulted would probably have been one with the frontiers of Russia extended to the west and an eastward extension at the expense of Turkey, which would have included Russian possession of Constantinople. Germany would have been partially dismembered, with France gaining permanent possession of the Rhineland, as was provided for by a secret treaty between France and Russia in March 1917, and a weakened and federal Austria-Hungary would probably have survived.

With the USA's intervention in the war came disagreement over Allied war aims, as President Woodrow Wilson's basis for peace as expressed in his Fourteen Points was aimed at a 'peace without victory' and set store by objectives such as democracy, transparent diplomacy, national self-determination, and a new world order in which there would be an international framework for peace keeping, a League of Nations. Although his aims have often been viewed as idealistic, Wilson was determined to remould the international order in a way that would register American political, economic and military power.

The Armistice agreements, drawn up by Allied conferences in Paris in October 1918 and attended by an American delegation led by President Wilson's representative, Colonel House, pre-empted many of the decisions made at the Peace Conference the following year. The decision to keep Germany as a unified state and largely intact was implicit in the conclusion of the Armistice at a time when a German state and army were still in being. After this, it was too late to implement any of the plans favoured by the French for the dismemberment of Germany. It was also agreed in Paris that the Brest-Litovsk and Bucharest Treaties should be annulled and German troops withdrawn to the 1914 border. The evacuation of Russian Poland by the Germans gave the Poles the opportunity to merge with Austrian Galicia and thus form an embryonic Polish state. The armistice with Austria took place as the Austro Hungarian Empire was disintegrating. The Serbs, Croats and Slovenes under Austrian rule had declared their independence and were to proclaim their union with Serbia on 1 December, but the emergent new kingdom, which aspired to possession of much of the same previously Austrian territory as Italy, was dealt heavy blows when the Paris Conference provided for the handing over of the ships of the Austro-Hungarian navy to Italy and for Italian troops to occupy land on the Adriatic coast along a line almost identical to that which had been promised to Italy by the 1915 Treaty of London.

Wilson had been against any Allied occupation of Germany but gave way under French pressure, and it was agreed that Allied forces would occupy the left bank of the Rhine and bridgeheads on the right bank. He had also been against a punitive settlement, but by allowing the second point of his fourteen, 'restoration of the invaded territories', to be interpreted by the Allies as 'damage done to the civilian population of the Allies and their property', opened the door to what was to be the most criticised clause of the Versailles Settlement, reparations.

The Armistice agreements clothed harsh conditions in the raiment of Wilsonian morality. It was, 'an ambiguous contract and the European Allies paid lip-service to Wilson's intentions'.[1] Further punishment came with the decision to continue the blockade, which, as the Royal Navy now controlled the Baltic, squeezed the German economy and the living standards of Germans more tightly than ever. As a result, the winter of 1918–19 was a cold and hungry experience for the German population.

When the representatives of the Allied powers gathered in Paris in January 1919, they had the greatest opportunity to create a new and more stable European order since that other conference of victorious allies at the Congress of Vienna at the end of the Napoleonic Wars. Russia and Germany were still extant, but temporarily feeble, and the victorious powers had a brief opportunity, while Russia and Germany were weak, in which to lay the foundations of a stable Europe. They did not use this opportunity wisely.

The central problem was what to do about Germany, still potentially the most powerful state in Europe. A.J.P. Taylor argued that, the decision to grant an armistice to the German government, 'ultimately led to the Second World War'.[2] Taylor's argument is in line with the widely held view that the establishment of a the German Empire in 1871 had fundamentally overturned the pre-existing European balance of power in Europe, and that any unified German state was bound to seek to dominate the continent, a view which was much later to be put forward by a number of German historians, led by Fritz Fischer. Taylor was correct in that the Armistice had made it impossible to pursue the policy advocated during the war by some, mainly French, statesmen of both depriving Germany of territory and dividing it into a number of separate states, thus permanently putting an end to its great power status. An alternative was to accept that the Germany which might develop out of defeat would be democratic and prepared to live in amity with its neighbours and would be assisted in this by a generally lenient settlement which encouraged its early economic recovery. After a long and desperate war in which much of France had been occupied for four years and both Britain and France had suffered enormous losses and considerable hardship, such an alternative was never likely to appeal to the governments or the people of the two Entente partners. As an authority on the Versailles Settlement has written:

> It was a wise precept of Machiavelli that the victor should either conciliate his enemy or destroy him. The Treaty of Versailles did neither. It did not pacify Germany, still less permanently weaken her, appearances notwithstanding, but left her scourged, humiliated and resentful. It was neither a Wilson peace nor a Clemenceau peace, but a witches' brew concocted of the least palatable ingredients of each, which though highly distasteful to Germany, was by no means fatal.[3]

The terms which Germany was, eventually, forced to accept by the Treaty of Versailles seem at first sight harsh enough. The Germans certainly thought so and liberal, though not general, opinion in Britain and America soon began to regret the supposed harshness of the terms. Germany was labelled the guilty party for having caused the war, was forced to pay reparations, and limits were imposed on the size of its armed forces. It also lost territory: Alsace Lorraine was returned to France, a small amount of territory went to Belgium and part of Schleswig went to Denmark; to the east a large tract of territory went to the new Poland, while the Baltic port of Danzig became a 'free city'. The French agreed to German sovereignty continuing over both banks of the Rhine on two conditions; the first was the demilitarisation of German territory west of the Rhine and the continued presence of Allied troops on the west bank and the bridgeheads agreed at the Armistice; the second was a Treaty of Guarantee from the United States and Britain, signed on the same day as the Treaty of Versailles, of military support if Germany attacked France.

Clemenceau, as might have been expected, fought hard to ensure that French demands for future security against any revival of Germany were accepted, even if factions in France led by Foch thought he did not press hard enough. The French position was weakened as the British, determined to demobilise and end conscription as soon as possible, gradually withdrew their support and Lloyd George, so keen to punish Germany at the time of the 1918 British General Election, became more conciliatory. The French could expect little support from Woodrow Wilson, who had crossed the

Atlantic for the conference, and who, although he accepted that Germany bore the main responsibility for the war, was suspicious of British and French aims. Clemenceau, realising the necessity of maintaining British support and not falling out with the Americans, had to modify French demands. In the end, France gained little security and had lost the comfort it had enjoyed before 1917 of an ally to the East. France could depend only on itself. When the Anglo-American guarantee of assistance in the event of an attack by Germany was abandoned by the Americans, Britain made it clear that it would not bind itself to observe the guarantee unilaterally.

The peace settlement as a whole is often referred to as the Versailles Settlement, but the Versailles Treaty with Germany was only one of five treaties, the others being St Germain with Austria, Neuilly with Bulgaria, Trianon with Hungary, and Sèvres with Turkey. These treaties, with the exception of Sèvres, which was stillborn, made for a great change in the map of Europe. Even if the Allies had wished to preserve the Austro-Hungarian Empire, as they had probably wished to do in 1917, it was too late by the beginning of 1919. Not only had the Empire disintegrated but nationalist exiles from the Habsburg domains, aided by liberal academics and journalists, had been effective in gaining support in Western capitals for the replacement of the multi-national empire by national states. Allied statesmen, especially Wilson, were thus sympathetic to the idea at the same time as national groups were setting up councils designed to be blueprints for national states.

Allied statesmen had, however, two other aims which cut across their support for the idea of national self-determination: the desire to punish Germany and her erstwhile allies, and the need to create buffer states on Germany's eastern borders. These three inharmonious guidelines influenced the Treaty of St Germain with Austria, the Treaty of Trianon with Hungary, and the Treaty of Neuilly with Bulgaria, as well as the Treaty of Versailles with Germany. A further complication was the promises made to allies during the war; those made to Italy in the Treaty of London were a particular problem as they reduced flexibility and divided Britain, France and Italy from the Americans when it came to Italy's borders, which the Italian prime minister, Vittorio Orlando, was determined to push outwards at the expense of the new Yugoslavia, as the Kingdom of the Serbs, Croats and Slovenes was to become in 1929.

Never a realistic objective in east-central Europe, where there was a patchwork of nationalities, national self-determination was applied unevenly: the new and much reduced Austria was forbidden to unite with Germany, regardless of the wishes of its German population;

the Sudetenland Germans were incorporated into the new state of Czechoslovakia; and the South Tyrol passed to Italy without a plebiscite. Victors were rewarded and ex-enemies punished, with Hungary suffering harsh treatment in its loss of territory, largely populated by Magyars, to Romania, Czechoslovakia, and Serbia's successor, Yugoslavia. Unlucky Bulgaria, already reduced in size at the end of the Balkan Wars, lost territory to Yugoslavia and Thrace to Greece, while Romania emerged more swollen in size than for its future good. The historian H.A.L. Fisher, a member of the Lloyd George coalition, later defended these territorial provisions, arguing that the new map of Europe was drawn closely in line with the views of populations, but did concede that the treaties had 'left sore places'.[4] He was writing in 1935, just before the soreness became very evident.

The Treaty of Sèvres with Turkey, signed on 10 August 1920, was the last of treaties with the defeated powers to be signed. The entry of the Ottoman Empire into the war had led to a number of secret agreements among the Allies over its long-anticipated dismemberment. The ambitions of Britain and France to gain control of large tracts the Empire's former territories in the Middle East were to be largely satisfied. Largely due to American pressure, it was decided that, rather than become colonies of the Entente powers, the areas which Britain and France had agreed to control by their secret Sykes–Picot agreement should become mandated territories, which was meant to ensure that autonomous national development would take place under great-power supervision. Syria became a French mandate, Palestine and Mesopotamia British mandates and the Arabian peninsula became an independent Arab state. Britain and France had clashed as to control over Syria. Britain had the troops on the ground and had set up an administration under the Hashemite prince, Faisal, but Lloyd George, fearing the damage to Anglo-French relations, gave way and Syria and Lebanon became French protectorates, while Faisal was compensated with the new Kingdom of Iraq.

The situation in the Turkish heartlands was very different. The provisions of Sèvres would have led to a small and weak Turkish state which would have lost its Armenian provinces to an independent Armenia; eastern Thrace would have gone to Greece, and the Greeks were also to administer Smyrna and surrounding eastern Anatolia. Even what remained of Turkey was to be subject to a commission composed of British, French and Italian representatives. The treaty was signed by the government of the Sultan but even before this a resurgent Turkish national movement led by Mustafa Kemal (Atatürk) was challenging his authority. Kemal, by a combination of successful generalship and skilful diplomacy, was able to overturn the least acceptable features of Sèvres. Armenian independence and a Greek invasion were smashed by force of arms, and a succession of treaties with the Soviet Union, Italy and France isolated Britain, which remained the only upholder of Sèvres. The Treaty of Lausanne of July 1923 revised Sèvres in Turkey's favour and was to outlast all the other post-war settlements.

The provisions of the Versailles Peace Settlement did not extend to the greater part of eastern Europe. The Allies did not recognise the Bolshevik regime in Russia and were engaged in trying to destroy it. So far as eastern Europe was concerned, the post-war map of Europe was decided, not by diplomats in morning suits, but by a series of wars which were as confused and complex as they were bloody. The consecutive defeats of Russia and Germany meant that not only did Finland and the Baltic states win their independence by force of arms, but that Poland gained a vast increase in her eastern frontiers after her war with Russia in 1919–21. It was the simultaneous weakness of Germany and the Soviet Union that allowed these states to establish their inter-war positions, but neither Germany nor the Soviet Union were content with the new status quo. The afterglow of Brest-Litovsk fascinated German politicians and the Soviet Union was not reconciled to the loss of territory. There was always the danger that the pariah powers might get together to reorder Eastern Europe once more.

The Versailles settlement has found few admirers. The failure of the United States Congress to ratify the Treaty of Versailles dealt both the treaty and the League of Nations, whose foundation it provided for, immediate and powerful blows. The settlement has been seen as at best marking a lengthy armistice between two world wars or between the first and second stages of one long European war. Yet, it is possible to argue, as does David Stevenson, that the settlement with Germany was 'more flexible than its critics acknowledged and could either have accommodated a lasting reconciliation with the new republican regime in Germany or ensured that it remained militarily harmless'; that it did neither, he suggests, was due, fundamentally, to the disunity of the Allies.[5]

Conclusion: The War in European Memory

Interpretations of the causes of the war, its course and consequences had begun even before the war had ended and such interpretations, together with attitudes towards the conflict, have inevitably changed as perspectives have altered with time.

At the war's end, the desire to grieve for and remember the dead or the 'fallen', which was a more frequently used word, was, after relief that the war was over, the main reaction among victors and defeated alike. One result was a massive exercise in the reification of the sacrifice as memorials to the war-dead were erected, ranging from Lutyens' magnificent Cenotaph in Whitehall to war memorials, some 54,000 of them, all over Britain in every city, town and village. Throughout the British Empire, dominions, colonies and the Indian Empire erected their own memorials. The French also erected great national and small village memorials, while the Germans built a massive monument to their 1914 victory at Tannenberg. Memorials were no innovation, but the scale of their building was. What was new was the desire to bury each of the dead in his own grave, as far as possible. Such a desire was common to all of the countries which had fought in the war, but fulfilment of the wish was often not possible for many soldiers had already been buried in mass graves or lay where they had fallen. The great ossiaries at Douaumont, near Verdun, and at Caporetto contain thousands of anonymous corpses (identification tags were not usually worn by soldiers) and German soldiers had also been buried singly or in numbers in graves on French or Belgian territory or in the vast spaces fought over on the Eastern Front. Those who could not be identified were represented by the symbolic 'Unknown Soldier' (in France the 'Unknown Warrior'). The work of the Imperial War Graves Commission began before the war ended and its task of finding the dead and burying them has not yet finished.

The war has been seen by many historians as having created a cultural divide between pre- and post-war society, but, as Jay Winter has argued in respect of nearly all the memorials, not just the great memorials such as the Cenotaph and at Thiepval on the Somme, the architectural language of mourning was usually traditional. He challenges the view that an effect of the war was to bring about the triumph of modernism in the arts and culture and, with specific reference to mourning and remembrance, argues that, 'the strength of what may be termed 'traditional forms, in art, poetry and ritual, lay in their power to mediate bereavement'.[6] Indeed, when not informed by the traditional in high art, mourning was often expressed in older manifestations of popular culture, the shrines in streets which came during the war to mark the deaths of those who had lived there or, in Germany, the revival of the mediaeval tradition of *Nagelfiguren* (figure of nails) as a way of honouring the dead. Modernism was good at expressing anger, dislocation and despair, but traditional modes, 'provided a way of remembering which enabled the bereaved to live with their losses and perhaps to leave them behind'.

The attitudes to the war of those in the victorious states and those in the defeated were, nevertheless, despite a common grief and need to mourn, very different. Sacrifice can be justified by victory, but is made bitter by defeat. Until the autumn of 1918, the bulk of the German population had believed that victory was in sight; when defeat quickly followed, acquiescence was not the universal reaction. Any confidence the statesmen at Versailles may have had that the new Germany of the Weimar Republic would consider that Germany had been the aggressor and its defeat the just consequence of aggression were to be confounded. It is often forgotten that, if it was Adolf Hitler's methods of overturning Versailles that led to World War II, his aims were shared by almost all German political leaders in the 1920s and early 30s. If Germany could not celebrate victory, it could celebrate *a* victory and Tannenberg became the focus for patriots, while the ancient and modern came together with the great wooden statue of Hindenburg into which admirers hammered nails.

The perspective from post-1945 was different, in that the First World War viewed from across the Second was distanced and seemed less relevant. Popular attitudes were, however, little changed: Germans could, in contrast to the Second World War, still defend Germany's role in the First; British and French attitudes were also largely unchanged, perhaps confirmed by experience of another war with Germany.

It was during the 1960s that significant changes in attitudes took place. A number of German historians came to attribute blame for the war upon Germany, while conversely Alan Clark's book *The Donkeys* (1961) encouraged in Britain a general denigration, not just of British generals but of patriotic accounts of World War 1. Franco-German rapprochement and a leading partnership in the developing European Union resulted in efforts by governments to mellow the memories and attitudes of their countrymen. A more general change was the emergence of a European generation which had never known war and for whom patriotism was for football matches. This was henceforward to make it difficult for many to comprehend national cohesion and the determination of men to continue to fight under appalling conditions. Fascination with an increasingly distant war continued, however, to grow: tours of battlefields became ever more popular, military histories found widening readerships, and what had been Armistice Day and was now Remembrance Day experienced a revival.

The centenary of the outbreak of the war and the ways in which it was commemorated provide, therefore, an interesting test of attitudes and understanding of the war. France spent some 60 million euros on events, but the approach of President Hollande gave out mixed messages, The war, he has said, showed 'the strength of a nation when it stands together' and France's war demonstrated French and Republican values, yet Bastille Day in 2014 should, he said, 'be, above all a demonstration for peace'. The President of Germany was invited, somewhat bizarrely, to the commemoration of Germany's declaration of war on France on 3 July 1914. Soviet Russia had never made much of what to it was an imperialist war, nor has Putin's Russia great plans for commemorating its beginning or the great battles which followed. In Germany, Angela Merkel had no commemoration events in her diary and German comment concentrated on the way the war on the Eastern Front was ignored. The USA, which has a Centennial Commission, was, naturally, biding its time for April 1917. This left Britain and the ex-Dominions, with the latter commemorating the hundred anniversary of the beginning of the war and making plans for the anniversaries of many of the greatest battles, in so many of which Canadian, South African, Australian and New Zealand and Indian forces played a prominent part. It was in Britain, however, that, as the centenary of the summer crisis of 1914 approached, a war for the memory of the conflict began among historians, journalists and politicians.

Should the eventual victory of Britain and her allies be celebrated? Or was a war which had seen Europe torn apart and had cost the Allies and their enemies some ten million soldiers, overwhelmingly young men, killed, not a suitable subject for patriotic satisfaction? Should it rather be commemorated with ecumenical regret? Controversy arose over the causes of the war, the reasons for British involvement, the justice of the Allied cause, and the quality of the nation's wartime political and military leadership.

Historians duelled in print and on television, with Max Hastings[7] insisting that Britain was correct to go to war to prevent an arrogant and autocratic Germany dominating Europe and Niall Ferguson rebutting him with the view that the worst that could have resulted from a German victory over France and Russia was a German dominated European common market. The then Education Secretary, Michael Gove, widened the argument when he criticised the way the history of the war was taught in schools, thus incurring the wrath of schoolteachers, *The Guardian* newspaper and Regius Professor Sir Richard Evans.

It seemed apparent that, in Britain at any rate, the anniversary of the beginning of the war would not be the end of verbal and literary conflict and that, for the next four years, not only would the media examine, commemorate or bewail as, one after another, the centenaries of the campaigns and battles of the war succeeded each other, but that historians and commentators were going to fight their own long war, a war for its place in history.

Notes

Chapter 1: Why Did It Begin?

1. See Michael Howard, 'A Thirty Years War? The Two World Wars in Historical Perspective', *Transactions of the Royal Historical Society*, 6th series (1993), Vol. 3, pp. 171–184.
2. A.J.P.Taylor, *The Struggle for Mastery in Europe 1848–1918* (1954), p. xix.
3. Taylor, p. 319.
4. David Stevenson, *The First World War and International Politics* (1988), p. 6.
5. Gordon Martel, *The Origins of the First World War* (1996), pp. 18–19.
6. Fritz Fischer, *Germany's War Aims in the First World War* (1967) and Imanuel Geiss, *German Foreign Policy, 1871–1914* (1976).
7. John Charmley, *Splendid Isolation? Britain and the Balance of Power 1874–1914* (1999), p. 250.
8. Norman Stone, *World War I: A Short History* (2007), p. 9.
9. Christopher Clark, *The Sleepwalkers: How Europe Went to War in 1914* (2013), pp. 153–9.
10. Charmley, p. 311.
11. Martel, p. 67.
12. William Mulligan, *The Origins of the First World War* (2010), p. 51.
13. Charmley, p. 223.
14. Samuel R. Williamson Jr, 'The Origins of the War', in Arthur Marwick, Clive Emsley and Wendy Simpson (eds.), *Total War and Historical change: Europe 1914–1955* (2001), p. 73.
15. Benedict Anderson, *Imagined Communities* (1991).
16. Norman Angell, *The Great Illusion* (1910).
17. Viscount Grey of Falloden, *Twenty-Five Years, 1892–1916*, vol 1 (1925), p. 89.
18. Annika Mombauer, *Helmuth von Moltke and the Origins of the First World War* (2001).
19. Mulligan, p. 122.

20. Clark, *Sleepwalkers*, p. 191.
21. H. J. Mackinder, *The Geographical Journal*, (April 1904), Vol. 23, No. 4 (pp. 421–437).
22. See Paul Kennedy, *Strategy and Diplomacy* (1983), Chapter 2, 'Mahan versus Mackinder'.
23. Mombauer, p. 103.
24. Terence Zuber, *The Real German War Plan 1904–14* (2011).
25. John Keegan, *The First World War* (1998), p. 39.
26. Margaret MacMillan, *The War that Ended Peace* (2013) p. 347.
27. Mombauer, p. 216.
28. David Stevenson, *Armaments and the Coming of War* (1996); David Hermann, *The Arming of Europe and the Making of the First World War* (1996).
29. Clark, *Sleepwalkers*.
30. See Sean McMeekin, *The Russian Origins of the First World War* (2011).
31. Taylor, p. 258.
32. Clark, *Sleepwalkers*.
33. Sean McMeekin, *The Russian Origins of the First world War* (2011).
34. Samuel R. Williamson Jr, *Austria-Hungary and the Origins of the First World War* (1991).

Chapter 2:   How It Began

1. For an assessment of Princip see Tim Butcher, *The Trigger: Unveiling the Legend of the Assassin who led the World to War* (2014).
2. David Fromkin, *Europe's Last Summer* (2004), p. 155.
3. John Keegan, *The First World War* (1998), p. 59.
4. Samuel R. Williamson Jr, *Austria-Hungary and the Origins of the First World War* (1991), p. 197.
5. Margaret MacMillan, *The War That Ended Peace* (2013), p. 331.
6. Annika Mombauer and Wilhelm Deist (eds.), *The Kaiser, New Research on William II's Role in Imperial Germany* (2003), p. 199.
7. Fritz Fischer, *Germany's Aims in the First World War* (English-language edition, 1967).
8. A strong case for this argument is made by Annika Mombauer, *von Moltke and the Origins of the First World War*.
9. Fromkin, p. 91.
10. Quoted in Mombauer and Deist, p. 198.
11. Sean McMeekin, *The Russian Origins of the First World War* (2011).
12. Sean McMeekin, *July 1914. Countdown to War* (2013), p. 142.
13. *Ibid.* p. 144.
14. Annika Mombauer, *Helmuth von Moltke and the Origins of the First World War* (2001) p. 215.
15. Clark, p. 466.
16. Clark, p. 484.

17. McKeekin, *Russian Origins*.
18. Fritz Fellner, 'Austria-Hungary', in Keith Wilson (ed.), *Decisions for War* (1995), p. 22.
19. McMeekin, *July 1914*, p. 227.
20. *Ibid.*, p. 242.
21. Imanuel Geiss, 'The outbreak of the First World War and German war aims', *Journal of Contemporary History* (1966), vol. 1, No. 3, pp. 75–91.
22. Annika Mombauer, *Total War and Social Change: Europe 1914–1955*, Book 4 of Open University course AA312 (2000), p. 167.
23. MacMillan, p. 592.
24. A variation on the philosophic fallacy, 'Morton's fork'.
25. John Charmley, *Splendid Isolation? Britain and the Balance of Power 1874–1914* (1999), pp. 347–8.
26. Fromkin, p. 31.
27. Niall Ferguson, *The Pity of War* (1999), pp. 64–5.
28. Beaverbrook, *Politicians and War 1914–1916* (1932), pp. 22–3.
29. Keith Wilson, 'Britain', in Keith Wilson (ed.), *Decisions for War* (1995).
30. Kenneth O. Morgan, *Lloyd George* (1974), p. 81.
31. Travis L. Crosby, *The Unknown Lloyd George* (2014), p. 174.
32. *Ibid.*, p. 23.
33. Ferguson, p. 163.
34. Ben Macintyre, 'One Last battle over how we mark the First World War', *The Times*, 27 April 2013.
35. Ferguson, pp. 168–73.
36. Charmley, *Splendid Isolation*.
37. Paul Kennedy, *The Rise and Fall of the Great Powers* (1998).
38. Clark, *Sleepwalkers*, p. 546.
39. *Ibid.*, p. 546.
40. *Ibid.*, p. 547.
41. McMeekin, *Russian Origins*, pp. 122–3.

Chapter 3:   War Fever?

1. Barbara Tuchman, *The Proud Tower: A Portrait of the World before the War, 1890–1914* (1966), p. xiv.
2. Arno J. Meyer, *The Persistence of the old Regime* (1981) p. 304.
3. Modris Eksteins, *Rites of Spring: The Great War and the Birth of the Modern Age* (1989), p. 82.
4. Niall Ferguson, 'Germany and the Origins of the First World War: New Perspectives', *Historical Journal* (1992), vol. 35, p. 741.
5. Tuchman, p. 343.
6. David Fromkin, *Europe's Last Summer* (2004), p. 40.
7. Michael Neiberg, *Dance of the Furies. Europe and the Outbreak of World War1* (2011).

8. See, for instance, J.J. Becker, *The Great War and the French people* (1983).
9. Niall Ferguson, *The Pity of War* (1999), p. 105.
10. Catriona Pennell, *A Kingdom United: Popular Responses to the Outbreak of the First World War* (2012).
11. Neiberg, p. 119.

Chapter 4:   Elusive Victory

1. Britain had, of course plans for the disposition of the Royal Navy in the event of a war, and the CID had made arrangements for an Expeditionary Force which could be used in France, but such arrangements could not be seen as comparable to the plans made for war with identified potential enemies by the continental powers.
2. Annika Mombauer, *Helmuth von Moltke and the Origins of the First World War* (2001), pp. 101–2.
3. The development of the lorry was, as yet, not very advanced and those that the armies of 1914 possessed were not reliable. The Germans had some 4,000 lorries available for their offensive in France but two-thirds of them broke down during the advance.
4. David Stevenson, *1914–1918: The history of the First World War* (2004), p. 54.
5. Stevenson, p. 55.
6. Norman Stone, *World War I: A Short History* (2007), p. 37.
7. Hew Strachan, *The First World War: A New Illustrated History* (2003), p. 57.
8. Stevenson, p. 58.
9. Hew Strachan, *The First World War*, vol. 1 *To Arms* (2001), p. 261.
10. There has been debate as to whether the idea of the loss of these 'innocents', often portrayed as young students, was not, at least partly, a patriotic myth (the 'Langemarck Myth'). Certainly the percentage of *young* Germans killed was exaggerated and there was much retrospective embroidering.
11. See Gordon A. Craig, 'The World war 1 Alliance of the Central Powers in Retrospect; The Military Cohesion of the Alliance' (1965), *Journal of Modern History*, vol. 37, pp. 336–344.
12. Stevenson, p. 66.
13. See John Keegan, *The First World War* (1998), p. 162.
14. Hew Strachan, *To Arms*, p. 334.
15. Archduke Friedrich was the nominal commander but in practice it was Conrad who made the decisions.
16. Basil Liddell Hart, *The History of the Great War* (1930), p. 147.
17. Norman Stone, *The Eastern Front, 1914–17* (1973), p. 80.
18. Stevenson, p. 71.
19. Stone, *Eastern Front*, p. 44.
20. Keegan, p. 179.
21. Keegan, pp. 27–80.

22. J.M. Roberts *Europe 1880–1945* (3rd edn, 2000), p. 283.
23. Robert Massie, *Castles of Steel: Britain Germany and the Winning of the Great War at Sea* (2003), p. 418.
24. See Massie, p. 217.
25. The *Emden*'s Captain Karl von Müller was lionised by the British, almost as much as the German, press for his daring exploits.
26. Strachan, *To Arms*, p. 75.
27. Stevenson, p. 130.
28. Strachan, p. 148.

Chapter 5:   The Widened War

1. Zouave regiments were mainly composed of conscripts from French settlers in Algeria and Tunisia; Spahis were cavalry regiments recruited from the indigenous populations of Algeria, Morocco and Tunisia.
2. John Keegan, *The First World War* (1998), p. 229.
3. See p. **73**.
4. Edward Paice, *Tip and Run: The Untold Tragedy of the First World War in Africa* (2007).
5. Hew Strachan, *The First World War*, vol. 1 *To Arms* (2001), p. 67.
6. Battleships being built for Chile and Brazil were taken over by the Royal Navy at the same time.
7. See U. Trumpener, *Germany and the Ottoman Empire 1914–1918* (1968).
8. Sean McMeekin, *The Russian Origins of the First World War* (2011), p. 110.
9. McMeekin, p. 114.
10. Strachan, p. 137.
11. Christopher Clark, *The Sleepwalkers: How Europe Went to War in 1914* (2013), p. 348.
12. McMeekin, *Russian Origins*, p. 120.
13. *Ibid.*, p. 125.
14. The number of French casualties is often forgotten, but as many as 47,000 were killed or wounded, as compared to 43,000 British of whom about a quarter were Australian or New Zealand troops.
15. Strachan, p. 110.
16. Strachan, p. 154.

Chapter 6:   Home Fronts and the Test of War

1. Ferguson, p. 148.
2. Catriona Pennell, *A Kingdom United. Popular Responses to the Outbreak of the First World War* (2012).
3. Niall Ferguson, *The Pity of War* (1999), p. 199.

4. Gerard J. De Groot, 'The First World War as Total War', in Martin Pugh (ed.), *A Companion to Modern European History'* (1997), p. 266.
5. A measurement of ground and air munitions.
6. J.M. Winter, *The Great War and the British People* (1985).
7. Ferguson, p. 257.
8. Norman Stone, *World War I: A Short History* (2007), p. 35.
9. See David Runciman, *The Confidence Trap. A History of Democracy in Crisis from World War 1 to the Present* (2013).
10. See R. Knight, *Britain Against Napoleon: The Organisation of Victory 1793–1815* (2013).
11. Figures taken from Ferguson, p. 321.
12. K. Burke, *Britain, America and the Sinews of War, 1914–19* (1985) p. 64.
13. Rod Kedward, *La Vie En Bleu* (2007), pp. 79–82.
14. Ferguson, p. 275.
15. See Christopher Cappozzola, *Uncle Sam Wants You. World War 1 and the Making of the Modern American Citizen* (2008).
16. See A. Marwick, *The Deluge: British Society in the First World War* (1965) and Stefan Andreski, *Military Organisations and Society* (1968).
17. G.R. Searle, *A New England: Peace and War 1886–1918* (2004), p. 794.
18. Corporal W.H. Shaw, quoted in Lyn MacDonald, *1914–18:Voices and Images of the Great War* (1988), p. 217.
19. Jerry White, *Zeppelin Nights: London in the First World War* (2014), p. 48.
20. Kedward, p. 66.
21. White, *Zeppelin Nights*.
22. Rosie Kennedy, *The Children's War: Britain 1914–15* (2013).
23. David Monger, *Patriotism and Propaganda in First World War Britain: the National War Aims Committee and Civilian Morale* (2012).
24. Ferguson, p. 222.
25. Hilary Roberts, 'Photography in the Great War', in Mark Hoborn and Hilary Roberts (eds.), *The Great War* (2013).
26. Peter Jelavich, 'German culture in the Great War', in A. Roshwald and R. Stites (eds.), *European Culture in the Great War: The Arts, Entertainment and Propaganda 1914–1918* (1989), p. 42.

Chapter 7:   The Problems of the Offensive

1. Niall Ferguson, *The Pity of War* (1999), Chapter 9.
2. David Stevenson, *1914–1918: The history of the First World War* (2004), p. 154.
3. David French, 'The meaning of attrition, 1914–1916', *The English Historical Review* (1988), vol CIII, No. 407, pp. 385–405.
4. Quoted in Hew Strachan, *The First World War*, vol. 1 *To Arms* (2001), p. 174.
5. John Keegan, *The First World War* (1998), p. 213.
6. Keegan, p. 310.

7. Richard Holmes, *The Little Field Marshal: A Life of Sir John French* (1981), p. 307.
8. Strachan, p. 140.

Chapter 8:   1916, The Killing Fields

1. Hew Strachan, *The First World War*, vol. 1 *To Arms* (2001), p. 160.
2. Emily Mayhew, *Wounded: From Battlefield to Blighty* (2013).
3. Niall Ferguson, *The Pity of War* (1999), pp. 295–6.
4. John Keegan, *The First World War* (1998), pp. 297–8.
5. See Keegan, pp. 299–300. The authenticity of this 'Christmas Memorial' document has, according to David Stevenson, *1914–18*, p. 162, been challenged. It may have been fabricated by von Falkenhayn himself.
6. Keegan, p. 300.
7. Strachan, pp. 182–3.
8. Stevenson, p. 163.
9. Anthony Clayton, *Paths of Glory: The French Army 1914–18* (2003), p. 120.
10. Norman Stone, *The Eastern Front, 1914–17* (1973), p. 231.
11. John Terraine, *Douglas Haig: The Educated Soldier* (1963), p. 182.
12. Saul David, *100 Days To Victory: How the Great War Was Fought And Won* (2013), p. 256.
13. Mayhew, p. 262.
14. Stevenson, p. 171.
15. Keegan, pp. 315–16.
16. Ferguson, p. 294.
17. Robert Blake (ed.), *The Private Papers of Douglas Haig 1914–19* (1952), p. 154.
18. Terraine, p. 230.
19. Ferguson, p. 293.
20. Stevenson, p. 171.
21. The Germans in general were slow to realise the implications of the internal combustion engine for warfare. Not only were they late in realising the possibilities of the tank, but they lagged behind the French and British in the production of lorries and military vehicles.

Chapter 9:   1917, Germany's Victory in the East

1. David Stevenson, *1914–1918: The history of the First World War* (2004), p. 263.
2. Stevenson, p. 173.
3. This is particularly true in the case of Canada, whose troops made an enormous contribution to British Empire forces in battle after battle, a contribution which is too little recognised in popular memories of the war in Britain.

4. The role of the 'tunnellers' mainly miners turned soldiers, has only recently been recognised. Sebastian Faulks's novel *Birdsong* (1993) drew attention to their important work of tunnelling under the enemy lines and planting explosives.
5. John Keegan, *The First World War* (1998), p. 352.
6. See Saul David, *100 Days to Victory: How the Great War Was Fought And Won*, pp. 327–31, and Keegan, pp. 355–7.
7. Michael Florinsky, *The End of the Russian Empire* (1931).
8. Bernard Waites , Unit 8, 'The Nature of the First World War', in *Total War and Social Change 1914–1955* (Open University course AA312), p. 19.
9. Desmond Young, *Rommel* (1973), p. 37.
10. Hew Strachan, *The First World War*, vol. 1 *To Arms* (2001), p. 250.
11. For an account of the telegram's interception, see Taylor Downing, *Secret Warriors: Key Scientists, Code-Breakers and Propagandists of the Great War* (2014), pp. 139–146.
12. Norman Stone, *World War I: A Short History* (2007), p. 113.

Chapter 10:   The War at Sea

1. David Stevenson, *1914–1918: The history of the First World War* (2004), p. 252.
2. John Keegan, *The First World War* (1998), p. 282.
3. Robert K. Massie, *Castles of Steel: Britain Germany and the Winning of the Great War at Sea* (2003), p. 669.
4. Quoted in Niall Ferguson, *The Pity of War* (1999), p. 284.
5. G.R. Searle, *A New England. Peace and War, 1886–1918*, (2004), p. 708.
6. David Stevenson, *With Our Backs to the Wall: Victory and Defeat in 1918* (2011), p. 315.
7. *Ibid.*, pp. 314–5.
8. *Ibid.*, pp. 222–3.
9. Hew Strachan, *The First World War*, vol. 1 *To Arms* (2001), p. 223.
10. Massie, p. 738.

Chapter 11:   The Final Struggle

1. David Stevenson, *With Our Backs to the Wall. Victory and defeat in 1918* (2011), p. **30**.
2. Norman Stone, *World War I: A Short History* (2007), p. 5.
3. Quoted in Niall Ferguson, *The Pity of War* (1999), p. 316.
4. Niall Ferguson, 'Germany and the Origins of the First World War: New Perspectives', *Historical Journal* (1992), vol. 35.3, p. 744.
5. The Germans suffered comparable casualties but had done disproportionate damage to the smaller army.

6. The Portuguese had entered the war largely in the hope of gaining support for the maintenance of the their empire in Africa.

7. John Terraine, *Douglas Haig: The Educated Soldier* (1963), pp. 424–5.

8. Stone, p. 136.

9. Dennis Winter, *Haig's Command. A Reassessment*, (2001).

10. For a discussion of the Maurice Debate, see Travis L. Crosby, *The Unkown Lloyd George* (2014), pp. 231–2.

11. David Stevenson, *1914–1918: The History of the First World War* (2004), p. 411.

12. Stevenson, *Backs to the Wall*, quoting General Albrecht von Thaer, p. 416.

13. Travis L. Crosby, *The Unknown Lloyd George* (2014), p. 233.

14. Stevenson, *Backs to the Wall*, p. 84.

15. Ferguson, p. 288.

16. M. Kitchen, *The Silent Dictatorship: The Politics of the German High Command under Hindenburg and Ludendorff* (1976).

17. See Ferguson for casualty figures, pp. 294–7.

18. Peter Hart, *1918: A Very British Victory* (2008).

19. John Keegan, *The First World War* (1998), p. 442.

20. Ferguson, p. 314.

21. Isobel V. Hull, 'The End of the Monarchy', in Annika Mombauer and Wilhelm Deist (eds.), *The Kaiser: New Research on Wilhelm II's Role in Imperial Germany* (2003), p. 245.

22. Hew Strachan, *The First World War*, vol. 1 *To Arms* (2001), p. 321.

23. Ferguson, p. 314.

Chapter 12: The Peace That did not Bring an End to War

1. David Stevenson, *The First World War and International Politics*, (1988), p. 235.

2. A.J.P. Taylor, *The Origins of the Second World War* (1961).

3. A. Lentin, *Lloyd George, Woodrow Wilson and the Guilt of Germany* (1985), p. 132.

4. H.A.L. Fisher, *A History of Europe*, vol. III (1936), p. 1169.

5. David Stevenson, *1914–1918: The History of the First World War* (2004), p. 506.

6. Jay Winter, *Sites of Memory, Sites of Mourning. The Great War in European Cultural History* (1995), p. 5.

7. Author of *Catastrophe: Europe Goes to War 1914* (2013).

Further Reading

The literature on the First World war is vast. The following list is a select guide to further reading in published secondary sources in English rather than a comprehensive bibliography.

General Histories of the war

David Stevenson, *1914–1918: The History of the First World War* (2004), is a fine and comprehensive account of all aspects of the war. Hew Strachan, *The First World War* (2006), is one of the best short histories and is accessible and masterful in its explanations of complex developments, while Norman Stone, *World War I: A Short History* (2007), provides a broad, often witty and always insightful, sweep through the war's history. Niall Ferguson, *The Pity of War* (1999), is not a narrative but, is an analysis of major debates, and is particularly strong on the economic dimension of the war, it challenges many established views.

War Atlases

The Palgrave Concise Historical Atlas of the First World War (2005) by William Philpott, the maps in Norman Lowe's *Mastering Modern World History* (2013) and *Atlas of the First World War* (1970, 2nd edn 1994) by Martin Gilbert, are valuable guides to the course of the war and help understanding of its campaigns and battles.

Origins and causes of the war

William Mulligan, *The Origins of the First World War* (2010) and Gordon Martel *The Origins of the First World War* (1987) provide perceptive guides and an introduction to the debates and literature. A.J.P. Taylor's *The*

Struggle For Mastery In Europe 1848–1918 (1954) remains essential reading for an understanding of the diplomatic history of the late nineteenth and early twentieth century. Among recent studies of the causes of the war are: Christopher Clark, *The Sleepwalkers: How Europe Went To War in 1914* (2013); David Fromkin, *Europe's Last Summer: Why the World Went to War in 1914* (2004); Max Hastings, *Catastrophe: Europe Goes To War,1914* (2013), argues that Britain had little choice but to go to war in the face of German expansionism, while Sean McMeekin, *July 1914: Countdown to War* (2013) lays much of the blame on Russia. Margaret MacMillan, *The War That Ended Peace: How Europe Abandoned Peace For the First World War* (2013) is a wide-ranging account of the drift towards war. S.R. Williamson, *Austria Hungary and the Origins of the First World War* (1991) provides a good account of the often neglected role of Austria-Hungary, and Fritz Fischer, *Germany's Aims in the First World War* (1967) remains highly influential. Fischer's arguments for German responsibility are powerfully reinforced by Annika Mombauer in *Helmuth von Moltke and the Origins of the First World War* (2001).

Military Histories

John Keegan, *The First World War* (1998) manages in a single volume to give a clear description of main campaigns and succeeds in the difficult task of making complex battles understandable. Saul David, *100 Days to Victory: How the Great War was Fought and Won* (2013) provides very useful succinct and informed accounts of the major battles of the war.

Other valuable military studies are:

Hart, Peter, *1918: A Very British Victory* (2008)
Holmes, Richard, *The Little Field Marshal: A Life of Sir John French* (1981)
Horne, Alastair, *The Price of Glory: Verdun 1916* (1978)
Lloyd, Nick, *Hundred Days: The End of the Great War* (2013)
Massie, Robert. K, *Castles of Steel. Britain, Germany and the Winning of the Great War at Sea* (2003)
Philpott, William, *Attrition: Fighting the First World War* (2014)
Stone, Norman, *The Eastern Front, 1914–1917* (1975)
Terraine, John, *Douglas Haig: The Educated Soldier* (1963).

Peacemaking

Excellent books on the Versailles Settlement are, A. Lentin, *The Versailles Peace settlement* (2003) and Alan Sharp, *The Versailles settlement: Peacemaking after the First world War 1919–23* (2008). David Stevenson's *The First World*

War and International Politics (1988) puts Versailles into the wider context of diplomatic history of the war, and Margaret MacMillan's *Peacemakers: The Paris Conference of 1919 and its Attempt to End the War* (2002) is an enjoyable study of the machinations and decisions of the diplomats at Versailles.

Other Further Reading

For European society and culture in 1914 see, Michael Neiberg, *Dance of the Furies: Europe and the Outbreak of World War 1* (2011); Barbara Tuchman, *The Proud Tower: A Portrait of the World Before the War 1890–1914* (1966); Modris Eksteins, *Rites of Spring: The Great War and the Birth of the Modern Age* (1989).

For the effects of the war *on* Britain, Jeremy Paxman, *Great Britain's Great War* (2013) is eminently readable and well-researched, while the impact of the war on London is described by Jerry White in *Zeppelin Nights: London in the First World War* (2014). The first chapters of Rod Kenward's, *La Vie en Bleu: France and the French since 1900* (2005) describe the war's effects on French society.

Martin Kitchen, *The Silent Dictatorship: The Politics of the German High Command under Hindenburg and Ludendorff* (1976), suggests that under the impact of war the German High Command eschewed conservative monarchism and turned to militarised, nationalist autocracy. *A People's Tragedy* (1997), by Orlando Figes, deals with that other great consequence of the war, the Bolshevik Revolution and its aftermath.

The reactions of post-war European societies to the death toll of the war are described by Jay Winter, Sites of Memory, *Sites of Mourning: The Great War in European Cultural History* (1995).

Index

Franco-Prussian War, 5, 6
French, Field Marshal Sir John, 56–7, 120–2
Franz Ferdinand, Archduke, 27–31, 36, 44
Franz Josef, Emperor, 33, 46, 143, 157
Fromkin, David (historian), 44, 48

Gallipoli, 90–4, 119, 159
Gaza, battles of, 159, 185
Geiss, Imanuel (historian), 35
George V, King, 46, 111, 122
Germany
    armistice and Versailles settlement, 187-94, 195, 197
    army, 19, 54–5, 67, 100–101, 135, 175,179–80, 186–9
    blockade and submarine warfare, 69, 71, 77, 118, 157, 165, 169, 171–6, 169
    defeat, 181–2, 183–7
    foreign policy, 6, 7–14, 53
    memory of war, 61, 197–9
    military strategy, 8, 12, 19–20, 58, 62, 68, 116–17, 141–3, 174–181, 182–3
    navy, 70–75, 160–72
    SPD (Social Democratic Party), 30, 44, 50, 114, 187, 189
Gough, General Sir Hubert, 155, 177
Grey, Sir Edward, 2, 13, 16, 33, 36–41, 80, 86
Greece, 3, 24–5, 43, 87, 89–90, 92–5, 154, 196

Haig, Field Marshal Sir Douglas, 120–24, 133–6, 138, 141, 144–5, 153–6, 158, 178–9, 184, 186–7, 189
Haldane, Richard, 39
Hamilton, General Sir Ian, 90
Hankey, Lt Colonel Maurice, 170, 180
Hindenburg, Field Marshal Paul von, 64, 65, 67–8, 79, 102, 114, 117, 120, 123–4, 130, 136, 142, 158, 168, 174–6, 180–83, 186, 199,
Holland, 19, 111, 189
home fronts, 97–114, 137–8
    economies and production, 13, 14-15, 44–5, 50, 53, 97–106, 116, 157, 171, 175–6, 182
    industrial relations, 44, 48, 104–5, 108, 109, 151,

morale, 77, 111–13
propaganda, 34–5, 111–12
Hoyos, Count, 29, 33

imperialism, 14, 18
Indian Empire, 81, 83, 88, 145, 185, 198
Ireland, 36, 48, 72, 134
Isonzo, battles of, 121, 125, 130, 150, 153
Izvolski, Alexander, 17, 23
Italy, 43, 47, 84, 92-3, 97, 99, 111, 121, 143, 150-51, 157, 169, 184
    during war, 97, 99, 111, 121, 127, 130, 144, 150-51, 153, 157, 173, 184
    entry into war, 43, 53, 79, 90, 92-3
    foreign policy, 6-7, 8, 24, 25, 38, 53, 84, 90, 95, 195, 197
    war aims and gains, 79, 92-3, 95, 187, 191, 192, 195-6

Japan, 10–11, 80, 171
    Anglo-Japanese Alliance (1902), 11, 41, 80
    Russo-Japanese War (1905), 11, 18, 21, 52, 95, 147
Jellicoe, Admiral Sir John,74, 153, 160–6, 170
Jutland, battle of, 69–70, 125, 137, 162–5
Joffre, General Joseph, 20, 55–6, 58, 60, 118, 120, 129, 131, 133, 141

Karl I, Emperor, 143, 158, 184
Kemal, Mustapha, 90, 196
Kennedy, Paul (historian), 41
Kitchener, Lord, 52, 57, 100, 106, 108, 119, 122, 124, 127, 134, 138
Konigsberg, 63–4
Kuhlmann, Richard von, 176–7, 181–2

Lansdowne, Lord, 37, 139
Lawrence, T.E., 3, 185
Lenin, Vladimir, 15, 18
Lettow-Vorbeck, Colonel Paul von, 82–3
Libya, 24
Liege, siege of, 55, 60, 64
Liman von Sanders, General Otto, 25, 85
Lloyd George, David, 14, 39–40, 94, 102, 109, 114, 119, 137–8, 144–5, 154, 158, 170, 176, 178–80, 185, 194, 196,
Loos, battle of, 122
London, conference of, (1912), 24